MARK TWAIN'S

SPEECHES

The Beauty And The Chivalry Of New Orleans

American Artists Edition

THE COMPLETE WORKS OF MARK TWAIN

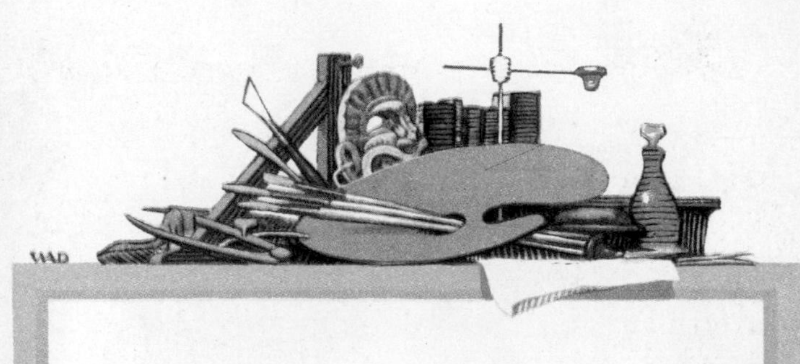

MARK TWAIN'S SPEECHES

HARPER & BROTHERS
NEW YORK

Mark Twain's Speeches

Printed in the United States of America

I-D

CONTENTS

PAGE

AN APPRECIATION, BY WILLIAM DEAN HOWELLS v
INTRODUCTION, BY ALBERT BIGELOW PAINE vii
ON SPEECH-MAKING REFORM 1
THE SANDWICH ISLANDS 7
THE AMERICAN VANDAL 21
WOMAN—AN OPINION 31
AMERICANS AND THE ENGLISH 34
ABOUT LONDON 37
THE LADIES 42
LICENSE OF THE PRESS 46
THE WEATHER 53
THE BABIES 58
THE STORY OF A SPEECH 63
UNCONSCIOUS PLAGIARISM 77
ACCIDENT INSURANCE 80
ON AFTER-DINNER SPEAKING 83
PLYMOUTH ROCK AND THE PILGRIMS 86
ON ADAM 93
SPEECH OF SAMUEL L. CLEMENS 98
ADVICE TO YOUTH 104
SPEECH 109
TURNCOATS 113
A TRIBUTE 117
CONSISTENCY 120

CONTENTS

PAGE

Henry M. Stanley 131
On Stanley and Livingstone 133
General Grant's Grammar 135
The Old-fashioned Printer 138
Yale College Speech 142
Welcome Home (1889) 145
On Foreign Critics 150
Mistaken Identity 154
Daly Theatre 157
Lotos Club Dinner in Honor of Mark Twain 161
An Undelivered Speech 164
Die Schrecken der Deutschen Sprache 168
The Horrors of the German Language 169
German for the Hungarians 176
To the Whitefriars 178
Authors' Club 185
The Day We Celebrate 187
Theoretical and Practical Morals 190
Henry Irving 193
Welcome Home (1900) 197
Galveston Orphan Bazaar 204
Literature 207
Disappearance of Literature 209
Public Education Society 211
Municipal Government 214
Municipal Corruption 218
Votes for Women 222
University Settlement Society 225

CONTENTS

PAGE

On Lincoln's Birthday 228
Osteopathy 232
Business 235
Dinner to Hamilton W. Mabie 239
The Dinner to Mr. Choate 242
Sixty-seventh Birthday 244
Seventieth Birthday 254
Russian Sufferers 263
Joan of Arc 269
Taxes and Morals 276
Layman's Sermon 281
Morals and Memory 284
When in Doubt, Tell the Truth 292
Introducing Doctor van Dyke 296
Billiards 302
"Mark Twain's First Appearance" 303
In Aid of the Blind 306
Spelling and Pictures 315
Copyright 323
Educating Theatre-goers 330
The Educational Theatre 333
Books, Authors, and Hats 335
Independence Day 344
The Savage Club Dinner 350
Charity and Actors 357
Fulton Day, Jamestown 359
The Alphabet and Simplified Spelling 364
Compliments and Degrees 368

CONTENTS

PAGE

BOOKSELLERS 375
EDUCATION AND CITIZENSHIP 378
DINNER TO WHITELAW REID 382
COURAGE 386
QUEEN VICTORIA 387
ROGERS AND RAILROADS 389

AN APPRECIATION

THESE speeches will address themselves to the minds and hearts of those who read them, but not with the effect they had with those who heard them; Clemens himself would have said, not with half the effect. I have noted elsewhere how he always held that the actor doubled the value of the author's words; and he was a great actor as well as a great author. He was a most consummate actor, with this difference from other actors, that he was the first to know the thoughts and invent the fancies to which his voice and action gave the color of life. Representation is the art of other actors; his art was creative as well as representative; it was nothing at second hand.

I never heard Clemens speak when I thought he had quite failed; some burst or spurt redeemed him when he seemed flagging short of the goal, and, whoever else was in the running, he came in ahead. His near-failures were the error of a rare trust to the spontaneity in which other speakers confide, or are believed to confide, when they are on their feet. He knew that from the beginning of oratory the orator's spontaneity was for the silence and solitude of the closet where he mused his words to an imagined audience; that this was the use of orators from Demosthenes and Cicero up and down. He studied every word and syllable, and memorized them by a system of mnemonics peculiar to himself, consisting of an arbitrary arrangement of things on a table—knives, forks, salt cellars; inkstands, pens, boxes, or whatever was at hand—which stood for points and clauses and climaxes, and were at once indelible diction and constant suggestion. He studied every tone and every gesture, and he forecast the result with the real audience from its result with that imagined audience. Therefore, it was beautiful to see him and to hear him; he rejoiced in the pleasure he gave and the blows of surprise which he dealt; and because he had his end in mind, he knew when to stop.

I have been talking of his method and manner; the matter the reader has here before him; and it is good matter, glad, honest, kind, just.

W. D. Howells.

INTRODUCTION

MARK TWAIN made his first speech when he was about twenty years old, at a printers' "banquet," in Keokuk, Iowa. No fragment of this early effort has survived the years, but his hearers long recalled it as a hilarious performance which promptly qualified him for membership in a debating society, where he became the chief star. Doubtless he spoke on other festival occasions of the moment, and one wishes that some slight remnant of those beginnings might have been preserved.

Keokuk was a brief incident in Mark Twain's career. He was presently piloting on the Mississippi River, where he was much regarded as a story-teller by his associates, but if he ever spoke at a pilots' dinner or at one of their meetings no record of the fact is discoverable. It was not until he had left the river several years behind him and had become a sage-brush journalist, reporting the Nevada legislature, that we learn of another public appearance, this time as Governor of the Third House, a burlesque organization to which he delivered in person his first (and last) "annual message." The Third House threw open its doors to the public for the event, levying a tax of a dollar on each admission, for the benefit of the church. Very likely this was

Mark Twain's first appearance before a mixed audience, and if the memory of those present may be trusted his speech that night was the "greatest effort of his life." Such a verdict is to be taken with a liberal allowance for the enthusiasm and setting of the occasion, and while we may regret that no sample of that celebrated address has come down to us, we may console ourselves in the thought that perhaps it is just as well for its renown that this is so. Mark Twain had at this time written very little that would bear the test of years, and it seems probable that his memorable message was for that day and date only.

But now came a change—a large and important change—in Mark Twain's intellectual life. One might call it a "sea change," for it followed a trip to the Sandwich Islands, where he had remained for a period of four months, a considerable portion of that time in almost daily intercourse with America's distinguished statesman, Anson Burlingame, who had stopped there on his way to China. Burlingame's example, companionship, and advice, coming when it did, were in the nature of a revelation to Samuel Clemens, who returned to San Francisco, consciously or not, the inhabitant of a new domain. His Sandwich Island letters to the Sacramento Union had been nothing remarkable, but the lecture he was persuaded to deliver a few months after his return indicates a mental awakening, a growth in vigor and poetic utterance that cannot be measured by comparison with his earlier writings because it is not of the same realm. Fortunately, some considerable portions of this first lecture have been preserved, and the reader may judge for himself what the Mark Twain of that day—he was then thirty-one—had to say when, as he tells us, he appeared, "quaking in every limb," the fear of failure in his heart. The story of that evening, as set down in *Roughing It*, is very good history, and need not be repeated here. He subsequently delivered the lecture the length of the Pacific coast, and finally at Cooper Union in New York, just before sailing on the Quaker City Holy Land excursion.

The result of the *Quaker City* venture was a series of travel letters of quite a new sort, and Mark Twain returned to find himself famous. Temporarily in Washington, he was all at once in the midst of receptions and dinners and much in demand as a speech-maker. One example only of that time has survived—his reply to the toast of "Woman" at a banquet of the "Washington Correspondents' Club." It does not seem particularly brilliant, as we read it to-day, but it must have been so regarded at the moment, for no less an authority than Vice-President Schuyler Colfax pronounced it, "the best after-dinner speech ever made." Doubtless it was a refreshing departure from the prosy or clumsy-witted efforts common to that period.

It is not the purpose here to set down a history of Mark Twain's speech-making career. He was fully launched, now, and the end would not come until the final years of his life, his prestige and popularity steadily growing until in those later days he occupied a position which none thought even to approach. It may be worth while, however, to record something of his methods of preparation and delivery.

In the beginning he carefully wrote out his speeches, learned them by heart, and practiced them in the seclusion of his chamber. Later on he frequently trusted himself to speak without any special preparation or notes, confident of picking up an idea from the toastmaster's introduction or from some previous speaker, usually asking to be placed third on the list. But if the occasion was an important one he wrote his speech and rehearsed it in the old way. His manner of delivery did not change with the years, except to become more finished, and to seem less so, for it was his naturalness, his apparent lack of all art, that was his greatest charm. One of those who attended his earliest lectures spoke of his exaggerated drawl of that day, his habit of loosely lounging about the stage, his apparent indifference to the audience. His later art was of the sort that made the hearer forget that he was not being personally entertained by a new and wonderful friend, who had come there for his particular benefit. One listener has written that he sat "simmering with laughter" through what he thought was a sort of introduction, waiting for the traditional lecture to begin, when presently with a bow the lecturer disappeared and it was over. The listener looked at his watch—he had been there for more than an hour.

His manner gave the impression of being entirely unstudied, yet no one better than Mark Twain knew the value of every gesture and particularly of every pause. He used to say, "The right word may be effective, but no word was ever as effective as a rightly timed pause." In his speech on "Speech-making Reform," with which this volume opens, he has given us, in semi-burlesque, a summary of his own methods.

Mark Twain's speeches, as here collected, are rather loosely separated into three periods: the first division beginning with his San Francisco lecture, continuing through those years when his conquest of the world of letters had not yet lost its novelty, when his blood was quick, when the gods were still kind and his words in the main a lilt of good-natured foolery. The middle period covers those years when the affairs of men and nations began to make a larger appeal, when political abuses and the injustice of class began to stir him to active rebellion and to righteous, even if violent, attitudes of reform. The final group is of those later days when, full of honors yet saddened by bereavement and the uncertainty of life's adventures, he had become the philosopher and sage whose voice was sought on every public question, whose humor was more gentle, whose judgments had become mellowed and were all the more welcome for that reason. The conclusion of the Seventieth Birthday address and of the Liverpool speech are perhaps the most perfect examples of his after-dinner art.*

Not to have heard Mark Twain is to have missed

*The closing paragraphs of the Liverpool speech were repeated at the end of a speech made at the Lotos Club, N.Y., January 11, 1908, and will be found so placed in this volume.

much of the value of his utterance. He had immeasurable magnetism and charm, his face, surrounded by its great mass of hair, pure white in old age, was one of unusual beauty, having in repose that gravity and pathos of which his whimsical humor and flickering smile were the break. No one could resist him—probably nobody ever tried to do so.

ALBERT BIGELOW PAINE.

THE EARLY PERIOD

ON SPEECH-MAKING REFORM

After-dinner Speech, About 1884

LIKE many another well-intentioned man, I have made too many speeches. And like other transgressors of this sort, I have from time to time reformed, binding myself, by oath, on New Year's Days, to never make another speech. I found that a new oath holds pretty well; but that when it is become old and frayed out and damaged by a dozen annual retyings of its remains, it ceases to be serviceable; any little strain will snap it. So, last New Year's Day I strengthened my reform with a money penalty, and made that penalty so heavy that it has enabled me to remain pure from that day to this. Although I am falling once more, now, I think I can behave myself from this out, because the penalty is going to be doubled ten days hence. I see before me and about me the familiar faces of many poor, sorrowing fellow sufferers, victims of the passion for speech making—poor, sad-eyed brothers in affliction, who, fast in the grip of this fell, degrading, demoralizing vice, have grown weak with struggling, as the years drifted by, and at last have all but given up hope. To them I say, in this last final obituary of mine, don't give up—don't do it; there is still hope for you. I beseech you, swear one more oath, and back it up with cash. I do not say this to all, of course; for there are some among you who are past reform; some who, being long accustomed to success and to the delicious intoxication of the applause which follows it, are too wedded to their dissipation to be capable now or hereafter of abandoning it. They have thoroughly learned the deep art of speech making, and they suffer no longer from those misgivings and embarrassments and apprehensions which are really the only things that ever make a speech maker want to reform. They have learned their art by long observation and slowly compacted experience; so now they know what they did not know at first, that the best and most telling speech is not the actual impromptu one, but the counterfeit of it; they know that that speech is most worth listening to which has been carefully prepared in private and tried on a plaster cast, or an empty chair, or any other appreciative object that will keep quiet until the speaker has got his matter and his delivery limbered up so that they will seem impromptu to an audience. The expert knows that. A touch of indifferent grammar flung in here and there, apparently at random, has a good effect—often restores the confidence of a suspicious audience. He arranges these errors in private; for a really random error wouldn't do any good; it would be sure to fall in the wrong place. He also leaves blanks here and there—leaves them where genuine impromptu remarks can be dropped in, of a sort that will add to the natural aspect of the speech without breaking its line of march. At the banquet he listens to the other speakers, invents happy turns upon remarks of theirs, and sticks these happy turns into his blanks for impromptu use by and by when he shall be called up. When this expert rises to his feet, he looks around over the house with the air of a man who has just been strongly impressed by something. The uninitiated cannot interpret his aspect; but the initiated can.

They know what is coming. When the noise of the clapping and stamping has subsided this veteran says: "Aware that the hour is late, Mr. Chairman, it was my intention to abide by a purpose which I framed in the beginning of the evening—to simply rise and return my duty and thanks, in case I should be called upon, and then make way for men more able and who have come with something to say. But, sir, I was so struck by General Smith's remark concerning the proneness of evil to fly upward, that"—etc., etc., etc., and before you know it he has slidden smoothly along on his compliment to the general, and out of it and into his set speech, and you can't tell, to save you, where it was nor when it was that he made the connection. And that man will soar along, in the most beautiful way, on the wings of a practiced memory, heaving in a little decayed grammar here, and a little wise tautology there, and a little neatly counterfeited embarrassment yonder, and a little finely acted stumbling and stammering for a word, rejecting this word and that, and finally getting the right one, and fetching it out with ripping effect, and with the glad look of a man who has got out of a bad hobble entirely by accident—and wouldn't take a hundred dollars down for that accident; and every now and then he will sprinkle you in one of those happy turns on something that has previously been said; and at last, with supreme art, he will catch himself, when in the very act of sitting down, and lean over the table and fire a parting rocket, in the way of an afterthought, which makes everybody stretch his mouth as it goes up, and dims the very stars in heaven when it explodes. And yet that man has been practicing that afterthought and that attitude for about a week.

Well, you can't reform that kind of a man. It's a case of Eli joined to his idols. Let him alone. But there is one sort that can be reformed. That is the genuine impromptu speaker. I mean the man who "didn't expect to be called upon and isn't prepared," and yet goes waddling and warbling along, just as if he thought it wasn't any harm to commit a crime so long as it wasn't premeditated. Now and then he says, "but I must not detain you longer"; every little while he says, "Just one word more and I am done"—but at these times he always happens to think of two or three more unnecessary things and so he stops to say them. Now that man has no way of finding out how long his windmill is going. He likes to hear it creak, and so he goes on creaking, and listening to it, and enjoying it, never thinking of the flight of time; and when he comes to sit down at last and look under his hopper, he is the most surprised person in the house to see what a little bit of a grist he has ground and how unconscionably long he has been grinding it. As a rule, he finds that he hasn't said anything—a discovery which the unprepared man ought always to make, and does usually make—and has the added grief of making it at second hand, too.

This is a man who can be reformed. And so can his near relative, who now rises out of my reconstructed past—the man who provisions himself with a single prepared bite of a sentence or so, and trusts to luck to catch quails and manna as he goes along. This person frequently gets left. You can easily tell when he has finished his prepared bit and begun on the impromptu part. Often the prepared portion has been built during the banquet; it may consist of ten sentences, but it oftener consists of two—oftenest of all, it is but a single sentence; and it has seemed so happy and pat and bright and good that the creator of it, the person that laid it, has been sitting there cackling privately over it and admiring it and petting it and shining it up and imagining how fine it is going to "go," when, of course, he ought to have been laying another one, and still another one, and maybe a basketful, if it's a fruitful day; yes, and he is thinking that when he comes to hurl that egg at the house there is going to be such electric explosion of applause that the inspiration of it will fill him instantly with ideas and clothe the ideas in brilliant language, and that an impromptu speech will result which will be infinitely finer than anything he could have deliberately prepared. But there are two damaging things which he is leaving out of the calculation: one is the historical fact that a man is never called up as soon as he thinks he is going to be called up, and that every speech that is injected into the proceedings ahead of him gives his fires an added chance to cool; and the other thing which he is forgetting is that he can't sit there and keep saying that fine sentence of his over and over to himself for three quarters of an hour without by and by getting a trifle tired of it and losing somewhat of confidence in it.

When at last his chance comes and he touches off his pet sentence, it makes him sick to see how shamefacedly and apologetically he has done it, and how compassionate the applause is, and how sorry everybody feels; and then he bitterly thinks what a lie it is to call this a free country, where none but the unworthy and the undeserving may swear. And at this point, naked and blind and empty, he swallows off into his *real* impromptu speech; stammers out three or four incredibly flat things, then collapses into his seat, murmuring, "I wish I was in ——" He doesn't say where, because he doesn't. The stranger at his left, says, "Your opening was very good"; stranger at his right says, "I liked your opening"; man opposite says, "Opening very good indeed—*very* good"; two or three other people mumble something about his opening. People always feel obliged to pour some healing thing on a crippled man that way. They mean it for oil; they think it *is* oil; but the sufferer recognizes it for aquafortis.

THE SANDWICH ISLANDS

EXTRACTS FROM MARK TWAIN'S FIRST LECTURE, ORIGINALLY DELIVERED AT MAGUIRE'S ACADEMY OF MUSIC, SAN FRANCISCO, OCTOBER 2, 1866. MANY TIMES REPEATED IN THIS COUNTRY AND GREAT BRITAIN

TO cut the matter short the Sandwich Isles are 2,100 miles southwest from San Francisco, but why they were put away out there in the middle of the Pacific, so far away from any place and in such an inconvenient locality, is no business of ours—it was the work of Providence and is not open to criticism. The subject is a good deal like many others we should like to inquire into, such as, What mosquitoes were made for, etc., but under the circumstances we naturally feel a delicacy about doing it. They are a dozen in number, of volcanic origin—eight of them inhabited and four of them the most marvelously productive sugar land in the known world. Eighty years ago there was a population of 400,000 on the islands, but only 50,000 now. The Kanaka race is rapidly passing away. . . .

It is said by some, and believed, that Kanakas won't lie, but I know they *will* lie—lie like auctioneers—lie like lawyers—lie like patent-medicine advertisements—they will *almost* lie like *newspaper* men. They will lie for a dollar when they could get a dollar and a half for telling the truth. They *never* tell a traveler the right road or right distance to a place. Christian Kanakas will go into court and swear on the Bible and then stand up and lie till the lights burn blue around them, and then go home and go through a lot of purifying idolatrous ceremonies and the thing is all straight. There is only one way of getting them to tell the truth, on the stand or anywhere else—and that it to swear them on the Great Shark God, which seems to have been the most potent personage in their idolatrous mythology. In old times, when the priests fancied that the shark god was angry or out of sorts about anything and stood in need of a sacrifice to compose his spirits, they used to go forth and lasso a poor wretch of a plebeian native and cast him into the sea where the sharks could devour him. And to this day, in the island of Hawaii, they fear and respect this deity, and when they swear by him they keep the oath and tell the truth. And yet the unsagacious judges go on swearing such witnesses on the Scriptures—and refuse to profit by our keener judgment. When we have a Chinese witness on an important case we swear him on a butchered chicken.

And cheat? They will cheat anybody. They used to be arrant thieves in old times, and now they are arrant rascals—arrant knaves. They measure a stranger by the eye, and begin to average him as soon as he gets into their cabin. If he knows the language and is only *pretending* to be a stranger, he will hear them comment on him and his probable errand very freely. They will wonder if he is a missionary—and shake their heads and say no, looks too worldly for a missionary; and wonder if he is a Californian—no, not quick-motioned enough for a Californian; and so on. If they determine that you are a missionary, they will offer to have family prayers; if they decide that you are a Californian, they will proceed to swindle you. To them, anybody who doesn't live in the islands is usually a Californian, no matter where he comes from. If you merely want to stay all night, stay and welcome, eat their poi and raw fish and welcome, make yourself at home—for theirs is the freest hospitality in the world. It is customary to pay them, but the offer must come from *you;* they would never ask it. But if you want to *trade*, if you want to *buy* anything, they will manage to get ahead of you, somehow or other, nearly every time. They have always got a sore-back horse lying around somewhere to sell to the stranger. They will sell him a young chicken and then cook him one that remembered Noah's ark and the Deluge. A Kanaka will hire a stranger a horse for a dollar, and then demand $2.50 when he gets back, and say he doesn't know anything about the original bargain—his *brother* made it and then went to the country. These niggers have generally got a brother nigger on the fence—or in the country.

These natives are strange people—they can die whenever they want to—don't mind dying any more than a jilted Frenchman. When they take a notion to die, they *die*, no matter whether anything matters or not; they will lie right down sometimes and say they are going to die, and can't be persuaded otherwise—have got ready to die, made up their minds to die, and *will* die, in spite of all.

A gentleman in Hawaii asked his servant if he wouldn't like to die and have a big funeral. He said yes, and looked happy, and the next morning the overseer came and said, "That boy of yours laid down and died last night and said you were going to give him a fine funeral."

They are more civilized and Christianized than they used to be, but still they believe an enemy can offer incantations to the idols and pray them to death. Three Kanakas on one whaleship that left the islands last year died one after the other, from no apparent cause, and each said it was no use to try to save them, for they knew some enemy at home was praying them to death. I know there is something in it—albeit it is rank idolatry—and I sincerely feel for these poor creatures. Even in this Christian city I went to church last Sunday and came mighty near getting prayed to death myself.

The Kanakas are passionately fond of dogs—not great, magnificent Newfoundlands or stately mastiffs or graceful greyhounds—but a species of little, puny, cowardly, sneaking, noisy cur that a white man would condemn to death on general principles. They love these puppies better than they love one another—better than their children or their religion. They feed them—stuff them—with poi and fish, from their own calabashes when the supply is scanty, and even the family must go hungry. They sleep with them; they don't mind the fleas. Men and women carry these dogs in their arms, always. If they have got to walk a mile, the dog must be carried—or five miles, for that matter—while the little children walk. The dog travels in the schooners with them. I have seen a puppy hugged and caressed by a mother, and her little, tired, sore-footed child cuffed and slapped for stumbling to the ground and crying. When the woman rides on horseback, she often carries the puppy in front of her on the horse; and when the man rides—they nearly always go in a keen gallop—the puppy stands up behind the saddle, "thortships," as a sailor would say, and sways gently to and fro to the motion of the horse. No danger of its falling; it is educated to ride thus from earliest puppyhood. They passionately love and tenderly care for the puppy, and feed it from their own hands until it is a full-grown dog—and then they cook it and eat it.

I did not eat any dog. I ate raw salt pork and poi, and that was bad enough, but I was lost in the woods and hungry.

I do not see where old Kanehameha got his fierce warriors. He was a great warrior, you know—a Kanaka Napoleon—and in the old times when the feudal system prevailed and the islands were so divided up that there was an average of three kings to an acre, he held four aces once and took them all in and combined the whole concern under one sovereignty. He fought many great battles, but I cannot think where he got his fighting material, for certainly the Kanakas of the present day are the most peaceable, inoffensive, unwarlike creatures imaginable. One would as soon expect a rabbit to fight as one of these. You often see them quarreling

—doubling their fists and striking them together, and making frightful grimaces, and hurling curses and the deadliest insults at one another, even striking out savagely within an inch of one another's faces—and just as you think blood is going to flow, just as you think there is going to be a Kanaka for breakfast, it all ends in smoke. They go off growling and viciously shaking their heads. The army of the Hawaiian Islands consists of two hundred men (they have got a Secretary of War there—and a Secretary of the Navy, too, for that matter, but not any ships; and a Minister of Finance also—Harris—and if he stays there they won't have any money shortly). The army consists of two hundred men, but it is not on a war footing, now, happily. Some of the muskets haven't got any locks to them, and the others haven't got any ramrods.

Kanakas are fond of horses, and they have got plenty of them. They seldom walk anywhere; they nearly always ride. Whenever you see a lot of men and women at work in a sugar plantation, you will see as many horses hitched at hand for them to ride a quarter of a mile home on. These horses are worth on an average about seven dollars and a half apiece (you can often buy them for less, though), and they have to pay a government tax of a dollar a head on them. But that doesn't matter. A Kanaka with an income of fifty dollars a year will keep half a dozen horses, if it breaks him. And he is as unkind and as unmerciful to his horse as he is disgustingly fond of his puppy. His horse is seldom well fed and is always hard ridden. And they can make a horse go when a white man can't. If there is any of that capacity in a horse the Kanaka will get it out. I once rode over a mountain in Mani with a white man whose horse was so lean and spiritless and worthless that he could not be persuaded or spurred out of a walk, and he kept going to sleep, besides—at least he seemed to. But the man said that when he got to Maaleo Bay he would find one of his own horses there—a blooded animal that could outstrip the wind. He got his blooded animal, and gave the slow horse to a Kanaka boy and told him to follow. Then he put his blooded steed to his utmost speed to show him off. But the Kanaka, without spur or whip, or scarcely any appearance of urging, sailed by us on the old plug, and stayed ahead, and in eight miles he beat us out of sight. I never could understand how those savages managed to make those wretched horses travel so. They are wild, free riders, and perfectly at home in the saddle—they call it a saddle, a little vile English spoon of a thing with a girth that never is tight enough to touch the horse and sometimes without any girth at all. With their loose ideas, they never cinch a Californian's horse tight enough to suit him.

When a Kanaka rides through the country, he stops fifteen or twenty minutes at every single cabin he comes to, and has a chat. Consequently their horses early acquire an inveterate habit of stopping, and they cannot be cured of it. If you attempt to keep them in the road and go on about your business, they grow frantic and kick up and charge around fiercely, and finally take the bits in their mouths and carry you to the cabin by main force. I rode Kanaka horses nearly altogether. When I made the tour of that pleasant country I hadn't any business at any of the roadside cabins, but I stopped at them all. The horses wanted to stop, and I had to put up with it. That is how I happen to have such an intimate knowledge of the country and the people.

The Kanaka women all ride, and ride well and gracefully. They ride as women *should* ride—astride. To ride sidewise tires the horse, makes his back sore and his footing insecure, and endangers the life of the rider. A sidesaddle is always turning and spilling its precious freight into the mud or on the rocks and bruising the limbs or breaking the neck of the same. For a woman to ride sidewise is to do an awkward, ungainly, absurd, and to the last degree foolish and perilous thing.

Kanakas are cruel by nature. They will put a live chicken in the hot embers merely to see it caper about. They used to be cruel to themselves before the missionaries came. They used to tear and burn their flesh, or shave their heads, or pluck out their eyes, or knock out a couple of their front teeth, when a great chief died. And if their bereavement were particularly sore and hard to bear, they would go out and murder a neighbor. There was no law against it. The largest liberty in the matter of mourning was permitted. But the missionaries have done away with all that.

Down there in the islands they have exploded one of our most ancient and trusted maxims. It was a maxim that we have all of us implicitly believed in and revered—and now it turns out to be a swindling humbug. *Be virtuous and you will be happy.* The Kanakas are not virtuous—neither men, women, nor children—and yet they are the happiest creatures the sun shines on. They are as happy as the day is long. They wail and carry on grievously when a friend or relative dies, but it is all a pretense; they do precisely the same thing when a friend returns from a month's absence. In both instances the tears are manufactured to order and the joy and sorrow counterfeited. A woman returns from a distance and a lot of her female friends will huddle around her on the ground and twine their arms about her and weep and whine and blubber and howl for an hour—and they would cheerfully repeat the same thing the next day if she died, and dance the hula-hula into the bargain. It is rarely that they show any genuine tribulation. Theirs is a state of placid happiness. All they want is unfettered liberty to eat, drink, sleep, sing, dance, swindle, lie, and pray, and then, whether school keeps or not is a matter of no interest to *them*.

The natives do everything wrong end foremost. When you meet one on horseback he turns out on the wrong side; they cinch a horse on the wrong side and mount him from the wrong side; their lineage and rank come down from the female ancestor instead of the male; the women smoke more than the men; the natives' English "no" generally means "yes"; they eat their fish raw, and bathe in the middle of the day; instead of keeping it from a patient that he is likely to die, they tell him early;

when they beckon to a person to come, they motion the hand in the opposite direction; the only native bird that has handsome feathers has only two, and they are under its wings instead of on top of its head; frequently a native cat has a tail only two inches long and has got a knot tied in the end of it; the native duck lives on the dry tops of mountains 5,000 feet high; the natives always stew chickens instead of baking them; they dance at funerals and sing a dismal heart-broken dirge when they are happy; and with atrocious perverseness they wash your shirts with a club and iron them with a brickbat.

In old times the Kanaka king was the owner of all the lands and supreme head of church and state. He was absolute. His word was superior to all law. His person was sacred. If a common man passed his house without prostrating himself, if he came near the king with his head wet, if he ventured to stand on a hillock that brought him higher than the level the king stood on, if his intangible and harmless shadow fell upon the king's royal person—that man had to die; there was no salvation for him. Thus sacred was the presence and the belongings of those naked, greasy, mud-colored, regal savages. The king had the power of life and death and liberty over all. He could place a *taboo* (prohibition) upon any spot or thing or person, and it was death for any man to molest it.

The high priest came next in authority—decreed the human sacrifices and captured the doomed men and butchered them. They regulated and bossed all such matters under the king. The chiefs came next.

They held the lands by feudal tenure from the king and owed him service, as in England in the old baronial days. The common Kanakas came next; they were the slaves of the chiefs—sweated and labored for them and were cruelly maltreated in return.

After these came the women, and they were the abject slaves of the men; they were degraded to the rank of brutes and beasts and considered to be no better; they were kept at hard labor and were beaten and contemptuously treated by their lords. By the *taboo* it was death for them to sit at the tables with their husbands, or to eat of the choice fruits of the lands, such as bananas, pineapples, etc., at any time. They seemed to have had a sort of dim knowledge of what came of women eating fruit in the Garden of Eden and they didn't feel justified in taking any more chances. And it is wisdom—unquestionably it is wisdom. Adam wasn't strict enough; Eve broke the *taboo*, and hence comes all this trouble. Can't be too particular about fruit—with women.

They were a rusty set all round, those Kanakas, in those days. But the missionaries came and knocked off the shackles from the whole race—broke the power of the king and the chiefs and set the common man free and elevated his wife to an equality with him, and got a patch of land set apart and secured to each to hold forever. And the missionaries set up schools and churches and printing presses and taught the people the Christian religion, after a fashion, and taught the whole nation to read and write with facility in the native tongue—and now I suppose there is not an uneducated Kanaka in the kingdom.

The natives of the Sandwich Islands are dark brown. Their tropical sun and the easy-going ways inherited from their ancestors have made them rather lazy, perhaps, but they are not vicious. Nor yet virtuous, altogether.

The missionaries have educated them and have about half civilized and half christianized them. You may well say, "Well done, good and faithful servants!" for mortal man could not have accomplished more with such material to work upon.

The native women in the rural districts wear a single long, loose garment, but the men don't. They don't wear anything to speak of. They would cheerfully wear a plug hat and a vest if they had them, but they haven't. . . .

If you would see magnificent scenery—scenery on a mighty scale—and get scenery which charms with its softness and delights you with its unspeakable beauty, at the same moment that it deeply impresses you with its grandeur and its sublimity, you should go to the islands.

Each island is a mountain—or two or three mountains. They begin at the seashore—in a torrid climate where the cocoa palm grows, and the coffee tree, the mango, orange, banana, and the delicious chirinoya; they begin down there in a sweltering atmosphere, rise with a grand and gradual sweep till they hide their beautiful regalia of living green in the folds of the drooping clouds, and higher and higher yet they rise among the mists till their emerald forests change to dull and stunted shrubbery, then to scattering constellations of the brilliant silver sword, then higher yet to dreary, barren desolation—no trees, no shrubs, nothing but torn and scorched and blackened piles of lava; higher yet, and then, towering toward heaven, above the dim and distant *land*, above the waveless sea, and high above the rolling plains of clouds themselves, stands the awful summit, wrapped in a mantle of everlasting ice and snow and burnished with a tropical sunshine that fires it with a dazzling splendor! Here one may stand and shiver in the midst of eternal winter and look down upon a land reposing in the loveliest hues of a summer that hath no end.

Such is Mauna Loa—16,000 feet high by recent and accurate measurement, and such is Mauna Kea, 14,000 feet high. . . .

The natives are indifferent to volcanic terrors. During the progress of an eruption they ate, drank, bought, sold, planted, builded, apparently indifferent to the roar of consuming forests, the sight of devouring fire, the startling detonations, the hissing of escaping steam, the rending of the earth, the shivering and melting of gigantic rocks, the raging and dashing of the fiery waves, the bellowings and unearthly mutterings coming up from a burning deep. They went carelessly on, amid the rain of ashes, sand, and fiery scintillations, gazing vacantly on the ever-varying appearance of the atmosphere, murky, black, livid, blazing, the sudden rising of lofty pillars of flame, the upward curling of ten thousand columns of smoke, and their majestic roll in dense and lurid clouds. All these moving phenomena were regarded by them as the fall of a shower or the running of a brook; while to others they were as the tokens of a burning world, the departing heavens, and a coming judge. . . .

THE AMERICAN VANDAL

EXTRACTS FROM A LECTURE WIDELY DELIVERED BY MARK TWAIN FOLLOWING HIS RETURN FROM THE "QUAKER CITY" EXCURSION, NOVEMBER, 1867, AND PRIOR TO THE PUBLICATION OF THE "INNOCENTS ABROAD," JULY, 1869

I AM to speak of the American Vandal this evening, but I wish to say in advance that I do not use this term in derision or apply it as a reproach, but I use it because it is convenient; and duly and properly modified, it best describes the roving, independent, free-and-easy character of that class of traveling Americans who are *not* elaborately educated, cultivated, and refined, and gilded and filigreed with the ineffable graces of the first society. The best class of our countrymen who go abroad keep us well posted about their doings in foreign lands, but their brethren vandals cannot sing their own praises or publish their adventures.

The American Vandal gallops over England, Scotland, Spain, and Switzerland, and finally brings up in Italy. He thinks it is the proper thing to visit Genoa, the stately old City of Palaces, whose vast marble edifices almost meet together over streets so narrow that three men can hardly walk abreast in them, and so crooked that a man generally comes out of them about the same place he went in. He only stays in Genoa long enough to see a few celebrated things and get some fragments of stone from the house Columbus was born in—for your genuine Vandal is an intolerable and incorrigible relic gatherer. It is estimated that if all the fragments of stone brought from Columbus's house by travelers were collected together they would suffice to build a house fourteen thousand feet long and sixteen thousand feet high—and I suppose they would.

Next he hurries to Milan and takes notes of the Grand Cathedral (for he is always taking notes). Oh, I remember Milan and the noble cathedral well enough—that marble miracle of enchanting architecture. I remember how we entered and walked about its vast spaces and among its huge columns, gazing aloft at the monster windows all aglow with brilliantly colored scenes in the life of the Savior and his followers. And I remember the side-shows and curiosities there, too. The guide showed us a coffee-colored piece of sculpture which he said was considered to have come from the hand of Phidias, since it was not possible that any other man, of any epoch, could have copied nature with such faultless accuracy. The figure was that of a man without a skin; with every vein, artery, muscle, every fiber and tendon and tissue of the human frame, represented in minute detail. It looked natural, because it looked somehow *as if it were in pain.* A skinned man *would be likely to look that way*—unless his attention were occupied by some other matter. . . .

The Vandal goes to see the ancient and most celebrated painting in the world, "The Last Supper."

We all know it in engravings: the disciples all sitting on side of a long, plain table and Christ with bowed head in the center—all the last suppers in the world are copied from this painting. It is so damaged now, by the wear and tear of three hundred years, that the figures can hardly be distinguished. The Vandal goes to see this picture—which all the world praises—looks at it with a critical eye, and says it's a perfect old nightmare of a picture and he wouldn't give forty dollars for a million like it (and I indorse his opinion), and then he is done with Milan.

He paddles around the Lake of Como for a few days, and then takes the cars. He is bound for Venice, the oldest and the proudest and the princeliest republic that ever graced the earth. We put on a good many airs with our little infant of a Republic of a century's growth, but we grow modest when we stand before this gray, old imperial city that used to laugh the armies and navies of half the world to scorn, and was a haughty, invincible, magnificent Republic for fourteen hundred years! The Vandal is bound for Venice! He has a long, long, weary ride of it; but just as the day is closing he hears some one shout, "Venice!" and puts his head out of the window, and sure enough, afloat on the placid sea, a league away, lies the great city with its towers and domes and steeples drowsing in a golden mist of sunset!

Have you been to Venice, and seen the winding canals, and the stately edifices that border them all along, ornamented with the quaint devices and sculptures of a former age? And have you seen the great Cathedral of St. Mark's—and the Giant's Staircase—and the famous Bridge of Sighs—and the great Square of St. Mark's—and the ancient pillar with the winged lion of St. Mark that stands in it, whose story and whose origin are a mystery—and the Rialto, where Shylock used to loan money on human flesh and other collateral?

I had begun to feel that the old Venice of song and story had departed forever. But I was too hasty. When we swept gracefully out into the Grand Canal and under the mellow moonlight the Venice of poetry and romance stood revealed. Right from the water's edge rose palaces of marble; gondolas were gliding swiftly hither and thither and disappearing suddenly through unsuspected gates and alleys; ponderous stone bridges threw their shadows athwart the glittering waves. There were life and motion everywhere, and yet everywhere there was a hush, a stealthy sort of stillness, that was suggestive of secret enterprises of bravos and of lovers; and clad half in moonbeams and half in mysterious shadows, the grim old mansions of the republic seemed to have an expression about them of having an eye out for just such enterprises as these. At that same moment music came stealing over the waters—Venice was complete.

Our Vandals hurried away from Venice and scattered abroad everywhere. You could find them breaking specimens from the dilapidated tomb of Romeo and Juliet at Padua—and infesting the picture galleries of Florence—and risking their necks on the Leaning Tower of Pisa—and snuffing sulphur fumes on the summit of Vesuvius—and burrowing among the exhumed wonders of Herculaneum and Pompeii—and you might see them with spectacles on, and blue cotton umbrellas under their arms, benignantly contemplating Rome from the venerable arches of the Coliseum.

And finally we sailed from Naples, and in due time anchored before the Piræus, the seaport of Athens in Greece. But the quarantine was in force, and so they set a guard of soldiers to watch us and would not let us go ashore. However, I and three other Vandals took a boat, and muffled the oars, and slipped ashore at 11.30 at night, and dodged the guard successfully. Then we made a wide circuit around the slumbering town, avoiding all roads and houses—for they'd about as soon hang a body as not for violating the quarantine laws in those countries. We got around the town without any accident, and then struck out across the Attic Plain, steering straight for Athens—over rocks and hills and brambles and everything—with Mt. Helicon for a landmark. And so we tramped for five or six miles. The Attic Plain is a mighty uncomfortable plain to travel in, even if it *is* so historical. The armed guards got after us three times and flourished their gleaming gun barrels in the moonlight, because they thought we were stealing grapes occasionally—and the fact is we *were*—for we found by and by that the brambles that tripped us up so often were grape-vines—but these people in the country didn't know that we were quarantine-blockade runners, and so they only scared us and jawed Greek at us, and let us go, instead of arresting us.

We didn't care about Athens particularly, but we wanted to see the famous Acropolis and its ruined temples, and we did. We climbed the steep hill of the Acropolis about one in the morning and tried to storm that grand old fortress that had scorned the battles and sieges of three thousand years. We had the garrison out mighty quick—four Greeks—and we bribed them to betray the citadel and unlock the gates. In a moment we stood in the presence of the noblest ruins we had ever seen—the most elegant, the most graceful, the most imposing. The renowned Parthenon towered above us, and about us were the wreck of what were once the snowy marble Temples of Hercules and Minerva, and another whose name I have forgotten. Most of the Parthenon's grand columns are still standing, but the roof is gone.

As we wandered down the marble-paved length of this mighty temple, the scene was strangely impressive. Here and there in lavish profusion were gleaming white statues of men and women, propped against blocks of marble, some of them armless, some without legs, others headless, but all looking mournful and sentient and startlingly human! They rose up and confronted the midnight intruder on every side; they stared at him with stony eyes from unlooked-for nooks and recesses; they peered at him over fragmentary heaps far down the desolate corridors; they barred his way in the midst of the broad forum, and solemnly pointed with handless arms the way from the sacred fane; and through the roofless temple the moon looked down and banded the floor and darkened the scattered fragments and broken statues with the slanting shadows of the columns!

What a world of ruined sculpture was about us! Stood up in rows, stacked up in piles, scattered broadcast over the wide area of the Acropolis, were hundreds of crippled statues of all sizes and of the most exquisite workmanship; and vast fragments of marble that once belonged to the entablatures, covered with bas-reliefs representing battles and sieges, ships of war with three and four tiers of oars, pageants and processions—everything one could think of.

We walked out into the grass-grown, fragment-strewn court beyond the Parthenon. It startled us every now and then, to see a stony white face stare suddenly up at us out of the grass, with its dead eyes. The place seemed alive with ghosts. We half expected to see the Athenian heroes of twenty centuries ago glide out of the shadows and steal into the old temple they knew so well and regarded with such boundless pride.

The full moon was riding high in the cloudless heavens now. We sauntered carelessly and unthinkingly to the edge of the lofty battlements of the citadel, and looked down, and, lo! a vision! And such a vision! Athens by moonlight! All the beauty in all the world combined could not rival it! The prophet that thought the splendors of the New Jerusalem were revealed to him, surely saw this instead. It lay in the level plain right under our feet—all spread abroad like a picture—and we looked down upon it as we might have looked from a balloon.

We saw no semblance of a street, but every house, every window, every clinging vine, every projection, was as distinct and sharply marked as if the time were noonday; and yet there was no glare, no glitter, nothing harsh or repulsive—the silent city was flooded with the mellowest light that ever streamed from the moon, and seemed like some living creature wrapped in peaceful slumber. On its farther side was a little temple whose delicate pillars and ornate front glowed with a rich luster that chained the eye like a spell; and, nearer by, the palace of the king reared its creamy walls out of the midst of a great garden of shrubbery that was flecked all over with a random shower of amber lights—a spray of golden sparks that lost their brightness in the glory of the moon and glinted softly upon the sea of dark foliage like the palled stars of the Milky Way! Overhead, the stately columns, majestic still in their ruin; underfoot, the dreaming city; in the distance the silver sea—not on the broad earth is there another picture half so beautiful!

We got back to the ship safely, just as the day was dawning. We had walked upon pavements that had been pressed by Plato, Aristotle, Demosthenes, Socrates, Phocion, Euclid, Xenophon, Herodotus, Diogenes, and a hundred others of deathless fame, and were satisfied. We got to stealing grapes again on the way back, and half a dozen rascally guards with muskets and pistols captured us and marched us in the center of a hollow square nearly to the sea—till we were beyond all the graperies. Military escort—ah, I never traveled in so much state in all my life.

What, sir, would the people of the earth be without woman? They would be scarce, sir, almighty scarce. Then let us cherish her; let us protect her; let us give her our support, our encouragement, our sympathy, ourselves—if we get a chance.

But, jesting aside, Mr. President, woman is lovable, gracious, kind of heart, beautiful—worthy of all respect, of all esteem, of all deference. Not any here will refuse to drink her health right cordially in this bumper of wine, for each and every one has personally known and loved, and honored the very best one of them all—his own mother.

AMERICANS AND THE ENGLISH

Address for a Gathering of Americans in London, July 4, 1872

MR. CHAIRMAN AND LADIES AND GENTLEMEN,—I thank you for the compliment which has just been tendered me, and to show my appreciation of it I will not afflict you with many words. It is pleasant to celebrate in this peaceful way, upon this old mother soil, the anniversary of an experiment which was born of war with this same land so long ago, and wrought out to a successful issue by the devotion of our ancestors. It has taken nearly a hundred years to bring the English and Americans into kindly and mutually appreciative relations, but I believe it has been accomplished at last. It was a great step when the two last misunderstandings were settled by arbitration instead of cannon. It is another great step when England adopts our sewing machines without claiming the invention—as usual. It was another when they imported one of our sleeping cars the other day. And it warmed my heart more than I can tell, yesterday, when I witnessed the spectacle of an Englishman ordering an American sherry cobbler of his own free will and accord—and not only that, but with a great brain and a level head reminding the barkeeper not to forget the strawberries. With a common origin, a common language, a common literature, a common religion, and—common drinks, what is longer needful to the cementing of the two nations together in a permanent bond of brotherhood?

This is an age of progress, and ours is a progressive land. A great and glorious land, too—a land which has developed a Washington, a Franklin, a William M. Tweed, a Longfellow, a Motley, a Jay Gould, a Samuel C. Pomeroy, a recent Congress which has never had its equal (in some respects), and a United States Army which conquered sixty Indians in eight months by tiring them out—which is much better than uncivilized slaughter, God knows. We have a criminal jury system which is superior to any in the world; and its efficiency is only marred by the difficulty of finding twelve men every day who don't know anything and can't read. And I may observe that we have an insanity plea that would have saved Cain. I think I can say, and say with pride, that we have some legislatures that bring higher prices than any in the world.

I refer with effusion to our railway system, which consents to let us live, though it might do the opposite, being our owners. It only destroyed three thousand and seventy lives last year by collisions, and twenty-seven thousand two hundred and sixty by running over heedless and unnecessary people at crossings. The companies seriously regretted the killing of these thirty thousand people, and went so far as to pay for some of them—voluntarily, of course, for the meanest of us would not claim that we possess a court treacherous enough to enforce a law against a railway company. But, thank Heaven, the railway companies are generally disposed to do the right and kindly thing without compulsion. I know of an instance which greatly touched me at the time. After an accident the company sent home the remains of a dear distant old relative of mine in a basket, with the remark, "Please state what figure you hold him at—and return the basket." Now there couldn't be anything friendlier than that.

But I must not stand here and brag all night. However, you won't mind a body bragging a little about his country on the Fourth of July. It is a fair and legitimate time to fly the eagle. I will say only one more word of brag—and a hopeful one. It is this. We have a form of government which gives each man a fair chance and no favor. With us no individual is born with a right to look down upon his neighbor and hold him in contempt. Let such of us as are not dukes find our consolation in that. And we may find hope for the future in the fact that as unhappy as is the condition of our political morality to-day, England has risen up out of a far fouler since the days when Charles I. ennobled courtesans and all political places was a matter of bargain and sale. There is hope for us yet.*

* At least the above is the speech which I was *going* to make, but our minister, General Schenck, presided, and after the blessing, got up and made a great, long, inconceivably dull harangue, and wound up by saying that inasmuch as speech making did not seem to exhilarate the guests much, all further oratory would be dispensed with during the evening, and we could just sit and talk privately to our elbow neighbors and have a good, sociable time. It is known that in consequence of that remark forty-four perfected speeches died in the womb. The depression, the gloom, the solemnity that reigned over the banquet from that time forth will be a lasting memory with many that were there. By that one thoughtless remark General Schenck lost forty-four of the best friends he had in England. More than one said that night: "And this is the sort of person that is sent to represent us in a great sister empire!"

ABOUT LONDON

Address at a Dinner Given by the Savage Club, London, September 28, 1872

Reported by Moncure D. Conway in the Cincinnati Commercial.

IT affords me sincere pleasure to meet this distinguished club, a club which has extended its hospitalities and its cordial welcome to so many of my countrymen. I hope [and here the speaker's voice became low and fluttering] you will excuse these clothes. I am going to the theater; that will explain these clothes. I have other clothes than these. Judging human nature by what I have seen of it, I suppose that the customary thing for a stranger to do when he stands here is to make a pun on the name of this club, under the impression, of course, that he is the first man that that idea has occurred to. It is a credit to our human nature, not a blemish upon it; for it shows that underlying all our depravity (and God knows and you know we are depraved enough) and all our sophistication, and untarnished by them, there is a sweet germ of innocence and simplicity still. When a stranger says to me, with a glow of inspiration in his eye, some gentle, innocuous little thing about "Twain and one flesh," and all that sort of thing, I don't try to crush that man into the earth—no. I feel like saying: "Let me take you by the hand, sir; let me embrace you; I have not heard that pun for weeks." We will deal in palpable puns. We will call parties named King "Your Majesty," and we will say to the Smiths that we think we have heard that name before somewhere. Such is human nature. We cannot alter this. It is God that made us so for some good and wise purpose. Let us not repine. But though I may seem strange, may seem eccentric, I mean to refrain from punning upon the name of this club, though I could make a very good one if *I* had time to think about it—a week.

I cannot express to you what entire enjoyment I find in this first visit to this prodigious metropolis of yours. Its wonders seem to me to be limitless. I go about as in a dream—as in a realm of enchantment—where many things are rare and beautiful, and all things are strange and marvelous. Hour after hour I stand—I stand spellbound, as it were—and gaze upon the statuary in Leicester Square. [Leicester Square being a horrible chaos, with the relic of an equestrian statue in the center, the king being headless and limbless, and the horse in little better condition.] I visit the mortuary effigies of noble old Henry VIII., and Judge Jeffreys, and the preserved gorilla, and try to make up my mind which of my ancestors I admire the most. I go to that matchless Hyde Park and drive all around it, and then I start to enter it at the Marble Arch—and—am induced to "change my mind." [Cabs are not permitted in Hyde Park—nothing less aristocratic than a private carriage.] It is a great benefaction—is Hyde Park. There, in his hansom cab, the invalid can go—the poor, sad child of misfortune—and insert his nose between the railings, and breathe the pure, health-giving air of the country and of heaven. And if he is a swell invalid, who isn't obliged to depend upon parks for his country air, he can drive inside—if he owns his vehicle. I drive round and round Hyde Park, and the more I see of the edges of it the more grateful I am that the margin is extensive.

And I have been to the Zoölogical Gardens. What a wonderful place that is! I never have seen such a curious and interesting variety of wild animals in any garden before—except "Mabille." I never believed before there were so many different kinds of animals in the world as you can find there—and I don't believe it yet. I have been to the British Museum. I would advise you to drop in there some time when you have nothing to do for—five minutes—if you have never been there. It seems to me the noblest monument that this nation has yet erected to her greatness. I say to her, our greatness—as a nation. True, she has built other monuments, and stately ones, as well; but these she has uplifted in honor of two or three colossal demigods who have stalked across the world's stage, destroying tyrants and delivering nations, and whose prodigies will still live in the memories of men ages after their monuments shall have crumbled to dust—I refer to the Wellington and Nelson monuments, and—the Albert memorial.

The library at the British Museum I find particularly astounding. I have read there hours together, and hardly made an impression on it. I revere that library. It is the author's friend. I don't care how mean a book is, it always takes one copy. [A copy of every book printed in Great Britain must by law be sent to the British Museum, a law much complained of by publishers.] And then every day that author goes there to gaze at that book, and is encouraged to go on in the good work. And what a touching sight it is of a Saturday afternoon to see the poor, careworn clergymen gathered together in that vast reading-room cabbaging sermons for Sunday. You will pardon my referring to these things. Everything in this monster city interests me, and I cannot keep from talking, even at the risk of being instructive. People here seem always to express distance by parables. To a stranger it is just a little confusing to be so parabolic—so to speak. I collar a citizen, and I think I am going to get some valuable information out of him. I ask him how far it is to Birmingham, and he says it is twenty-one shillings and sixpence. Now we know that doesn't help a man who is trying to learn. I find myself downtown somewhere, and I want to get some sort of idea where I am—being usually lost when alone—and I stop a citizen and say: "How far is it to Charing Cross?" "Shilling fare in a cab," and off he goes. I suppose if I were to ask a Londoner how far it is from the sublime to the ridiculous, he would try to express it in coin. But I am trespassing upon your time with these geological statistics and historical reflections. I will not longer keep you from your orgies. 'Tis a real pleasure for me to be here, and I thank you for it. The name of the Savage Club is associated in my mind with the kindly interest and the friendly offices which you lavished upon an old friend of mine who came among you a stranger, and you opened your English hearts to him and gave him welcome and a home—Artemus Ward. Asking that you will join me, I give you his memory.

THE LADIES

DELIVERED AT THE ANNIVERSARY FESTIVAL, 1872, OF THE SCOTTISH CORPORATION OF LONDON

Mr. Clemens replied to the toast "The Ladies."

I AM proud, indeed, of the distinction of being chosen to respond to this especial toast to "The Ladies," or to women if you please, for that is the preferable term, perhaps; it is certainly the older, and therefore the more entitled to reverence. I have noticed that the Bible, with that plain, blunt honesty which is such a conspicuous characteristic of the Scriptures, is always particular to never refer to even the illustrious mother of all mankind as a "lady," but speaks of her as a woman. It is odd, but you will find it is so. I am peculiarly proud of this honor, because I think that the toast to women is one which, by right and by every rule of gallantry, should take precedence of all others—of the army, of the navy, of even royalty itself—perhaps, though the latter is not necessary in this day and in this land, for the reason that, tacitly, you do drink a broad general health to all good women when you drink the health of the Queen of England and the Princess of Wales. I have in mind a poem just now which is familiar to you all, familiar to everybody. And what an inspiration that was, and how instantly the present toast recalls the verses to all our minds when the most noble, the most gracious, the purest, and sweetest of all poets says:

> "Woman! O woman!——er——
> Wom——"

However, you remember the lines; and you remember how feeling, how dainty, how almost imperceptibly the verses raise up before you, feature by feature, the ideal of a true and perfect woman, and how, as you contemplate the finished marvel, your homage grows into worship of the intellect that could create so fair a thing out of mere breath, mere words. And you call to mind now, as I speak, how the poet, with stern fidelity to the history of all humanity, delivers this beautiful child of his heart and his brain over to the trials and sorrows that must come to all, sooner or later, that abide in the earth, and how the pathetic story culminates in that apostrophe—so wild, so regretful, so full of mournful retrospection. The lines run thus:

> "Alas!—alas!—a—alas!
> — — Alas! — — — — alas!"

—and so on. I do not remember the rest; but, taken together, it seems to me that poem is the noblest tribute to woman that human genius has ever brought forth—and I feel that if I were to talk hours I could not do my great theme completer or more graceful justice than I have now done in simply quoting that poet's matchless words. The phases of the womanly nature are infinite in their variety. Take any type of woman, and you shall find in it something to respect, something to admire, something to love.

And you shall find the whole joining you heart and hand. Who was more patriotic than Joan of Arc? Who was braver? Who has given us a grander instance of self-sacrificing devotion? Ah! you remember well, what a throb of pain, what a great tidal wave of grief swept over us all when Joan of Arc fell at Waterloo. Who does not sorrow for the loss of Sappho, the sweet singer of Israel? Who among us does not miss the gentle ministrations, the softening influences, the humble piety of Lucretia Borgia? Who can join in the heartless libel that says woman is extravagant in dress when he can look back and call to mind our simple and lowly mother Eve arrayed in her modification of the Highland costume? Sir, women have been soldiers, women have been painters, women have been poets. As long as language lives the name of Cleopatra will live. And not because she conquered George III.—but because she wrote those divine lines:

> "Let dogs delight to bark and bite,
> For God hath made them so."

The story of the world is adorned with the names of illustrious ones of our own sex—some of them sons of St. Andrew, too—Scott, Bruce, Burns, the warrior Wallace, Ben Nevis—the gifted Ben Lomond, and the great new Scotchman, Ben Disraeli.* Out of the great plains of history tower whole mountain ranges of sublime women—the Queen of Sheba, Josephine, Semiramis, Sairey Gamp; the list is endless—but I

* Mr. Benjamin Disraeli, at that time Prime Minister of England, had just been elected Lord Rector of Glasgow University, and had made a speech which gave rise to a world of discussion.

will not call the mighty roll, the names rise up in your own memories at the mere suggestion, luminous with the glory of deeds that cannot die, hallowed by the loving worship of the good and the true of all epochs and all climes. Suffice it for our pride and our honor that we in our day have added to it such names as those of Grace Darling and Florence Nightingale. Woman is all that she should be—gentle, patient, long-suffering, trustful, unselfish, full of generous impulses. It is her blessed mission to comfort the sorrowing, plead for the erring, encourage the faint of purpose, succor the distressed, uplift the fallen, befriend the friendless—in a word, afford the healing of her sympathies and a home in her heart for all the bruised and persecuted children of misfortune that knock at its hospitable door. And when I say, God bless her, there is none among us who has known the ennobling affection of a wife, or the steadfast devotion of a mother but in his heart will say, Amen!

LICENSE OF THE PRESS

In a talk before the Monday Evening Club of Hartford, in 1873, Mark Twain set forth with some vigor Newspaper Sins and omissions incident to the period following the Civil War.

(First paragraph missing)

. . . IT (the press) has scoffed at religion till it has made scoffing popular. It has defended official criminals, on party pretexts, until it has created a United States Senate whose members are incapable of determining what crime against law and the dignity of their own body *is*, they are so morally blind, and it has made light of dishonesty till we have as a result a Congress which contracts to work for a certain sum and then deliberately steals additional wages out of the public pocket and is pained and surprised that anybody should worry about a little thing like that.

I am putting all this odious state of things upon the newspaper, and I believe it belongs there—chiefly, at any rate. It is a free press—a press that is more than free—a press which is licensed to say any infamous thing it chooses about a private or a public man, or advocate any outrageous doctrine it pleases. It is tied in *no* way. The public opinion which *should* hold it in bounds it has itself degraded to its own level. There are laws to protect the freedom of the press's speech, but none that are worth anything to protect the people from the press. A libel suit simply brings the plaintiff before a vast newspaper court to be tried before the law tries him, and reviled and ridiculed without mercy. The touchy Charles Reade can sue English newspapers and get verdicts; he would soon change his tactics here; the papers (backed by a public well taught by themselves) would soon teach him that it is better to suffer any amount of misrepresentation than go into our courts with a libel suit and make himself the laughing stock of the community.

It seems to me that just in the ratio that our newspapers increase, our morals decay. The more newspapers the worse morals. Where we have one newspaper that does good, I think we have fifty that do harm. We *ought* to look upon the establishment of a newspaper of the average pattern in a virtuous village as a calamity.

The difference between the tone and conduct of newspapers to-day and those of thirty or forty years ago is *very* noteworthy and very sad—I mean the average newspaper (for they had bad ones then, too). In those days the average newspaper was the champion of right and morals, and it dealt conscientiously in the truth. It is not the case now. The other day a reputable New York daily had an editorial defending the salary steal and justifying it on the ground that Congressmen were not paid enough—as if that were an all-sufficient excuse for stealing. That editorial put the matter in a new and perfectly satisfactory light with many a leather-headed reader, without a doubt. It has become a sarcastic proverb that a thing must be true if you saw it in a newspaper. That is the opinion intelligent people have of that lying vehicle in a nutshell. But the trouble is that the stupid people—who constitute the grand overwhelming majority of this and all other nations—*do* believe and *are* moulded and convinced by what they get out of a newspaper, and there is where the harm lies.

Among us, the newspaper is a tremendous power. It can make or mar any man's reputation. It has perfect freedom to call the best man in the land a fraud and a thief, and he is destroyed beyond help. Whether Mr. Colfax is a liar or not can never be ascertained now—but he will rank as one till the day of his death—for the newspapers have so doomed him. Our newspapers—*all* of them, without exception—glorify the "Black Crook" and make it an opulent success—they could have killed it dead with one broadside of contemptuous silence if they had wanted to. *Days Doings* and *Police Gazettes* flourish in the land unmolested by the law, because the *virtuous* newspapers long ago nurtured up a public laxity that loves indecency and never cares whether laws are administered or not.

In the newspapers of the West you can use the *editorial voice* in the editorial columns to defend any wretched and injurious dogma you please by paying a dollar a line for it.

Nearly all newspapers foster Rozensweigs and kindred criminals and send victims to them by opening their columns to their advertisements. You all know that.

In the Foster murder case the New York papers made a weak pretense of upholding the hands of the Governor and urging the people to sustain him in standing firmly by the law; but they printed a whole page of sickly, maudlin appeals to his clemency as a paid advertisement. And I suppose they would have published enough pages of abuse of the Governor to destroy his efficiency as a public official to the end of his term if anybody had come forward and paid them for it—as an advertisement. The newspaper that obstructs the law on a trivial pretext, for money's sake, is a dangerous enemy to the public weal.

That awful power, the public opinion of a nation, is created in America by a horde of ignorant, self-complacent simpletons who failed at ditching and shoemaking and fetched up in journalism on their way to the poorhouse. I am personally acquainted with hundreds of journalists, and the opinion of the majority of them would not be worth tuppence in private, but when they speak in print it is the *newspaper* that is talking (the pygmy scribe is not visible) and *then* their utterances shake the community like the thunders of prophecy.

I know from personal experience the proneness of journalists to lie. I once started a peculiar and picturesque fashion of lying myself on the Pacific coast, and it is not dead there to this day. Whenever I hear of a shower of blood and frogs combined, in California, or a sea serpent found in some desert, there, or a cave frescoed with diamonds and emeralds (*always* found by an Injun who died before he could finish telling where it was), I say to myself I am the father of this child—I have got to answer for this lie. And habit is everything—to this day I am liable to lie if I don't watch all the time.

The license of the press has scorched every individual of us in our time, I make no doubt. Poor Stanley was a very god, in England, his praises in every man's mouth. But nobody said anything about his lectures—they were charitably quiet on that head, and were content to praise his higher virtues. But our papers tore the poor creature limb from limb and scattered the fragments from Maine to California—merely because he couldn't lecture well. His prodigious achievement in Africa goes for naught — the man is pulled down and utterly destroyed—but *still* the persecution follows him as relentlessly from city to city and from village to village as if he had committed some bloody and detestable crime. Bret Harte was suddenly snatched out of obscurity by our papers and throned in the clouds—all the editors in the land stood out in the inclement weather and adored him through their telescopes and swung their hats till they wore them out and then borrowed more; and the first time his family fell sick, and in his trouble and harassment he ground out a rather flat article in place of another heathen Chinee, that hurrahing host said, "Why, this man's a fraud," and then they began to reach up there for him. And they got him, too, and fetched him down, and walked over him, and rolled him in the mud, and tarred and feathered him, and then set him up for a target and have been heaving dirt at him ever since. The result is that the man has had only just nineteen engagements to lecture this year, and the audience have been so scattering, too, that he has never discharged a sentence yet that hit two people at the same time. The man is ruined—never can get up again. And yet he is a person who has great capabilities, and might have accomplished great things for our literature and for himself if he had had a happier chance. And he made the mistake, too, of doing a pecuniary kindness for a starving beggar of our guild—one of the journalistic shoemaker class—and that beggar made it his business as soon as he got back to San Francisco to publish four columns of exposures of crimes committed by his benefactor, the least of which ought to make any decent man blush. The press that admitted that stuff to its columns had too much license.

In a town in Michigan I declined to dine with an editor who was drunk, and he said, in his paper, that my lecture was profane, indecent, and calculated to encourage intemperance. And yet that man never heard it. It might have reformed him if he had.

A Detroit paper once said that I was in the constant habit of beating my wife and that I still kept this recreation up, although I had crippled her for life and she was no longer able to keep out of my way when I came home in my usual frantic frame of mind. Now scarcely the half of that was true. Perhaps I ought to have sued that man for libel—but I knew better. All the papers in America—with a few creditable exceptions—would have found out then, to *their* satisfaction, that I was a wife beater, and they would have given it a pretty general airing, too.

Why *I* have published vicious libels upon people *myself*—and ought to have been hanged before my time for it, too—if I *do* say it myself, that shouldn't.

But I will not continue these remarks. I have a sort of vague general idea that there is too much liberty of the press in this country, and that through the absence of all wholesome restraint the newspaper has become in a large degree a national *curse*, and will probably damn the Republic yet.

There *are* some excellent virtues in newspapers, some powers that wield vast influences for good; and I could have told all about these things, and glorified them exhaustively—but that would have left you gentlemen nothing to say.

THE WEATHER

Address at the New England Society's Seventy-first Annual Dinner, New York City

The next toast was: "The Oldest Inhabitant—The Weather of New England."

Who can lose it and forget it?
Who can have and regret it?

"Be interposer 'twixt us Twain."
—Merchant of Venice.

I REVERENTLY believe that the Maker who made us all makes everything in New England but the weather. I don't know who makes that, but I think it must be raw apprentices in the weather-clerk's factory who experiment and learn how, in New England, for board and clothes, and then are promoted to make weather for countries that require a good article, and will take their custom elsewhere if they don't get it. There is a sumptuous variety about the New England weather that compels the stranger's admiration—and regret. The weather is always doing something there; always attending strictly to business; always getting up new designs and trying them on the people to see how they will go. But it gets through more business in spring than in any other season. In the spring I have counted one hundred and thirty-six different kinds of weather inside of four-and-twenty hours. It was

I that made the fame and fortune of that man who had that marvelous collection of weather on exhibition at the Centennial, which so astounded the foreigners. He was going to travel all over the world and get specimens from all the climes. I said, "Don't you do it; you come to New England on a favorable spring day." I told him what we could do in the way of style, variety, and quantity. Well, he came and he made his collection in four days. As to variety, why, he confessed that he got hundreds of kinds of weather that he had never heard of before. And as to quantity—well, after he had picked out and discarded all that was blemished in any way, he not only had weather enough, but weather to spare; weather to hire out; weather to sell; to deposit; weather to invest; weather to give to the poor. The people of New England are by nature patient and forbearing, but there are some things which they will not stand. Every year they kill a lot of poets for writing about "Beautiful Spring." These are generally casual visitors, who bring their notions of spring from somewhere else, and cannot, of course, know how the natives feel about spring. And so the first thing they know the opportunity to inquire how they feel has permanently gone by. Old Probabilities has a mighty reputation for accurate prophecy, and thoroughly well deserves it. You take up the paper and observe how crisply and confidently he checks off what to-day's weather is going to be on the Pacific, down South, in the Middle States, in the Wisconsin region. See him sail along in the joy and pride of his power till he gets to New England, and see his tail drop. *He* doesn't know what the weather is going to be in New England. Well, he mulls over it, and by and by he gets out something about like this: Probably northeast to southwest winds, varying to the southward and westward and eastward, and points between, high and low barometer swapping around from place to place; probable areas of rain, snow, hail, and drought, succeeded or preceded by earthquakes, with thunder and lightning. Then he jots down a postscript from his wandering mind, to cover accidents. "But it is possible that the programme may be wholly changed in the meantime." Yes, one of the brightest gems in the New England weather is the dazzling uncertainty of it. There is only one thing certain about it: you are certain there is going to be plenty of it—a perfect grand review; but you never can tell which end of the procession is going to move first. You fix up for the drought; you leave your umbrella in the house and sally out, and two to one you get drowned. You make up your mind that the earthquake is due; you stand from under, and take hold of something to steady yourself, and the first thing you know you get struck by lightning. These are great disappointments; but they can't be helped. The lightning there is peculiar; it is so convincing, that when it strikes a thing it doesn't leave enough of that thing behind for you to tell whether— Well, you'd think it was something valuable, and a Congressman had been there. And the thunder. When the thunder begins to merely tune up and scrape and saw, and key up the instruments for the performance, strangers say, "Why, what awful thunder you have here!" But when the baton is raised and the real concert begins, you'll find that stranger down in the cellar with his head in the ash-barrel. Now as to the *size* of the weather in New England—lengthways, I mean. It is utterly disproportioned to the size of that little country. Half the time, when it is packed as full as it can stick, you will see that New England weather sticking out beyond the edges and projecting around hundreds and hundreds of miles over the neighboring States. She can't hold a tenth part of her weather. You can see cracks all about where she has strained herself trying to do it. I could speak volumes about the inhuman perversity of the New England weather, but I will give but a single specimen. I like to hear rain on a tin roof. So I covered part of my roof with tin, with an eye to that luxury. Well, sir, do you think it ever rains on that tin? No, sir; skips it every time. Mind, in this speech I have been trying merely to do honor to the New England weather—no language could do it justice. But, after all, there is at least one or two things about that weather (or, if you please, effects produced by it) which we residents would not like to part with. If we hadn't our bewitching autumn foliage, we should still have to credit the weather with one feature which compensates for all its bullying vagaries—the ice storm: when a leafless tree is clothed with ice from the bottom to the top—ice that is as bright and clear as crystal; when every bough and twig is strung with ice beads, frozen dewdrops, and the whole tree sparkles cold and white like the Shah of Persia's diamond plume. Then the wind waves the branches and the sun comes out and turns all those myriads of beads and drops to prisms that glow and burn and flash with all manner of colored fires, which change and change again with inconceivable rapidity from blue to red, from red to green, and green to gold—the tree becomes a spraying fountain, a very explosion of dazzling jewels; and it stands there the acme, the climax, the supremest possibility in art or nature, of bewildering, intoxicating, intolerable magnificence. One cannot make the words too strong.

THE BABIES

DELIVERED AT THE BANQUET, IN CHICAGO, GIVEN BY THE ARMY OF THE TENNESSEE TO THEIR FIRST COMMANDER, GENERAL U. S. GRANT, NOVEMBER, 1879[1]

The fifteenth regular toast was "The Babies.—As they comfort us in our sorrows, let us not forget them in our festivities."

I LIKE that. We have not all had the good fortune to be ladies. We have not all been generals, or poets, or statesmen; but when the toast works down to the babies, we stand on common ground. It is a shame that for a thousand years the world's banquets have utterly ignored the baby, as if he didn't amount to anything. If you will stop and think a minute—if you will go back fifty or one hundred years to your early married life and recontemplate your first baby—you will remember that he amounted to a good deal, and even something over. You soldiers all know that when that little fellow arrived at family headquarters you had to hand in your resignation. He took entire command. You became his lackey, his mere body-servant, and you had to stand around, too. He was not a commander who made allowances for time, distance, weather, or anything else. You had to execute his order whether it was possible or not. And there

[1] The story of the delivery of this speech may be found in Chapter CXXIII of *Mark Twain—A Biography.*

was only one form of marching in his manual of tactics, and that was the double-quick. He treated you with every sort of insolence and disrespect, and the bravest of you didn't dare to say a word. You could face the death storm at Donelson and Vicksburg, and give back blow for blow; but when he clawed your whiskers, and pulled your hair, and twisted your nose, you had to take it. When the thunders of war were sounding in your ears you set your faces toward the batteries, and advanced with steady tread; but when he turned on the terrors of his war-whoop you advanced in the other direction, and mighty glad of the chance, too. When he called for soothing-syrup, did you venture to throw out any side-remarks about certain services being unbecoming an officer and a gentleman? No. You got up and *got* it. When he ordered his pap bottle and it was not warm, did you talk back? Not you. You went to work and *warmed* it. You even descended so far in your menial office as to take a suck at that warm, insipid stuff yourself, to see if it was right—three parts water to one of milk, a touch of sugar to modify the colic, and a drop of peppermint to kill those immortal hiccoughs. I can taste that stuff yet. And how many things you learned as you went along! Sentimental young folks still take stock in that beautiful old saying that when the baby smiles in his sleep, it is because the angels are whispering to him. Very pretty, but too thin—simply wind on the stomach, my friend. If the baby proposed to take a walk at his usual hour, two o'clock in the morning, didn't you rise up promptly and remark, with a mental addition which would not improve a Sunday-school book *much*, that that was the very thing you were about to propose yourself? Oh! you were under good discipline, and as you went fluttering up and down the room in your undress uniform, you not only prattled undignified baby talk, but even tuned up your martial voices and tried to *sing!—Rock-a-by Baby in the Tree-top*, for instance. What a spectacle for an Army of the Tennessee! And what an affliction for the neighbors, too; for it is not everybody within a mile around that likes military music at three in the morning. And when you had been keeping this sort of thing up two or three hours, and your little velvet-head intimated that nothing suited him like exercise and noise, what did you do? You simply *went* on until you dropped in the last ditch. The idea that a *baby* doesn't *amount* to anything! Why, *one* baby is just a house and a front yard full by itself. *One* baby can furnish more business than you and your whole Interior Department can attend to. He is enterprising, irrepressible, brimful of lawless activities. Do what you please, you can't make him stay on the reservation. Sufficient unto the day is one baby. As long as you are in your right mind don't you ever pray for twins. Twins amount to a permanent riot. And there ain't any real difference between triplets and an insurrection.

Yes, it was high time for a toastmaster to recognize the importance of the babies. Think what is in store for the present crop! Fifty years from now we shall all be dead, I trust, and then this flag, if it still survive (and let us hope it may), will be floating over a Republic numbering 200,000,000 souls, according to the settled laws of our increase. Our present schooner of State will have grown into a political leviathan—a *Great Eastern*. The cradled babies of to-day will be on deck. Let them be well trained, for we are going to leave a big contract on their hands. Among the three or four million cradles now rocking in the land are some which this nation would preserve for ages as sacred things, if we could know which ones they are. In one of these cradles the unconscious Farragut of the future is at this moment teething—think of it!—and putting in a world of dead earnest, unarticulated, but perfectly justifiable profanity over it, too. In another the future renowned astronomer is blinking at the shining Milky Way with but a languid interest—poor little chap!—and wondering what has become of that other one they call the wet-nurse. In another the future great historian is lying—and doubtless will continue to lie until his earthly mission is ended. In another the future President is busying himself with no profounder problem of state than what the mischief has become of his hair so early; and in a mighty array of other cradles there are now some 60,000 future office-seekers, getting ready to furnish him occasion to grapple with that same old problem a second time. And in still one more cradle, somewhere under the flag, the future illustrious commander-in-chief of the American armies is so little burdened with his approaching grandeurs and responsibilities as to be giving his whole strategic mind at this moment to trying to find out some way to get his big toe into his mouth—an achievement which, meaning no disrespect, the illustrious guest of this evening turned *his* entire attention to some fifty-six years ago; and if the child is but a prophecy of the man, there are mighty few who will doubt that he *succeeded.*

THE STORY OF A SPEECH

An address delivered in 1877, and a review of it twenty-nine years later. The original speech was delivered at a dinner given by the publishers of The Atlantic Monthly *in honor of the seventieth anniversary of the birth of John Greenleaf Whittier, at the Hotel Brunswick, Boston, December 17, 1877.*

The Speech

THIS is an occasion peculiarly meet for the digging up of pleasant reminiscences concerning literary folk; therefore I will drop lightly into history myself. Standing here on the shore of the Atlantic and contemplating certain of its largest literary billows, I am reminded of a thing which happened to me thirteen years ago, when I had just succeeded in stirring up a little Nevadian literary puddle myself, whose spume-flakes were beginning to blow thinly Californiaward. I started an inspection tramp through the southern mines of California. I was callow and conceited, and I resolved to try the virtue of my *nom de guerre*.

I very soon had an opportunity. I knocked at a miner's lonely log cabin in the foot-hills of the Sierras just at nightfall. It was snowing at the time. A jaded, melancholy man of fifty, barefooted, opened the door to me. When he heard my *nom de guerre* he looked more dejected than before. He let me in—pretty reluctantly, I thought—and after the customary bacon and beans, black coffee and hot whiskey, I took a pipe. This sorrowful man had not said three words up to this time. Now he spoke up and said, in the voice of one who is secretly suffering, "You're the fourth—I'm going to move." "The fourth what?" said I. "The fourth literary man that has been here in twenty-four hours—I'm going to move." "You don't tell me!" said I; "who were the others?" "Mr. Longfellow, Mr. Emerson, and Mr. Oliver Wendell Holmes—consound the lot!"

You can easily believe I was interested. I supplicated—three hot whiskies did the rest—and finally the melancholy miner began. Said he:

"They came here just at dark yesterday evening, and I let them in, of course. Said they were going to the Yosemite. They were a rough lot, but that's nothing; everybody looks rough that travels afoot. Mr. Emerson was a seedy little bit of a chap, red-headed. Mr. Holmes was as fat as a balloon; he weighed as much as three hundred, and had double chins all the way down to his stomach. Mr. Longfellow was built like a prize-fighter. His head was cropped and bristly, like as if he had a wig made of hair-brushes. His nose lay straight down his face, like a finger with the end joint tilted up. They had been drinking, I could see that. And what queer talk they used! Mr. Holmes inspected this cabin, then he took me by the buttonhole, and says he:

"'Through the deep caves of thought
I hear a voice that sings,
Build thee more stately mansions,
O my soul!'

"Says I, 'I can't afford it, Mr. Holmes, and moreover I don't want to.' Blamed if I liked it pretty well, either, coming from a stranger, that way. However, I started to get out my bacon and beans, when Mr. Emerson came and looked on awhile, and then *he* takes me aside by the buttonhole and says:

"'Gives me agates for my meat;
Gives me cantharids to eat;
From air and ocean bring me foods,
From all zones and altitudes.'

"Says I, 'Mr. Emerson, if you'll excuse me, this ain't no hotel.' You see it sort of riled me—I warn't used to the ways of littery swells. But I went on a-sweating over my work, and next comes Mr. Longfellow and buttonholes me, and interrupts me. Says he:

"'Honor be to Mudjekeewis!
You shall hear how Pau-Puk-Keewis—'

"But I broke in, and says I, 'Beg your pardon, Mr. Longfellow, if you'll be so kind as to hold your yawp for about five minutes and let me get this grub ready, you'll do me proud.' Well, sir, after they'd filled up I set out the jug. Mr. Holmes looks at it, and then he fires up all of sudden and yells:

"'Flash out a stream of blood-red wine!
For I would drink to other days.'

"By George, I was getting kind of worked up. I don't deny it, I was getting kind of worked up. I turns to Mr. Holmes, and says I, 'Looky here, my fat friend, I'm a-running this shanty, and if the court knows herself, you'll take whisky straight or you'll go dry.' Them's the very words I said to him.

Now I don't want to sass such famous littery people, but you see they kind of forced me. There ain't nothing onreasonable 'bout me; I don't mind a passel of guests a-treadin' on my tail three or four times, but when it comes to *standing* on it it's different, 'and if the court knows herself,' I says, 'you'll take whisky straight or you'll go dry.' Well, between drinks they'd swell around the cabin and strike attitudes and spout; and pretty soon they got out a greasy old deck and went to playing euchre at ten cents a corner—on trust. I began to notice some pretty suspicious things. Mr. Emerson dealt, looked at his hand, shook his head, says:

> "'I am the doubter and the doubt—'

and ca'mly bunched the hands and went to shuffling for a new layout. Says he:

> "'They reckon ill who leave me out;
> They know not well the subtle ways I keep
> I pass and deal *again!*'

Hang'd if he didn't go ahead and do it, too! Oh, he was a cool one! Well, in about a minute things were running pretty tight, but all of a sudden I see by Mr. Emerson's eye he judged he had 'em. He had already corralled two tricks, and each of the others one. So now he kind of lifts a little in his chair and says:

> "'I tire of globes and aces!—
> Too long the game is played!'

—and down he fetched a right bower. Mr. Longfellow smiles as sweet as pie and says:

> "'Thanks thanks to thee, my worthy friend,
> For the lesson thou hast taught,'

—and blamed if he didn't down with *another* right bower! Emerson claps his hand on his bowie, Longfellow claps his on his revolver, and I went under a bunk. There was going to be trouble; but that monstrous Holmes rose up, wobbling his double chins, and says he, 'Order, gentlemen; the first man that draws, I'll lay down on him and smother him!' All quiet on the Potomac, you bet!

"They were pretty how-come-you-so by now, and they begun to blow. Emerson says, 'The nobbiest thing I ever wrote was "Barbara Frietchie."' Says Longfellow, 'It don't begin with my "Biglow Papers."' Says Holmes, 'My "Thanatopsis" lays over 'em both.' They mighty near ended in a fight. Then they wished they had some more company—and Mr. Emerson pointed to me and says:

"'Is yonder squalid peasant all
That this proud nursery could breed?'

He was a-whetting his bowie on his boot—so I let it pass. Well, sir, next they took it into their heads that they would like some music; so they made me stand up and sing "When Johnny Comes Marching Home" till I dropped—at thirteen minutes past four this morning. That's what I've been through, my friend. When I woke at seven, they were leaving, thank goodness, and Mr. Longfellow had my only boots on, and his'n under his arm. Says I, 'Hold on, there, Evangeline, what are you going to do with *them?*' He says, 'Going to make tracks with 'em; because:

"'Lives of great men all remind us
We can make our lives sublime;
And, departing, leave behind us
Footprints on the sands of time.'

As I said, Mr. Twain, you are the fourth in twenty-four hours—and I'm going to move; I ain't suited to a littery atmosphere."

I said to the miner, "Why, my dear sir, *these* were not the gracious singers to whom we and the world pay loving reverence and homage; these were impostors.'

The miner investigated me with a calm eye for awhile; then said he, "Ah! impostors, were they? Are *you?*"

I did not pursue the subject, and since then I have not traveled on my *nom de guerre* enough to hurt. Such was the reminiscence I was moved to contribute, Mr. Chairman. In my enthusiasm I may have exaggerated the details a little, but you will easily forgive me that fault, since I believe it is the first time I have ever deflected from perpendicular fact on an occasion like this.

The Story

January 11, 1906.

Answer to a letter received this morning:

DEAR MRS. H.,—I am forever your debtor for reminding me of that curious passage in my life. During the first year or two after it happened, I could not bear to think of it. My pain and shame were so intense, and my sense of having been an imbecile so settled, established and confirmed, that I drove the episode entirely from my mind—and so all these twenty-eight or twenty-nine years I have lived in the conviction that my performance of that time was coarse, vulgar, and destitute of humor. But your suggestion that you and your family found humor in it twenty-eight years ago moved me to look into the matter. So I commissioned a Boston typewriter to delve among the Boston papers of that bygone time and send me a copy of it.

It came this morning, and if there is any vulgarity about it I am not to discover it. If it isn't innocently and ridiculously funny, I am no judge. I will see to it that you get a copy.

What I have said to Mrs. H. is true. I did suffer during a year or two from the deep humiliations of the episode. But at last, in 1888, in Venice, my wife and I came across Mr. and Mrs. A. P. C., of Concord, Massachusetts, and a friendship began then of the sort which nothing but death terminates. The C.'s were very bright people and in every way charming and companionable. We were together a month or two in Venice and several months in Rome, afterward, and one day that lamented break of mine was mentioned. And when I was on the point of lathering those people for bringing it to my mind when I had gotten the memory of it almost squelched, I perceived with joy that the C.'s were indignant about the way that my performance had been received in Boston. They poured out their opinions most freely and frankly about the frosty attitude of the people who were present at that performance, and about the Boston newspapers for the position they had taken in regard to the matter. That position was that I had been irreverent beyond belief, beyond imagination. Very well; I had accepted that as a fact for a year or two, and had been thoroughly miserable about it whenever I thought of it—which was not frequently, if I could help it. Whenever I thought of it I wondered how I ever could have been inspired to do so unholy a thing. Well, the C.'s comforted me, but they did not persuade me to continue to think about the unhappy episode. I resisted that. I tried to get it out of my mind, and let it die, and I succeeded. Until Mrs. H.'s letter came, it had been a good twenty-five years since I had thought of that matter; and when she said that the thing was funny I wondered if possibly she might be right. At any rate, my curiosity was aroused, and I wrote to Boston and got the whole thing copied, as above set forth.

I vaguely remembered some of the details of that gathering—dimly I can see a hundred people—no, perhaps fifty—shadowy figures sitting at tables feeding, ghosts now to me, and nameless forevermore. I don't know who they were, but I can very distinctly see, seated at the grand table and facing the rest of us, Mr. Emerson, supernaturally grave, unsmiling; Mr. Whittier, grave, lovely, his beautiful spirit shining out of his face; Mr. Longfellow, with his silken white hair and his benignant face; Dr. Oliver Wendell Holmes, flashing smiles and affection and all good-fellowship everywhere like a rose-diamond whose facets are being turned toward the light first one way and then another—a charming man, and always fascinating, whether he was talking or whether he was sitting still (what *he* would call still, but what would be more or less motion to other people). I can see those figures with entire distinctness across this abyss of time.

One other feature is clear—Willie Winter (for these past thousand years dramatic editor of the *New York Tribune*, and still occupying that high post in his old age) was there. He was much younger then than he is now, and he showed it. It was always a pleasure to me to see Willie Winter at a banquet. During a matter of twenty years I was seldom at a banquet where Willie Winter was not also present, and where he did not read a charming poem written for the occasion. He did it this time, and it was up to standard: dainty, happy, choicely phrased, and as good to listen to as music, and sounding exactly as if it was pouring unprepared out of heart and brain.

Now at that point ends all that was pleasurable about that notable celebration of Mr. Whittier's seventieth birthday—because *I* got up at that point and followed Winter, with what I have no doubt I supposed would be the gem of the evening—the gay oration above quoted from the Boston paper. I had written it all out the day before and had perfectly memorized it, and I stood up there at my genial and happy and self-satisfied ease, and began to deliver it. Those majestic guests, that row of venerable and still active volcanoes, listened, as did everybody else in the house, with attentive interest. Well, I delivered myself of—we'll say the first two hundred words of my speech. I was expecting no returns from that part of the speech, but this was not the case as regarded the rest of it. I arrived now at the dialogue: "The old miner said, 'You are the fourth, I'm going to move.' 'The fourth what?' said I. He answered, 'The fourth littery man that has been here in twenty-four hours. I am going to move.' 'Why, you don't tell me,' said I. 'Who were the others?' 'Mr. Longfellow, Mr. Emerson, Mr. Oliver Wendell Holmes, consound the lot—'"

Now, then, the house's *attention* continued, but the expression of interest in the faces turned to a sort of black frost. I wondered what the trouble was. I didn't know. I went on, but with difficulty—I struggled along, and entered upon that miner's fearful description of the bogus Emerson, the bogus Holmes, the bogus Longfellow, always hoping—but with a gradually perishing hope—that somebody would laugh, or that somebody would at least smile, but nobody did. I didn't know enough to give it up and sit down, I was too new to public speaking, and so I went on with this awful performance, and carried it clear through to the end, in front of a body of people who seemed turned to stone with horror. It was the sort of expression their faces would have worn if I had been making these remarks about the Deity and the rest of the Trinity; there is no milder way in which to describe the petrified condition and the ghastly expression of those people.

When I sat down it was with a heart which had long ceased to beat. I shall never be as dead again as I was then. I shall never be as miserable again as I was then. I speak now as one who doesn't know what the conditions of things may be in the next world, but in this one I shall never be as wretched again as I was then. Howells, who was near me, tried to say a comforting word, but couldn't get beyond a gasp. There was no use—he understood the whole size of the disaster. He had good intentions, but the words froze before they could get out. It was an atmosphere that would freeze anything. If Benvenuto Cellini's salamander had been in that place he would not have survived to be put into Cellini's autobiography. There was a frightful pause. There was an awful silence, a desolating silence. Then the next man on the list had to get up—there was no help for it. That was Bishop—Bishop had just burst handsomely upon the world with a most acceptable novel, which had appeared in The *Atlantic Monthly*, a place which would make any novel respectable and any author noteworthy. In this case the novel itself was recognized as being, without extraneous help, respectable. Bishop was away up in the public favor, and he was an object of high interest, consequently there was a sort of national expectancy in the air; we may say our American millions were standing, from Maine to Texas and from Alaska to Florida, holding their breath, their lips parted, their hands ready to applaud, when Bishop should get up on that occasion, and for the first time in his life speak in public. It was under these damaging conditions that he got up to "make good," as the vulgar say. I had spoken several times before, and that is the reason why I was able to go on without dying in my tracks, as I ought to have done—but Bishop had had no experience. He was up facing those awful deities—facing those other people, those strangers—facing human beings for the first time in his life, with a speech to utter. No doubt it was well packed away in his memory, no doubt it was fresh and usable, until I had been heard from. I suppose that after that, and under the smothering pall of that dreary silence, it began to waste away and disappear out of his head like the rags breaking from the edge of a fog, and presently there wasn't any fog left. He didn't go on—he didn't last long. It was not many sentences after his first before he began to hesitate, and break, and lost his grip, and totter, and wobble, and at last he slumped down in a limp and mushy pile.

Well, the programme for the occasion was probably not more than one-third finished, but it ended there. Nobody rose. The next man hadn't strength enough to get up, and everybody looked so dazed, so stupefied, paralyzed, it was impossible for anybody to do anything, or even try. Nothing could go on in that strange atmosphere. Howells mournfully, and without words, hitched himself to Bishop and me and supported us out of the room. It was very kind—he was most generous. He towed us tottering away into some room in that building, and we sat down there. I don't know what my remark was now, but I know the nature of it. It was the kind of remark you make when you know that nothing in the world can help your case. But Howells was honest—he had to say the heart-breaking things he did say: that there was no help for this calamity, this shipwreck, this cataclysm; that this was the most disastrous thing that had ever happened in anybody's history—and then he added, "That is, for *you*—and consider what you have done for Bishop. It is bad enough in your case, you deserve to suffer. You have committed this crime, and you deserve to have all you are going to get. But here is an innocent man. Bishop had never done you any harm, and see what you have done to him. He can never hold his head up again. The world can never look upon Bishop as being a live person. He is a corpse."

That is the history of that episode of twenty-eight

years ago, which pretty nearly killed me with shame during that first year or two whenever it forced its way into my mind.

Now then, I take that speech up and examine it. As I said, it arrived this morning, from Boston. I have read it twice, and unless I am an idiot, it hasn't a single defect in it from the first word to the last. It is just as good as good can be. It is smart; it is saturated with humor. There isn't a suggestion of coarseness or vulgarity in it anywhere. What could have been the matter with that house? It is amazing, it is incredible, that they didn't shout with laughter, and those deities the loudest of them all. Could the fault have been with me? Did I lose courage when I saw those great men up there whom I was going to describe in such a strange fashion? If that happened, if I showed doubt, that can account for it, for you can't be successfully funny if you show that you are afraid of it. Well, I can't account for it, but if I had those beloved and revered old literary immortals back here now on the platform at Carnegie Hall I would take that same old speech, deliver it, word for word, and melt them till they'd run all over that stage. Oh, the fault must have been with *me*, it is not in the speech at all.

Yet, characteristically enough, Mark Twain had quite another opinion of this unfortunate speech. Reading it for the first time after the lapse of nearly thirty years, he said: "I find it gross, coarse—well,

I needn't go into particulars. I don't like any part of it, from beginning to end."

It was only on the second reading that the spirit and delight of his old first conception returned, causing him to completely reverse this opinion and write the words of approval, as quoted.[1]

[1] For some further history of this curious episode the reader is referred to Howell's "*My Mark Twain*" and to "*Mark Twain—a Biography*," by A. B. Paine.

UNCONSCIOUS PLAGIARISM

DELIVERED AT THE DINNER GIVEN BY THE PUBLISHERS OF "THE ATLANTIC MONTHLY" TO OLIVER WENDELL HOLMES, IN HONOR OF HIS SEVENTIETH BIRTHDAY, AUGUST 29, 1879[1]

I WOULD have traveled a much greater distance than I have come to witness the paying of honors to Doctor Holmes; for my feeling toward him has always been one of peculiar warmth. When one receives a letter from a great man for the first time in his life, it is a large event to him, as all of you know by your own experience. You never can receive letters enough from famous men afterward to obliterate that one, or dim the memory of the pleasant surprise it was, and the gratification it gave you. Lapse of time cannot make it commonplace or cheap.

Well, the first great man who ever wrote me a letter was our guest—Oliver Wendell Holmes. He was also the first great literary man I ever stole anything from—and that is how I came to write to him and he to me. When my first book was new, a friend of mine said to me, "The dedication is very neat." Yes, I said, I thought it was. My friend said, "I always admired it, even before I saw it in *The Innocents Abroad.*" I naturally said: "What do

[1] This speech was felt to be in the nature of atonement for the "*Atlantic* Birthday-dinner" speech of two years before.

you mean? Where did you ever see it before?" "Well, I saw it first some years ago as Doctor Holmes's dedication to his *Songs in Many Keys*." Of course, my first impulse was to prepare this man's remains for burial, but upon reflection I said I would reprieve him for a moment or two and give him a chance to prove his assertion if he could. We stepped into a book-store, and he did prove it. I had really stolen that dedication, almost word for word. I could not imagine how this curious thing had happened; for I knew one thing—that a certain amount of pride always goes along with a teaspoonful of brains, and that this pride protects a man from deliberately stealing other people's ideas. That is what a teaspoonful of brains will do for a man—and admirers had often told me I had nearly a basketful—though they were rather reserved as to the size of the basket.

However, I thought the thing out, and solved the mystery. Two years before, I had been laid up a couple of weeks in the Sandwich Islands, and had read and re-read Doctor Holmes's poems till my mental reservoir was filled up with them to the brim. The dedication lay on the top, and handy, so, by and by, I unconsciously stole it. Perhaps I unconsciously stole the rest of the volume, too, for many people have told me that my book was pretty poetical, in one way or another. Well, of course, I wrote Doctor Holmes and told him I hadn't meant to steal, and he wrote back and said in the kindest way that it was all right and no harm done; and added that he believed we all unconsciously worked over ideas gathered in reading and hearing, imagining they were original with ourselves. He stated a truth, and did it in such a pleasant way, and salved over my sore spot so gently and so healingly, that I was rather glad I had committed the crime, for the sake of the letter. I afterward called on him and told him to make perfectly free with any ideas of mine that struck him as being good protoplasm for poetry. He could see by that that there wasn't anything mean about me; so we got along right from the start. I have not met Doctor Holmes many times since; and lately he said— However, I am wandering wildly away from the one thing which I got on my feet to do; that is, to make my compliments to you, my fellow teachers of the great public, and likewise to say that I am right glad to see that Doctor Holmes is still in his prime and full of generous life; and as age is not determined by years, but by trouble and infirmities of mind and body, I hope it may be a very long time yet before any one can truthfully say, "He is growing old."

ACCIDENT INSURANCE—ETC.

Delivered in Hartford, at a Dinner to Cornelius Watford, of London

GENTLEMEN,—I am glad, indeed, to assist in welcoming the distinguished guest of this occasion to a city whose fame as an insurance center has extended to all lands, and given us the name of being a quadruple band of brothers working sweetly hand in hand—the Colt's arms company making the destruction of our race easy and convenient, our life-insurance citizens paying for the victims when they pass away, Mr. Batterson perpetuating their memory with his stately monuments, and our fire-insurance comrades taking care of their hereafter. I am glad to assist in welcoming our guest—first, because he is an Englishman, and I owe a heavy debt of hospitality to certain of his fellow-countrymen; and secondly, because he is in sympathy with insurance, and has been the means of making many other men cast their sympathies in the same direction.

Certainly there is no nobler field for human effort than the insurance line of business—especially accident insurance. Ever since I have been a director in an accident-insurance company I have felt that I am a better man. Life has seemed more precious. Accidents have assumed a kindlier aspect. Distressing special providences have lost half their horror. I look upon a cripple now with affectionate interest—as an advertisement. I do not seem to care for poetry any more. I do not care for politics—even agriculture does not excite me. But to me now there is a charm about a railway collision that is unspeakable.

There is nothing more beneficent than accident insurance. I have seen an entire family lifted out of poverty and into affluence by the simple boon of a broken leg. I have had people come to me on crutches, with tears in their eyes, to bless this beneficent institution. In all my experience of life, I have seen nothing so seraphic as the look that comes into a freshly mutilated man's face when he feels in his vest pocket with his remaining hand and finds his accident ticket all right. And I have seen nothing so sad as the look that came into another splintered customer's face when he found he couldn't collect on a wooden leg.

I will remark here, by way of advertisement, that that noble charity which we have named the HARTFORD ACCIDENT INSURANCE COMPANY* is an institution which is peculiarly to be depended upon. A man is bound to prosper who gives it his custom. No man can take out a policy in it and not get crippled before the year is out. Now there was one indigent man who had been disappointed so often with other companies that he had grown disheartened, his appetite left him, he ceased to smile—said life was but a weariness. Three weeks ago I got him to insure with us, and now he is the brightest, happiest

* The speaker was a director of the company named.

spirit in this land—has a good steady income and a stylish suit of new bandages every day, and travels around on a shutter.

I will say, in conclusion, that my share of the welcome to our guest is none the less hearty because I talk so much nonsense, and I know that I can say the same for the rest of the speakers.

Oliver Wendell Holmes

ON AFTER-DINNER SPEAKING

At a Dinner to Monsieur Frechette of Quebec, 1880

I HAVE broken a vow in order that I might give myself the pleasure of meeting my friend Frechette again. But that is nothing to brag about; a person who is rightly constructed will break a vow any time to meet a friend. Before I last met Monsieur Frechette, he had become the child of good fortune—that is to say, his poems had been crowned by the Academy of France; since I last met him he has become the child of good fortune once more—that is to say, I have translated his poems into English and written a eulogy of them in the French language to preface the work. He possessed a single-barrelled fame before; he will possess a double-barrelled fame now. For this reason: translations always reverse a thing and bring an entirely new side of it into view, thus doubling the property and making two things out of what was only one thing before. So, in my translation his pathetic poems have naturally become humorous, his humorous poems have become sad. Anybody who knows even the rudiments of arithmetic will know that Monsieur Frechette's poems are now worth exactly twice as much as they were before. I am glad to help welcome the laureate of Quebec to our soil; and I assure him that we will do our best to leave him no room to regret that he came.

Yes, as I was saying, I broke a vow. If it had been a trig, shiny, brand-new one, I should be sorry, of course, for it is always wrong and a pity to mistreat and injure good new property; but this was different; I don't regret this one, because it was an old ragged ramshackle vow that had seen so much service and been broken so often, and patched and spliced together in so many places, that it was become a disgraceful object, and so rotten that I could never venture to put any strain worth mentioning upon it. This vow was a vow which I first made eleven years ago, on a New-Year's Day that I would never make another after-dinner speech as long as I lived. It was as good a vow then as I ever saw; but I have broken it in sixty-four places, since, and mended it up fresh every New-Year's. Seven years ago I reformed in another way: I made a vow that I would lead an upright life—meaning by that that I would never deliver another lecture. I believe I have never broken that one; I think I can be true to it always, and thus disprove the Rev. Petroleum V. Nasby's maxim that "burglars and lecturers never reform." But this other vow has always been beyond my strength—I mean, I have always been beyond its strength. The reason is simple: it lies in the fact that the average man likes to hear himself talk, when he is not under criticism. The very man who sneers at your after-dinner speech when he reads it in next morning's paper, would have been powerfully moved to make just as poor a one himself if he had been present, with the encouraging champagne in him and the friendly, uncritical faces all about him.

But that discourteous man doesn't do all the sneering that is done over your speech; no, he does only a tenth of it—you do the other nine-tenths yourself. Your little talk, which sounded so fine and warbly and nice when you were delivering it in the mellow light of the lamps and in an enchanted atmosphere of applause and all-pervading good-fellowship, looks miserably pale and vapid and lifeless in the cold print of a damp newspaper next morning, with obituaries and cast-iron politics all around it and the hard gray light of day shining upon it and mocking at it. You do not recognize the corpse. You wonder if this is really that gay and handsome creature of the evening before. You look him over and find he certainly is those very remains. Then you want to bury him. You wish you could bury him privately.

PLYMOUTH ROCK AND THE PILGRIMS

ADDRESS AT THE FIRST ANNUAL DINNER, N. E. SOCIETY, PHILADELPHIA, DECEMBER 22, 1881

On calling upon Mr. Clemens to make response, President Rollins said:

"This sentiment has been assigned to one who was never *exactly* born in New England, nor, perhaps, were any of his ancestors. He is not *technically*, therefore, of New England descent. Under the painful circumstances in which he has found himself, however, he has done the best he could—he has had all his children born there,[1] and has made of *himself* a New England *ancestor*. He is a self-made man. More than this, and better even, in cheerful, hopeful, helpful literature he is of New England *ascent*. To *ascend* there in anything that's reasonable is difficult, for—confidentially, with the door shut—we all know that they are the brightest, ablest sons of that goodly land who never leave it, and it is among and above *them* that Mr. Twain has made his brilliant and permanent ascent—become a man of mark."

I RISE to protest. I have kept still for years, but really I think there is no sufficient justification for this sort of thing. What do you want to celebrate those people for?—those ancestors of yours of 1620—the *Mayflower* tribe, I mean. What do you want to celebrate *them* for? Your pardon: the gentleman at my left assures me that you are not celebrating the Pilgrims themselves, but the landing of the Pilgrims at Plymouth Rock on the 22d of December. So you

[1] A slight mistake: Mark Twain's children were born at Elmira, in the state of New York.

are celebrating their landing. Why, the other pretext was thin enough, but this is thinner than ever; the other was tissue, tinfoil, fish-bladder, but this is gold-leaf. Celebrating their landing! What was there remarkable about it, I would like to know? What can you be thinking of? Why, those Pilgrims had been at sea three or four months. It was the very middle of winter: it was as cold as death off Cape Cod there. Why shouldn't they come ashore? If they *hadn't* landed there would be some reason for celebrating the fact. It would have been a case of monumental leatherheadedness which the world would not willingly let die. If it had been *you*, gentlemen, you probably wouldn't have landed, but you have no shadow of right to be celebrating, in your ancestors, gifts which they did not exercise, but only transmitted. Why, to be celebrating the mere landing of the Pilgrims—to be trying to make out that this most natural and simple and customary procedure was an extraordinary circumstance—a circumstance to be amazed at, and admired, aggrandized and glorified, at orgies like this for two hundred and sixty years—hang it, a horse would have known enough to land; a horse— Pardon again; the gentleman on my right assures me that it was not merely the landing of the Pilgrims that we are celebrating, but the Pilgrims themselves. So we have struck an inconsistency here—one says it was the landing, the other says it was the Pilgrims. It is an inconsistency characteristic of you intractable and disputatious tribe, for you never agree about anything but Boston. Well, then, what do you want to celebrate those

Pilgrims for? They were a mighty hard lot—you know it. I grant you, without the slightest unwillingness, that they were a deal more gentle and merciful and just than were the people of Europe of that day; I grant you that they are better than their predecessors. But what of that?—that is nothing. People always progress. You are better than your fathers and grandfathers were (this is the first time I have ever aimed a measureless slander at the departed, for I consider such things improper). Yes, those among you who have not been in the penitentiary, if such there be, are better than your fathers and grandfathers were; but is that any sufficient reason for getting up annual dinners and celebrating you? No, by no means—by no means. Well, I repeat, those Pilgrims were a hard lot. They took good care of themselves, but they abolished everybody else's ancestors. I am a border-ruffian from the State of Missouri. I am a Connecticut Yankee by adoption. In me, you have Missouri morals, Connecticut culture; this, gentlemen, is the combination which makes the perfect man. But where are my ancestors? Whom shall I celebrate? Where shall I find the raw material?

My first American ancestor, gentlemen, was an Indian—an early Indian. Your ancestors skinned him alive, and I am an orphan. Later ancestors of mine were the Quakers William Robinson, Marmaduke Stevenson, *et al.* Your tribe chased them out of the country for their religion's sake; promised them death if they came back; for your ancestors had forsaken the homes they loved, and braved the perils of the sea, the implacable climate, and the savage wilderness, to acquire that highest and most precious of boons, freedom for every man on this broad continent to worship according to the dictates of his own conscience—and they were not going to allow a lot of pestiferous Quakers to interfere with it. Your ancestors broke forever the chains of political slavery, and gave the vote to every man in this wide land, excluding none!—none except those who did not belong to the orthodox church. Your ancestors—yes, they were a hard lot; but, nevertheless, they gave us religious liberty to worship as they required us to worship, and political liberty to vote as the church required; and so I the bereft one, I the forlorn one, am here to do my best to help you celebrate them right.

The Quaker woman Elizabeth Hooton was an ancestress of mine. Your people were pretty severe with her—you will confess that. But, poor thing! I believe they changed her opinions before she died, and took her into their fold; and so we have every reason to presume that when she died she went to the same place which your ancestors went to. It is a great pity, for she was a good woman. Roger Williams was an ancestor of mine. I don't really remember what your people did with him. But they banished him to Rhode Island, anyway. And then, I believe, recognizing that this was really carrying harshness to an unjustifiable extreme, they took pity on him and burned him. They were a hard lot! All those Salem witches were ancestors of mine! Your people made it tropical for them. Yes, they did;

by pressure and the gallows they made such a clean deal with them that there hasn't been a witch and hardly a halter in our family from that day to this, and that is one hundred and eighty-nine years. The first slave brought into New England out of Africa by your progenitors was an ancestor of mine—for I am of a mixed breed, an infinitely shaded and exquisite Mongrel. I'm not one of your sham meerschaums that you can color in a week. No, my complexion is the patient art of eight generations. Well, in my own time, I had acquired a lot of my kin—by purchase, and swapping around, and one way and another—and was getting along very well. Then, with the inborn perversity of your lineage, you got up a war, and took them all away from me. And so, again am I bereft, again am I forlorn; no drop of my blood flows in the veins of any living being who is marketable.

O my friends, hear me and reform! I seek your good, not mine. You have heard the speeches. Disband these New England societies—nurseries of a system of steadily augmenting laudation and hosannaing, which, if persisted in uncurbed, may some day in the remote future beguile you into prevaricating and bragging. Oh, stop, stop, while you are still temperate in your appreciation of your ancestors! Hear me, I beseech you; get up an auction and sell Plymouth Rock! The Pilgrims were a simple and ignorant race. They never had seen any good rocks before, or at least any that were not watched, and so they were excusable for hopping ashore in frantic delight and clapping an iron fence around this one.

But you, gentlemen, are educated; you are enlightened; you know that in the rich land of your nativity, opulent New England, overflowing with rocks, this one isn't worth, at the outside, more than thirty-five cents. Therefore, sell it, before it is injured by exposure, or at least throw it open to the patent-medicine advertisements, and let it earn its taxes.

Yes, hear your true friend—your only true friend—list to his voice. Disband these societies, hotbeds of vice, of moral decay—perpetuators of ancestral superstition. Here on this board I see water, I see milk, I see the wild and deadly lemonade. These are but steps upon the downward path. Next we shall see tea, then chocolate, then coffee—hotel coffee. A few more years—all too few, I fear—mark my words, we shall have cider! Gentlemen, pause ere it be too late. You are on the broad road which leads to dissipation, physical ruin, moral decay, gory crime, and the gallows! I beseech you, I implore you, in the name of your anxious friends, in the name of your impending widows and orphans, stop ere it be too late. Disband these New England societies, renounce these soul-blistering saturnalia, cease from varnishing the rusty reputations of your long-vanished ancestors—the super-high-moral old iron-clads of Cape Cod, the pious buccaneers of Plymouth Rock—go home, and try to learn to behave!

However, chaff and nonsense aside, I think I honor and appreciate your Pilgrim stock as much as you do yourselves, perhaps; and I indorse and adopt a sentiment uttered by a grandfather of mine once—a man of sturdy opinions, of sincere make of mind, and not given to flattery. He said: "People may talk as they like about that Pilgrim stock, but, after all's said and done, it would be pretty hard to improve on those people; and, as for me, I don't mind coming out flatfooted and saying there ain't any way to improve on them—except having them born in Missouri!"

ON ADAM

DELIVERED ABOUT 1880-85. (EXACT OCCASION UNKNOWN.)

I NEVER feel wholly at home and equal to the occasion except when I am to respond for the royal family, or the President of the United States. But I am full of serenity, courage, and confidence then, because I know by experience that I can drink standing "in silence" just as long as anybody wants me to. Sometimes I have gone on responding to those toasts with mute and diligent enthusiasm until I have become an embarrassment, and people have requested me to sit down and rest myself. But responding by speech is a sore trial to me. The list of toasts being always the same, one is always so apt to forget and say something that has already been said at some other banquet some time or other. For instance, you take the toast to—well, take any toast in the regulation lot, and you won't get far in your speech before you notice that everything you are saying is old; not only old, but stale; and not only stale, but rancid. At any rate, that is my experience. There are gifted men who have the faculty of saying an old thing in a new and happy way—they rub the old Aladdin lamp and bring forth the smoke and thunder, the giants and genii, the pomp and pageantry of all the wide and secret realms of enchantment—and these men are the saviors of the banquet; but for them it must have gone silent, as Carlyle would say, generations ago, and ceased from among the world's occasions and industries. But I cannot borrow their trick; I do not know the mystery of how to rub the old lamp the right way.

And so it has seemed to me that for the behoof of my sort and kind, the toast list ought to be reconstructed. We ought to have some of the old themes knocked out of it and a new one or two inserted in their places. There are plenty of new subjects, if we would only look around. And plenty of old ones, too, that have not been touched. There is Adam, for instance. Whoever talks about Adam at a banquet? All sorts of recent and ephemeral celebrities are held up and glorified on such occasions, but who ever says a good word for Adam? Yet why is he neglected, why is he ignored in this offensive way—can you tell me that? What has he done, that we let banquet after banquet go on and never give him a lift? Considering what we and the whole world owe him, he ought to be in the list—yes, and he ought to be away up high in the list, too. He ought to take precedence of the Press; yes, and the Army and Navy; and Literature; and the Day we Celebrate; and pretty much everything else. In the United States he ought to be at the very top—he ought to take precedence of the President; and even in the loyalist monarchy he ought at least to come right after the royal family. And be "drunk in silence and standing," too. It is his right; and, for one, I propose to stick here and *drink* him in silence and standing till I can't tell a ministering angel from a tax collector. This neglect has been going on too long. You always place Woman at the bottom of the toast list; it is but simple justice to place Adam at the top of it—for, if it had not been for the help of these two, where would you and your banquets be? Answer me that. You must excuse me for losing my temper and carrying on in this way; and in truth I would not do it if it were almost anybody but Adam; but I am of a narrow and clannish disposition, and I never can see a relative of mine misused without going into a passion. It is no trick for people with plenty of celebrated kin to keep cool when their folk are misused; but Adam is the only solitary celebrity in our family, and that man that misuses him has got to walk over my dead body, or go around, that is all there is to that. That is the way I feel about Adam. Years ago when I went around trying to collect subscriptions to build a monument to him, there wasn't a man that would give a cent; and generally they lost their temper because I interrupted their business, and they drove me away and said they didn't care A-dam for Adam—and in ninety-nine cases out of a hundred they got the emphasis on the wrong end of the word. Such is the influence of passion on a man's pronunciation. I tried Congress. Congress wouldn't build the monument. They wouldn't sell me the Washington monument, they wouldn't lend it to me temporarily while I could look around for another. I am negotiating for that Bastile yonder by the public square in Montreal, but they say they want to finish it first. Of course that ends the project, because there couldn't be any use of a monument after the man was forgotten. It is a pity, because I thought Adam might have pleasant associations with that building—he must have seen it in his time. But he shall have a monument yet, even if it be only a grateful place in the list of toasts; for to him we owe the two things which are most precious—Life and Death. Life, which the young, the hopeful, the undefeated hold above all wealth and all honors; and Death, the refuge, the solace, the best and kindliest and most prized friend and benefactor of the erring, the forsaken, the old, and weary, and broken of heart, whose burdens be heavy upon them, and who would lie down and be at rest.

I would like to see the toast list reconstructed, for it seems to me a needed reform; and as a beginning in this direction, if I can meet with a second, I beg to nominate Adam. I am not actuated by family considerations. It is a thing which I would do for any other member of our family, or anybody else's if I could honestly feel that he deserved it. But I do not. If I seem to be always trying to shove Adam into prominence, I can say sincerely that it is solely because of my admiration of him as a man who was a good citizen; a good husband at a time when he was not married; a good father at a time when he had to guess his way, having never been young himself; and would have been a good son if he had had the chance. He could have been governor if he had wanted to. He could have been postmaster-general, speaker of the house, he could have been anything he chose, if he had been willing to put himself up and stand a canvass. Yet he lived and died a private citizen, without a handle to his name, and he comes down to us as plain, simple Adam, and nothing more—a man who could have elected himself Major-General Adam or anything else as easy as rolling off a log. A man who comes down to us without a stain upon his name, unless it was a stain to take one apple when most of us would have taken the whole crop. I stand up for him on account of his sterling private virtues, and not because he happens to be a connection of mine.

SPEECH OF SAMUEL L. CLEMENS

THIRTEENTH ANNUAL REUNION OF THE ARMY OF THE POTOMAC, HELD IN HARTFORD, CONNECTICUT, JUNE 8, 1881

(Reported by the Hartford "Courant")

To the regular toast, "The Benefit of Judicious Training," Samuel L. Clemens (Mark Twain), responded as follows:—

"Let but the thoughtful civilian instruct the soldier in his duties, and the victory is sure."—Martin Farquhar Tupper on the Art of War.

MR. CHAIRMAN,—I gladly join with my fellow-townsmen in extending a hearty welcome to these illustrious generals and war-scarred soldiers of the Republic. This is a proud day for us, and, if the sincere desire of our hearts has been fulfilled, it has not been an unpleasant day for them. I am in full accord, sir, with the sentiment of the toast—for I have always maintained, with enthusiasm, that the only wise and true way is for the soldier to fight the battle and the unprejudiced civilian to tell him how to do it; yet when I was invited to respond to this toast and furnish this advice and instruction, I was almost as embarrassed as I was gratified; for I could bring to this great service but the one virtue of absence of prejudice and set opinion.

Still, but one other qualification was needed, and it was of only minor importance—I mean, knowledge of the subject—therefore I was not disheartened, for

I could acquire that, there being two weeks to spare. A general of high rank in this Army of the Potomac said two weeks was really more than I would need for the purpose—he had known people of my style who had learned enough in forty-eight hours to enable them to advise an army. Aside from the compliment, this was gratifying, because it confirmed the impression I had had before. He told me to go to the United States Military Academy at West Point—said in his flowery professional way that the cadets would "load me up." I went there and stayed two days, and his prediction proved correct. I make no boast on my own account—none; all I know about military matters I got from the gentlemen at West Point, and to them belongs the credit. They treated me with courtesy from the first; but when my mission was revealed, this mere courtesy blossomed into the warmest zeal. Everybody, officers and all, put down their work and turned their whole attention to giving me military information. Every question I asked was promptly and exhaustively answered. Therefore I feel proud to state that in the advice which I am about to give you, as soldiers, I am backed up by the highest military authority in the land, yes, in the world, if an American does say it—West Point!

To begin, gentlemen. When an engagement is meditated, it is best to feel the enemy first. That is, if it is night; for, as one of the cadets explained to me, you do not need to feel him in the daytime, because you can see him then. I never should have thought of that, but it is true—perfectly true. In the daytime the methods of procedure are various; but the best, it seems to me, is one which was introduced by General Grant. General Grant always sent an active young redoubt to reconnoitre and get the enemy's bearings. I got this from a high officer at the Point, who told me he used to be a redoubt on General Grant's staff and had done it often.

When the hour for the battle is come, move to the field with celerity—fool away no time. Under this head I was told of a favorite maxim of General Sheridan's. General Sheridan always said, "If the siege train isn't ready, don't wait; go by any train that is handy; to get there is the main thing." Now that is the correct idea. As you approach the field it is best to get out and walk. This gives you a better chance to dispose your forces judiciously for the assault. Get your artillery in position, and throw out stragglers to right and left to hold your lines of communication against surprise. See that every hodcarrier connected with the mortar battery is at his post. They told me at the Point that Napoleon despised mortar batteries and never would use them; he said that for real efficiency he wouldn't give a hatful of brickbats for a ton of mortar. However, that is all *he* knew about it.

Everything being ready for the assault, you want to enter the field with your baggage to the front. This idea was invented by our renowned guest, General Sherman. They told me General Sherman said the trunks and steamer chairs make a good protection for the soldiers, but that chiefly they attract the attention and rivet the interest of the enemy and this gives you an opportunity to whirl the other end of the column around and attack him in the rear. I have given a good deal of study to this tactic since I learned about it, and it appears to me it is a rattling-good idea. Never fetch on your reserves at the start. This was Napoleon's first mistake at Waterloo; next he assaulted with his bomb proofs and embrasures and ambulances, when he ought to have used a heavier artillery; thirdly, he retired his right by ricochet—which uncovered his pickets—when his only possibility of success lay in doubling up his center flank by flank and throwing out his chevaux-de-frise by the left oblique to relieve the skirmish line and confuse the enemy—and at West Point they said it would. It was about this time that the emperor had two horses shot under him. How often you see the remark that General So-and-So in such and such a battle had two or three horses shot under him. General Burnside and many great European military men—as I was informed by a high artillery officer at West Point, has justly characterized this as a wanton waste of projectiles, and he impressed upon me a conversation held in the tent of the Prussian chiefs at Gravelotte, in the course of which our honored guest just referred to—General Burnside—observed that if you can't aim a horse so as to hit the general with it, shoot it over him and you may bag somebody on the other side, whereas a horse shot under a general does no sort of damage. I agree cordially with General Burnside, and Heaven knows I shall rejoice to see the artillerists of this land and all lands cease from this wicked and idiotic custom.

At West Point they told me of another mistake at Waterloo, *viz.*, that the French were under fire from the beginning of the fight until the end of it, which was plainly a most effeminate and ill-timed attention to comfort, and a fatal and foolish division of military strength; for it probably took as many men to keep up the fires as it did to do the fighting. It would have been much better to have a small fire in the rear and let the men go there by detachments and get warm, and not try to warm up the whole army at once. All the cadets said that. An assault along the whole line was the one thing which could have restored Napoleon's advantages at this juncture; and he was actually rising in his stirrups to order it when a sutler burst at his side and covered him with dirt and debris; and before he could recover his lost opportunity Wellington opened a tremendous and devastating fire upon him from a monster battery of vivandières, and the star of the great captain's glory set, to rise no more. The cadet wept while he told me these mournful particulars.

When you leave a battlefield, always leave it in good order. Remove the wreck and rubbish and tidy up the place. However, in the case of a drawn battle, it is neither party's business to tidy up anything—you can leave the field looking as if the city government of New York had bossed the fight.

When you are traversing in the enemy's country in order to destroy his supplies and cripple his resources, you want to take along plenty of camp followers—the more the better. They are a tremendously effective arm of the service, and they inspire in the foe the liveliest dread. A West Point professor told me that the wisdon of this was recognized as far back as Scripture times. He quoted the verse. He said it was from the new revision and was a little different from the way it reads in the old one. I do not recollect the exact wording of it now, but I remember that it wound up with something about such-and-such a devastating agent being as "terrible as an army with bummers."

I believe I have nothing further to add but this: The West Pointer said a private should preserve a respectful attitude toward his superiors, and should seldom or never proceed so far as to offer suggestions to his general in the field. If the battle is not being conducted to suit him it is better for him to resign. By the etiquette of war, it is permitted to none below the rank of newspaper correspondent to dictate to the general in the field.

[While Mr. Clemens was speaking a band came down the street and struck up "Marching Through Georgia" in front of the hall. The remarks were interrupted. A voice in the hall started the words, others took it up, and the band finally joined in, producing a thrilling effect. Hardly had Mr. Clemens resumed when the outside band began "Auld Lang Syne," and, grasping the situation, he waved his hand in unison with the music, and the assemblage sang the words to the finish.]

ADVICE TO YOUTH

ABOUT 1882

BEING told I would be expected to talk here, I inquired what sort of a talk I ought to make. They said it should be something suitable to youth—something didactic, instructive, or something in the nature of good advice. Very well. I have a few things in my mind which I have often longed to say for the instruction of the young; for it is in one's tender early years that such things will best take root and be most enduring and most valuable. First, then, I will say to you, my young friends—and I say it beseechingly, urgingly——

Always obey your parents, when they are present. This is the best policy in the long run, because if you don't they will make you. Most parents think they know better than you do, and you can generally make more by humoring that superstition than you can by acting on your own better judgment.

Be respectful to your superiors, if you have any, also to strangers, and sometimes to others. If a person offend you, and you are in doubt as to whether it was intentional or not, do not resort to extreme measures; simply watch your chance and hit him with a brick. That will be sufficient. If you shall find that he had not intended any offense, come out frankly and confess yourself in the wrong when you struck him; acknowledge it like a man and say you didn't mean to. Yes, always avoid violence; in this age of charity and kindliness, the time has gone by for such things. Leave dynamite to the low and unrefined.

Go to bed early, get up early—this is wise. Some authorities say get up with the sun; some others say get up with one thing, some with another. But a lark is really the best thing to get up with. It gives you a splendid reputation with everybody to know that you get up with the lark; and if you get the right kind of a lark, and work at him right, you can easily train him to get up at half past nine, every time—it is no trick at all.

Now as to the matter of lying. You want to be very careful about lying; otherwise you are nearly sure to get caught. Once caught, you can never again be, in the eyes of the good and the pure, what you were before. Many a young person has injured himself permanently through a single clumsy and ill-finished lie, the result of carelessness born of incomplete training. Some authorities hold that the young ought not to lie at all. That, of course, is putting it rather stronger than necessary; still, while I cannot go quite so far as that, I do maintain, and I believe I am right, that the young ought to be temperate in the use of this great art until practice and experience shall give them that confidence, elegance, and precision which alone can make the accomplishment graceful and profitable. Patience, diligence, painstaking attention to detail—these are the requirements; these, in time, will make the student perfect;

upon these, and upon these only, may he rely as the sure foundation for future eminence. Think what tedious years of study, thought, practice, experience, went to the equipment of that peerless old master who was able to impose upon the whole world the lofty and sounding maxim that "truth is mighty and will prevail"—the most majestic compound fracture of fact which any of woman born has yet achieved. For the history of our race, and each individual's experience, are sown thick with evidence that a truth is not hard to kill and that a lie told well is immortal. There in Boston is a monument of the man who discovered anæsthesia; many people are aware, in these latter days, that that man didn't discover it at all, but stole the discovery from another man. Is this truth mighty, and will it prevail? Ah no, my hearers, the monument is made of hardy material, but the lie it tells will outlast it a million years. An awkward, feeble, leaky lie is a thing which you ought to make it your unceasing study to avoid; such a lie as that has no more real permanence than an average truth. Why, you might as well tell the truth at once and be done with it. A feeble, stupid, preposterous lie will not live two years—except it be a slander upon somebody. It is indestructible, then, of course, but that is no merit of yours. A final word: begin your practice of this gracious and beautiful art early—begin now. If I had begun earlier, I could have learned how.

Never handle firearms carelessly. The sorrow and suffering that have been caused through the innocent but heedless handling of firearms by the young!

Only four days ago, right in the next farmhouse to the one where I am spending the summer, a grandmother, old and gray and sweet, one of the loveliest spirits in the land, was sitting at her work, when her young grandson crept in and got down an old, battered, rusty gun which had not been touched for many years and was supposed not to be loaded, and pointed it at her, laughing and threatening to shoot. In her fright she ran screaming and pleading toward the door on the other side of the room; but as she passed him he placed the gun almost against her very breast and pulled the trigger! He had supposed it was not loaded. And he was right—it wasn't. So there wasn't any harm done. It is the only case of that kind I ever heard of. Therefore, just the same, don't you meddle with old unloaded firearms; they are the most deadly and unerring things that have ever been created by man. You don't have to take any pains at all with them; you don't have to have a rest, you don't have to have any sights on the gun, you don't have to take aim, even. No, you just pick out a relative and bang away, and you are sure to get him. A youth who can't hit a cathedral at thirty yards with a Gatling gun in three-quarters of an hour, can take up an old empty musket and bag his grandmother every time, at a hundred. Think what Waterloo would have been if one of the armies had been boys armed with old muskets supposed not to be loaded, and the other army had been composed of their female relations. The very thought of it makes one shudder.

There are many sorts of books; but good ones are

the sort for the young to read. Remember that. They are a great, an inestimable, an unspeakable means of improvement. Therefore be careful in your selection, my young friends; be very careful; confine yourselves exclusively to Robertson's Sermons, Baxter's *Saint's Rest*, *The Innocents Abroad*, and works of that kind.

But I have said enough. I hope you will treasure up the instructions which I have given you, and make them a guide to your feet and a light to your understanding. Build your character thoughtfully and painstaking upon these precepts, and by and by, when you have got it built, you will be surprised and gratified to see how nicely and sharply it resembles everybody else's.

SPEECH

At the Banquet of the International Congress of Wheelmen. (About 1884)

MR. CHAIRMAN,—I am not sure that I have voice enough to make myself heard over such a far-stretching landscape of humanity as this, but I will do what I can. I have been asked to tell, briefly, what bicycling is like, from the novice's point of view. I judge that this is for the instruction of the eight hundred guests, scattered through this vast assemblage, who are not wheelmen; for it is not likely that I could tell the rest of you anything about bicycling which you do not already know. As twelve speakers are to follow me, and as the weather is very warm and close, besides, I shall be careful to make quite sure of one thing at least—I will keep well within the ten-minute limit allowed each speaker.

It was on the 10th of May of the present year that a brace of curiously contrasted events added themselves to the sum of my experiences; for on that day I confessed to age by mounting spectacles for the first time, and in the same hour I renewed my youth, to outward appearance, by mounting a bicycle for the first time.

The spectacles stayed on.

THE MIDDLE PERIOD

TURNCOATS

With the nomination of James G. Blaine, in 1884, Mark Twain joined with a group of distinguished men in forming the "Mugwump" party which elected Grover Cleveland. During the campaign he made a number of speeches one of which follows:

IT seems to me that there are things about this campaign which almost amount to inconsistencies. The language may sound violent; if it does, it is traitor to my mood. The Mugwumps are contemptuously called turncoats by the Republican speakers and journals. The charge is true: we have turned our coats; we have no denials to make as to that. But does a man become of a necessity base because he turns his coat? And are there no Republican turncoats except the Mugwumps? Please look at the facts in the case candidly and fairly before sending us to political perdition without company.

Why are we called turncoats? Because we have changed our opinion. Changed it about what? About the greatness and righteousness of the principles of the Republican party? No, that is not changed. We believe in those principles yet; no one doubts this. What, then, is it that we have changed our opinion about? Why, about Mr. Blaine. That is the whole change. There is no other. Decidedly, we have done that, and do by no means wish to deny it. But when did we change it? Yesterday?—last week?—last summer? No—we changed it years and years ago, as far back as 1876. The vast bulk of the Republican party changed its opinion of him at the same time and in the same way. Will anybody be hardy enough to deny this? Was there more than a handful of really respectable and respect-worthy Republicans on the north Atlantic seaboard who did not change their opinion of Mr. Blaine at that time? Was not the Republican atmosphere—both private and journalistic—so charged with this fact that none could fail to perceive it?

Very well. Was this multitude called turncoats at that time? Of course not. That would have been an absurdity. Was any of this multitude held in contempt at that time, and derided and execrated, for turning his Blaine coat? No one thought of such a thing. Now, then, we who are called the Mugwumps turned our coats at that time, and they have remained so turned to this day. If it is shameful to turn one's coat once, what measure of scorn can adequately describe the man who turns it twice. If to turn one's coat once makes one a dude, a Pharisee, a Mugwump, and fool, where shall you find language rancid enough to describe a double turncoat? If to turn your coat, at a time when no one can impeach either the sincerity of the act or the cleanliness of your motives in doing it, is held to be a pathetic spectacle, what sort of spectacle is it when such a coat-turner turns his coat again, and this time under quite suggestively different circumstances?—that is to say, *after a nomination.* Do these double turncoats exist? And who are they? They are the bulk of the Republican party; and it

Mark Twain As Doctor Of Letters, University of Oxford, 1907

is hardly venturing too far to say that neither you nor I can put his finger upon a respectable member of that great multitude who can put a denial of it instantly into words and without blush or stammer. Here in Hartford they do not deny; they confess that they are double turncoats. They say they are convinced that when they formerly changed their opinion about Mr. Blaine they were wrong, and so they have changed back again. Which would seem to be an admission that to change one's opinion and turn one's coat is not necessarily a base thing to do, after all. Yet they call my tribe customary hard names in their next campaign speeches, just the same, without seeming to see any inconsistency or impropriety in it. Well, it is all a muddle to me. I cannot make out how it is or why it that is a single turncoat is a reptile and a double turncoat a bird of Paradise.

I easily perceive that the Republican party has deserted us and deserted itself; but I am not able to see that *we* have deserted anything or anybody. As for me, I have not deserted the Republican code of principles, for I propose to vote its ticket, with the presidential exception; and I have not deserted Mr. Blaine, for as regards him I got my free papers before he bought the property.

Personally I know that two of the best known of the Hartford campaigners for Blaine did six months ago hold as uncomplimentary opinions about him as I did then, and as I do to-day. I am told, upon what I conceive to be good authority, that the two or three other Connecticut campaigners of prominence of that ilk held opinions concerning him of that same uncomplimentary breed up to the day of the nomination. These gentlemen have turned their coats; and they now admire Blaine; and not calmly, temperately, but with a sort of ferocious rapture. In a speech the other night, one of them spoke of the author of the Mulligan letters—these strange Vassar-like exhibitions of eagerness, gushingness, timidity, secretiveness, frankness, naïveté, unsagacity, and almost incredible and impossible indiscretion—as the "first statesman of the age." Another of them spoke of "the three great statesmen of the age, Gladstone, Bismarck, and Blaine." Doubtless this profound remark was received with applause. But suppose the gentlemen had had the daring to read some of those letters first, appending the names of Bismarck and Gladstone to them; do not you candidly believe that the applause would have been missing and that in its place there would have been a smile which you could have heard to Springfield? For no one has ever seen a Republican mass meeting that was devoid of the perception of the ludicrous.

A TRIBUTE

This mock speech on the dead partisan written after the election of Grover Cleveland in 1884 was probably never delivered in public.

MR. CHAIRMAN,—That is a noble and beautiful ancient sentiment which admonishes us to speak well of the dead. Therefore let us try to do this for our late friend who is mentioned in the text. How full of life and strength and confidence and pride he was but a few short months ago; and, alas! how dead he is to-day! We that are gathered at these obsequies, we that are here to bury this dust, and sing the parting hymn, and say the comforting word to the widow and the orphan now left destitute and sorrowing by him, their support and stay in the post office, the consulship, the navy yard, and the Indian reservation—we knew him, right well and familiarly we knew him; and so it is meet that we, and not strangers, should take upon ourselves these last offices, lest his reputation suffer through explanations of him which might not explain him happily, and justifications of him which might not justify him conclusively. First, it is right and well that we censure him, in those few minor details wherein some slight censure may seem to be demanded; to the end that when we come to speak his praises the good he did may shine with all the more intolerable brightness by the contrast.

To begin, then, with the twilight side of his character: He was a slave; not a turbulent and troublesome, but a meek and docile, cringing and fawning, dirt-eating and dirt-preferring slave; and Party was his lord and master. He had no mind of his own, no will of his own, no opinion of his own; body and soul he was the property and chattel of that master, to be bought and sold, bartered, traded, *given* away, at his nod and beck—branded, mutilated, boiled in oil, if need were. And the desire of his heart was to make of a nation of freemen a nation of slaves like to himself; to bring to pass a time when it might be said that "all are for the Party, and none are for the State"; and the labors of his diligent hand and brain did finally compass his desire. For he fooled the people with plausible new readings of familiar old principles, and beguiled them to the degradation of their manhood and the destruction of their liberties. He taught them that the only true freedom of thought is to think as the party thinks; that the only true freedon of speech is to speak as the party dictates; that the only righteous toleration is toleration of what the party approves; that patriotism, duty, citizenship, devotion to country, loyalty to the flag, are all summed up in loyalty to party. Save the party, uphold the party, make the party victorious, though all things else go to ruin and the grave.

In these few little things he who lies here cold in death was faulty. Say we no more concerning them, but over them draw the veil of a charitable oblivion; for the good which he did far overpasses this little evil. With grateful hearts we may unite in praises and thanksgivings to him for one majestic fact of his life—that in his zeal for his cause he finally over-did it. The precious result was that a change came; and that change remains, and will endure, and on its banner is written——

"Not all are for the Party—*now* some are for the State."

CONSISTENCY

A paper read at the Hartford Monday Evening Club, following the Blaine-Cleveland campaign, 1884. *The proper emphasis for delivery was indicated on the author's manuscript.*

WE are continually warned to be consistent—by the pulpit, by the newspaper, by our associates. When we depart from consistency, we are reproached for it by these censors. When a man who has been born and brought up a Jew becomes a Christian, the Jews sorrow over it and reproach him for his inconstancy; all his life he has denied the divinity of Christ, but now he makes a lie of all his past; upon him rests the stigma of inconsistency; we can never be sure of him again. We put *in the deadly parallel columns* what he said *formerly* and what he says *now*, and his credit is *gone*. We say, Trust him *not;* we *know* him now; he will change *again;* and possibly *again* and yet *again;* he has no stability.

There are men called life-long Democrats, life-long Republicans. If one of these departs from his allegiance and votes the other ticket, the same thing happens as in the *Jew's* case. The man loses character. He is inconsistent. He is a traitor. His *past* utterances will be double columned with his *present* ones, and he is damned; also despised—even by his *new* political associates, for in theirs, as in *all* men's eyes, inconsistency is a treason and matter for scorn.

These are facts—common, every-day facts; and I have chosen them for that reason; facts known to everybody, facts which no one denies.

What is the most rigorous law of our being? *Growth.* No smallest atom of our moral, mental, or physical structure can stand still a *year.* It grows—it *must* grow; nothing can *prevent* it. It must grow downward *or* upward; it must grow smaller or larger, better or worse—it cannot stand still. In other words, we *change*—and *must* change, constantly, and keep on changing as long as we live. What, then, is the *true* gospel of consistency? *Change.* Who is the *really* consistent man? The man who changes. Since change is the law of his *being,* he cannot *be* consistent if he stick in a rut.

Yet, as the quoted facts show, there are those who would misteach us that to stick in a rut *is* consistency—and a *virtue;* and that to climb *out* of the rut is inconsistency—and a *vice.* They will grant you certain things, without murmur or dissent—as things which go without saying; truisms. They will grant that in time the crawling baby *walks* and must not be required to go *on crawling;* that in time the *youth* has *outgrown* the *child's jacket* and must not be required to crowd himself *into* it; they grant you that a child's *knowledge* is becoming and proper to the *child only* so they grant him a school and *teach* him, so that he may *change* and *grow;* they grant you that he must keep *on* learning—through youth and manhood and straight *on*—he must not be allowed to suppose that the knowledge of *thirty* can be any proper equipment for his *fiftieth* year; they will grant you that a young man's opinions about mankind and the universe are *crude*, and sometimes *foolish*, and they would not dream of requiring him to stick to them the rest of his life, lest by changing them he bring down upon himself the reproach of *inconsistency*. They will grant you *these*, and everything *else* you can think of, in the line of progress and change, until you get down to politics and religion; there they draw the *line*. These must suffer no change. Once a Presbyterian, *always* a Presbyterian, or you are inconsistent and a *traitor;* once a Democrat, *always* a Democrat, or you are inconsistent and a *traitor*—a turncoat.

It is curious logic. Is there but *one* kind of treason? No man *remains* the same sort of Presbyterian he was at *first*—the thing is *impossible*; time and various *influences modify* his Presbyterianism; it *narrows* or it *broadens*, grows *deeper* or *shallower*, but does not stand *still*. In some cases it grows so far beyond itself, upward *or* downward, that nothing is really *left of it* but the *name*, and perhaps an inconsequential *rag* of the original substance, the *bulk* being now Baptist or Buddhist or something. Well, if he go over to the Buddhists, he is a traitor. To whom? To what? No man can answer *those* questions rationally. Now if he does *not* go over what is he? Plainly a traitor to *himself*, a traitor to the best and the highest and the honestest that is *in* him. Which of these treasons is the blackest one—and the shamefulest? Which is the real and right consistency? To be consistent to a sham and an empty name, or consistent to the law of one's *being*, which is *change*, and in this case requires him to move forward and keep abreast of his best mental and moral progress, his highest convictions of the right and the true? Suppose this treason to the name of a church should carry him clear outside of *all* churches? Is that a blacker treason than to *remain?* So long as he is loyal to his best *self*, what should he care for *other* loyalties? It seems to me that a man should secure the *Well done, faithful servant*, of his own conscience *first* and foremost, and let all other loyalties go.

I have referred to the fact that when a man retires from his political party he is a *traitor*—that he is so *pronounced* in plain language. *That* is *bold*; so bold as to deceive many into the fancy that it is *true*. Desertion, treason—these are the terms applied. Their *military form* reveals the thought in the man's mind who uses them; to *him* a political party is an *army*. Well, *is* it? Are the two things identical? Do they even *resemble* each other? Necessarily a political party is not an army of conscripts, for *they* are in the ranks by *compulsion*. Then it must be a *regular* army, or an army of volunteers. *Is* it a *regular* army? No, for *these* enlist for a specified and well-understood *term* and can retire without reproach when the term is up. Is it an army of *volunteers* who have *enlisted for the war*, and may righteously be shot if they leave before the war is finished? No, it is not even an army in *that* sense. Those fine military terms are high-sounding, empty *lies*—and are no more rationally applicable to a political party than they would be to an oyster bed. The volunteer soldier comes to the recruiting office and strips himself, and proves that he is so many feet high, and has sufficiently good teeth, and no fingers gone, and is sufficiently sound in body *generally;* he is accepted, but *not* until he has sworn a deep *oath*, or made other solemn form of *promise*, to march under that flag until that war is done or his term of enlistment completed. What is the process when a *voter* joins a *party?* Must he prove that he is sound in *any* way, mind *or* body? Must he prove that *he knows* anything—whatever—is capable *of* anything? Does he take an oath or make a *promise* of any sort?—or doesn't he leave himself entirely *free?* If he were informed by the political boss that if he join it must be forever; that he must be that party's chattel and wear its brass collar the rest of his days, would not that *insult* him? It goes without saying. He would say some rude, unprintable thing and turn his back on that preposterous organization. But the political boss puts *no* conditions upon him at *all*; and his volunteer makes no promises, enlists for no stated *term*. He has in *no sense* become a part of an *army*, he is in no way restrained of his *freedom*. Yet he will presently find that his bosses and his newspapers have *assumed* just the reverse of that; that they have blandly arrogated to themselves an iron-clad military *authority* over him; and within twelve months, if he is an average man, he will have *surrendered* his liberty, and will actually be silly enough to believe that he cannot leave that party, for any cause whatever, without being a shameful *traitor*, a deserter, a legitimately dishonored *man*.

There you have the just measure of that freedom

of conscience, freedom of opinion, freedom of speech and action, which we hear so much inflated foolishness about, as being the precious possession of the Republic. Whereas, in *truth*, the surest way for a man to make of himself a target for almost universal scorn, obloquy, slander, and insult is to stop twaddling about these priceless independencies, and attempt to *exercise* one of them. If he is a preacher, half his congregation will clamor for his expulsion, and *will* expel him, except they find it will injure real estate in the neighborhood; if he is a mechanic, he will be discharged, promptly; if he is a lawyer, his clients will take their business elsewhere; if he is a doctor, his own dead will turn against him.

I repeat that the new party member who supposed himself independent will presently find that the party has somehow got a mortgage on his soul, and that within a year he will *recognize* the mortgage, deliver up his liberty, and actually believe he cannot retire from that party from *any* motive, howsoever high and right, in his *own* eyes, without shame and dishonor.

Is it possible for human wickedness to invent a doctrine more infernal and poisonous than this? Is there *imaginable* a baser servitude than it imposes? What slave is so degraded as the slave who is *proud* that he *is* a slave? What is the *essential difference* between a life-long *Democrat* and any other kind of life-long *slave?* Is it less humiliating to dance to the lash of *one* master than *another?*

This atrocious doctrine of allegiance to *party* plays directly into the hands of politicians of the *baser* sort—and doubtless for *that* it was borrowed—or stolen—from the monarchical system. It enables them to foist upon the country officials whom no self-respecting man would *vote* for, if he could but come to understand that loyalty to *himself* is his first and *highest* duty, not loyalty to any *party name*. The wire workers, convention packers, know they are not obliged to put up the *fittest* man for the office, for they know that the docile party will vote for any forked thing they *put up*, even though it do not even strictly *resemble* a *man*.

I am persuaded—convinced—that this idea of *consistency*—unchanging allegiance to *party*—has lowered the manhood of the whole *nation*—pulled it down and dragged it in the mud. When Mr. Blaine was nominated for the Presidency, I *knew* the man; no, I *judged* I knew him; I don't know him *now*, but at *that* time I *judged* I *knew* him; for my daily paper had been painting him black, and blacker, and blacker *still*, for a series of *years*, during which it had no call to speak anything but the *truth* about him, no call to be *malicious* toward him, no call to be otherwise than just simply and honestly *candid* about him, since he belonged to its *own party* and was not before the nation as a detectable candidate for anything. But within thirty days after the nomination that paper had him all painted up *white* again. *That* is not allegiance to one's best *self*, one's straitest *convictions*; it is allegiance to *party*. Nobody likes to eat a ton of black *paint*, and none but the *master* can make the slave *do* it. Was this paper *alone* at this singular feast? *No;* ten thousand *other* Republican newspapers sat down at the same table and worried down *their* ton apiece; and not any fewer than *100,000* more-or-less-prominent *politicians* sat down all over this country and worried down *their* ton apiece; and after long, long and bitter gagging, some *millions* of the *common* serfdom of the party sat down and worried down *their* ton apiece. *Paint?* It was *dirt*. Enough of it was eaten by the meek Republican party to build a railroad embankment from here to *Japan;* and it pains me to think that a year from now they will probably have to eat it all *over* again.

Well, there was a *lot* of queer feasting done in those days. One *learned in the law* pondered the Mulligan letters and other *frightful* literature, and rendered this impressive verdict: he said the evidence would not *convict* Mr. Blaine in a *court of law*, and so he would *vote* for him. He did not *say* whether the evidences would prove him *innocent* or not. *That* wasn't important.

Now, he knew that this verdict was absolutely inconclusive. He knew that it settled nothing, established nothing whatever, and was wholly valueless as a guide for his action, an answer to his questionings.

He knew that the merciful and righteous barriers raised up by the laws of our humane age for the shelter and protection of the possibly innocent, have often and over again protected and rescued the certainly *guilty*. He knew that in this way many and many a prisoner has gone unchastised from the court when judge and jury and the whole public believed with all their hearts that he was guilty. He knew—all credit not discredit to our age that it is so—that this result is so frequent, so almost commonplace, that the mere failure to satisfy the exacting forms of law and prove a man guilty in a *court*, is a hundred thousand miles from proving him innocent. You see a hiccoughing man wallowing in the gutter at two o'clock in the morning; you think the thing all over and weigh the details of it in your mind as you walk home, and with immeasurable wisdom arrive at the verdict that *you don't know he wasn't a Prohibitionist.* Of course you don't, and if you stop and think a minute you would realize that you don't know he *was*, either.

Well, a good clergyman who read the Mulligan and other published evidences was not able to *make* up *his* mind, but concluded to take refuge in the verdict rendered by the citizen learned in the *law;* take his intellectual and moral food at second-hand, though he doesn't *rank* as an intellectual infant, unable to chew his own moral and mental nourishment; he decided that an *apparently colored* person who couldn't be proven to be black *in the baffling crosslights of a court of law* was white enough for *him*, he being a little color blind, *anyway*, in matters where the *party* is concerned, and so *he* came reluctantly to the polls, with his redeeming blush on his countenance, and put in his vote.

I met a certain *other* clergyman on the *corner* the day after the nomination. He was very uncompromising. He said: "I *know* Blaine to the *core;* I have known him from boyhood *up;* and I know him to be utterly unprincipled and unscrupulous." Within six weeks after that, this clergyman was at a Republican *mass* meeting in the Opera House, and I think he presided. At *any* rate, he made a speech. If you did not know that the character depicted in it meant Mr. Blaine, you would suppose it meant—well, there isn't anybody down here on the *earth* that you can use as a comparison. It is praise, praise, praise; laudation, laudation, laudation; glorification, glorification, canonization. Conceive of the general crash and upheaval and ripping and tearing and readjustment of things that must have been going on in that man's moral and mental chaos for six weeks! What is any combination of inflammatory rheumatism and St. Vitus's dance to *this?* When the doctrine of allegiance to party can utterly up-end a man's moral constitution and make a temporary *fool* of him *besides*, what excuse are you going to offer for preaching it, teaching it, extending it, perpetuating it? Shall you say, the best good of the country demands allegiance to party? Shall you also say it demands that a man kick his truth and his conscience into the gutter, and become a mouthing lunatic, *besides?* Oh, no! you say; it does not demand *that.* But what if it *produce* that, in *spite* of you? There is no obligation upon a man to do things which he ought *not* to do, when *drunk*, but most men *will* do them, just the same, and so we hear no arguments about obligations in the matter; we only hear men warned to *avoid* the habit of *drinking;* get *rid* of the thing that can betray men into such things.

This is a funny business, all round. The same men who enthusiastically preach loyal consistency to church and party are always ready and willing and anxious to persuade a Chinaman or an Indian or a Kanaka to desert *his* Church, or a fellow-American to desert *his* party. The man who deserts to them is all that is high and pure and beautiful—apparently; the man who deserts from them is all that is foul and despicable. This is Consistency with a capital C.

With the daintiest and self-complacentest sarcasm the life-long loyalist scoffs at the Independent—or, as he calls him, with cutting irony, the Mugwump; makes himself too killingly funny for anything in this world about him. But—the Mugwump can stand it, for there is a great history at his back, stretching down the centuries, and he comes of a mighty ancestry. *He* knows that in the whole history of the race of men no single great and high and beneficent thing was ever done for the souls and bodies, the hearts and the brains, of the children of this world, but a Mugwump started it and Mugwumps carried it to victory. And their names are the stateliest in history: Washington, Garrison, Galileo, Luther, Christ. Loyalty to petrified opinions never yet broke a chain or freed a human soul in *this* world—and never *will*.

To return to the starting point: I am persuaded that the world has been tricked into adopting some false and most pernicious notions about *consistency*—and to such a degree that the average man has turned the rights and *wrongs* of things entirely *around*, and is *proud* to be "consistent," unchanging, immovable, fossilized, where it should be his humiliation that he is so.

HENRY M. STANLEY

ADDRESS DELIVERED IN BOSTON, NOVEMBER, 1886

Mr. Clemens introduced Mr. Stanley.

LADIES AND GENTLEMEN, if any should ask, Why is it that you are here as introducer of the lecturer? I should answer that I happened to be around and was asked to perform this function. I was quite willing to do so, and, as there was no sort of need of an introduction, anyway, it could be necessary only that some person come forward for a moment and do an unnecessary thing, and this is quite in my line. Now, to introduce so illustrious a name as Henry M. Stanley by any detail of what the man has done is clear aside from my purpose; that would be stretching the unnecessary to an unconscionable degree. When I contrast what I have achieved in my measurably brief life with what he has achieved in his possibly briefer one, the effect is to sweep utterly away the ten-story edifice of my own self-appreciation and leave nothing behind but the cellar. When you compare these achievements of his with the achievements of really great men who exist in history, the comparison, I believe, is in his favor. I am not here to disparage Columbus.

No, I won't do that; but when you come to regard the achievements of these two men, Columbus and Stanley, from the standpoint of the difficulties they encountered, the advantage is with Stanley and against Columbus. Now, Columbus started out to discover America. Well, he didn't need to do anything at all but sit in the cabin of his ship and hold his grip and sail straight on, and America would discover itself. Here it was, barring his passage the whole length and breadth of the South American continent, and he couldn't get by it. He'd got to discover it. But Stanley started out to find Doctor Livingstone, who was scattered abroad, as you may say, over the length and breadth of a vast slab of Africa as big as the United States.

It was a blind kind of search. He was the worst scattered of men. But I will throw the weight of this introduction upon one very peculiar feature of Mr. Stanley's character, and that is his indestructible Americanism—an Americanism which he is proud of. And in this day and time, when it is the custom to ape and imitate English methods and fashions, it is like a breath of fresh air to stand in the presence of this untainted American citizen who has been caressed and complimented by half of the crowned heads of Europe, who could clothe his body from his head to his heels with the orders and decorations lavished upon him. And yet, when the untitled myriads of his own country put out their hands in welcome to him and greet him, "Well done," through the Congress of the United States, that is the crown that is worth all the rest to him. He is a product of institutions which exist in no other country on earth—institutions that bring out all that is best and most heroic in a man. I introduce Henry M. Stanley.

ON STANLEY AND LIVINGSTONE

Mr. Clemens at dinner by the Whitefriars' Club, London, at the Mitre Tavern, in reply to the toast in his honor said:

GENTLEMEN, — I thank you very heartily indeed for this expression of kindness toward me. What I have done for England and civilization in the arduous affairs which I have engaged in (that is good: that is so smooth that I will say it again and again)—what I have done for England and civilization in the arduous part I have performed I have done with a single-hearted devotion and with no hope of reward. I am proud, I am very proud, that it was reserved for me to find Doctor Livingstone and for Mr. Stanley to get all the credit. I hunted for that man in Africa all over seventy-five or one hundred parishes, thousands and thousands of miles in the wilds and deserts all over the place, sometimes riding negroes and sometimes travelling by rail. I didn't mind the rail or anything else, so that I didn't come in for the tar and feathers. I found that man at Ujiji—a place you may remember if you have ever been there—and it was a very great satisfaction that I found him just in the nick of time. I found that poor old man deserted by his niggers and by his geographers, deserted by all of his kind except the gorillas—dejected, miserable, famishing, absolutely famishing—but he was eloquent. Just as I found him he had eaten his last elephant, and he said to me: "God knows where I shall get another." He had nothing to wear except his venerable and honorable naval suit, and nothing to eat but his diary.

But I said to him: "It is all right; I have discovered you, and Stanley will be here by the four-o'clock train and will discover you officially, and then we will turn to and have a reg'lar good time." I said: "Cheer up, for Stanley has got corn, ammunition, glass beads, hymn books, whisky, and everything which the human heart can desire; he has got all kinds of valuables, including telegraph poles and a few cart loads of money. By this time communication has been made with the land of Bibles and civilization, and property will advance." And then we surveyed all that country, from Ujiji, through Unanogo and other places, to Unyanyembe. I mention these names simply for your edification, nothing more—do not expect it—particularly as intelligence to the Royal Geographical Society. And then, having filled up the old man, we were all too full for utterance and departed. We have since then feasted on honors.

So far as I am personally concerned, I am here to stay a few months, and to see English people and to learn English manners and customs, and to enjoy myself; so the simplest thing I can do is to thank you for the toast you have honored me with and for the remarks you have made, and to wish health and prosperity to the Whitefriars' Club, and to sink down to my accustomed level.

GENERAL GRANT'S GRAMMAR

DELIVERED AT THE ARMY AND NAVY CLUB (1886)

LATELY a great and honored author, Matthew Arnold, has been finding fault with General Grant's English. That would be fair enough, maybe, if the examples of imperfect English averaged more instances to the page in General Grant's book than they do in Arnold's criticism on the book—but they do not. It would be fair enough, maybe, if such instances were commoner in General Grant's book than they are in the works of the average standard author—but they are not. In fact, General Grant's derelictions in the matter of grammar and constructions are not more frequent than such derelictions in the works of a majority of the professional authors of our time, and of all previous times—authors as exclusively and painstakingly trained to the literary trade as was General Grant to the trade of war. This is not a random statement; it is a fact, and easily demonstrable. I have a book at home called *Modern English Literature: Its Blemishes and Defects*, by Henry H. Breen, a countryman of Mr. Arnold. In it I find examples of bad grammar and slovenly English from the pens of Sydney Smith, Sheridan, Hallam, Whately, Carlyle, Disraeli, Allison, Junius, Blair, *Macaulay*, Shakespeare, Milton, Gibbon, Southey, Lamb, Landor, Smollet, Walpole, Walker (of the dictionary), Christopher North, Kirk White, Benjamin Franklin, Sir Walter Scott, and Mr. Lindley Murray (who made the grammar).

In Mr. Arnold's criticism on General Grant's book we find two grammatical crimes and more than several examples of very crude and slovenly English, enough of them to easily entitle him to a *lofty* place in the illustrious list of delinquents just named.

The following passage all by itself ought to elect him: "Meade suggested to Grant that he might wish to have immediately under him, Sherman, who had been serving with Grant in the West. He begged him not to hesitate if he thought it for the good of the service. Grant assured him that he had not thought of moving him, and in his memoirs, after relating what had passed, he adds," etc. To read that passage a couple of times would make a man dizzy; to read it four times would make him drunk.

Mr. Breen makes this discriminating remark: "To suppose that because a man is a poet or an historian, he must be correct in his grammar, is to suppose that an architect must be a joiner, or a physician a compounder of medicine." Mr. Breen's point is well taken. If you should climb the mighty Matterhorn to look out over the kingdoms of the earth, it might be a pleasant incident to find strawberries up there. But Great Scott! you don't climb the Matterhorn for strawberries!

People may hunt out what microscopic motes they please, but, after all, the fact remains and cannot be dislodged, that General Grant's book is a great, and in its peculiar department unique and unapproachable, literary masterpiece. In their line, there is no higher literature than those modest, simple memoirs. Their style is at least flawless and no man could improve upon it, and great books are weighed and measured by their style and matter, and not by the trimmings and shadings of their grammar.

There is that about the sun which makes us forget his spots, and when we think of General Grant our pulses quicken and his grammar vanishes; we only remember that this is the simple soldier, who, all untaught of the silken phrase makers, linked words together with an art surpassing the art of the schools and put into them a something which will still bring to American ears, as long as America shall last, the roll of his vanished drums and the tread of his marching hosts. What do we care for grammar when we think of those thunderous phrases: "unconditional and immediate surrender," "I propose to move immediately upon your works," "I propose to fight it out on this line if it takes all summer." Mr. Arnold would doubtless claim that that last phrase is not strictly grammatical, and yet it did certainly wake up this nation as a hundred million tons of A No. 1, fourth-proof, hard-boiled, hide-bound grammar from another mouth could not have done. And finally we have that gentler phrase, that one which shows you another true side of the man, shows you that in his soldier heart there was room for other than glory war mottoes and in his tongue the gift to fitly phrase them—"Let us have peace."

THE OLD-FASHIONED PRINTER

ADDRESS AT THE TYPOTHETÆ DINNER GIVEN AT DELMONICO'S, JANUARY 18, 1886, COMMEMORATING THE BIRTHDAY OF BENJAMIN FRANKLIN

Mr. Clemens responded to the toast "The Compositor."

THE chairman's historical reminiscences of Gutenberg have caused me to fall into reminiscences, for I myself am something of an antiquity. All things change in the procession of years, and it may be that I am among strangers. It may be that the printer of to-day is not the printer of thirty-five years ago. I was no stranger to him. I knew him well. I built his fire for him in the winter mornings; I brought his water from the village pump; I swept out his office; I picked up his type from under his stand; and, if he were there to see, I put the good type in his case and the broken ones among the "hell matter"; and if he wasn't there to see, I dumped it all with the "pi" on the imposing stone—for that was the furtive fashion of the cub, and I was a cub. I wetted down the paper Saturdays, I turned it Sundays—for this was a country weekly; I rolled, I washed the rollers, I washed the forms, I folded the papers, I carried them around at dawn Thursday mornings. The carrier was then an object of interest to all the dogs in town. If I had saved up all the bites I ever received, I could keep M. Pasteur busy for a year. I enveloped the papers that were for the mail—we had a hundred town subscribers and three hundred and fifty country ones; the town subscribers paid in groceries and the country ones in cabbages and cordwood—when they paid at all, which was merely sometimes, and then we always stated the fact in the paper, and gave them a puff; and if we forgot it they stopped the paper. Every man on the town list helped edit the thing—that is, he gave orders as to how it was to be edited; dictated its opinions, marked out its course for it, and every time the boss failed to connect he stopped his paper. We were just infested with critics, and we tried to satisfy them all over. We had one subscriber who paid cash, and he was more trouble than all the rest. He bought us once a year, body and soul, for two dollars. He used to modify our politics every which way, and he made us change our religion four times in five years. If we ever tried to reason with him, he would threaten to stop his paper, and, of course, that meant bankruptcy and destruction. That man used to write articles a column and a half long, leaded long primer, and sign them "Junius," or "Veritas," or "Vox Populi," or some other high-sounding rot; and then, after it was set up, he would come in and say he had changed his mind—which was a gilded figure of speech, because he hadn't any—and order it to be left out. We couldn't afford "bogus" in that office, so we always took the leads out, altered the signature, credited the article to the rival paper, in the next village, and put it in. Well, we did have one or two kinds of "bogus." Whenever there was a barbecue, or a circus, or a baptizing, we knocked off for half a day, and then to make up for short matter we would "turn over ads"—turn over the whole pages and duplicate it. The other "bogus" was deep philosophical stuff, which we judged nobody ever read; so we kept a galley of it standing, and kept on slapping the same old batches of it in, every now and then, till it got dangerous. Also, in the early days of the telegraph we used to economize on the news. We picked out the items that were pointless and barren of information and stood them on a galley, and changed the dates and localities, and used them over and over again till the public interest in them was worn to the bone. We marked the ads, but we seldom paid any attention to the marks afterward; so the life of a "td" ad and a "tf" ad was equally eternal. I have seen a "td" notice of a sheriff's sale still booming serenely along two years after the sale was over, the sheriff dead, and the whole circumstance become ancient history. Most of the yearly ads were patent-medicine stereotypes, and we used to fence with them.

I can see that printing office of prehistoric times yet, with its horse bills on the walls, its "d" boxes clogged with tallow, because we always stood the candle in the "k" box nights, its towel, which was not considered soiled until it could stand alone, and other signs and symbols that marked the establishment of that kind in the Mississippi Valley; and I can see, also, the tramping "jour," who flitted by in the summer and tarried a day, with his wallet stuffed with one shirt and a hatful of handbills, for if he couldn't get any type to set he would do a temperance lecture. His way of life was simple, his needs not complex; all he wanted was plate and bed and money enough to get drunk on, and he was satisfied. But it may be, as I have said, that I am among strangers, and sing the glories of a forgotten age to unfamiliar ears, so I will "make even" and stop.

YALE COLLEGE SPEECH

In June, 1888, Yale College conferred on Mark Twain the degree of Master of Arts. Later in the year he made the following address to the students.

I WAS sincerely proud and grateful to be made a Master of Arts by this great and venerable university, and I would have come last June to testify this feeling, as I do now testify it, but that the sudden and unexpected notice of the honor done me found me at a distance from home and unable to discharge that duty and enjoy that privilege.

Along at first, say for the first month or so, I did not quite know how to proceed, because of my not knowing just what authorities and privileges belonged to the title which had been granted me, but after that I consulted some students of Trinity, in Hartford, and they made everything clear to me. It was through them that I found out that my title made me head of the governing body of the university and lodged in me very broad and severely responsible powers. It is through trying to work these powers up to their maximum of efficiency that I have had such a checkered career this year. I was told that it would be necessary for me to report to you at this time, and, of course, I comply, though I would have preferred to put it off till I could make a better showing, for, indeed, I have been so pertinaciously hindered and obstructed at every turn by the faculty that it would be difficult to prove that the university is really in any better shape now than it was when I first took charge. In submitting my report I am sorry to have to begin it with the remark that respect for authority seems to be at a quite low ebb in the college. It is true that this has caused me pain, but it has not discouraged me. By advice, I turned my earliest attention to the Greek department. I told the Greek professor I had concluded to drop the use of the Greek written character, because it is so hard to spell with, and so impossible to read after you get it spelled. Let us draw the curtain there. I saw by what followed that nothing but early neglect saved him from being a very profane man. I ordered the professor of mathematics to simplify the whole system, because the way it was I couldn't understand it, and I didn't want things going on in the college in what was practically a clandestine fashion. I told him to drop the conundrum system; it was not suited to the dignity of a college, which should deal in facts, not guesses and suppositions; we didn't want any more cases of *if* A and B stand at opposite poles of the earth's surface and C at the equator of Jupiter, at what variations of angle will the left link of the moon appear to these different parties? I said you just let that thing alone; it's plenty time to get in a sweat about it when it happens. As like as not it ain't going to do any harm anyway. His reception of these instructions bordered on insubordination; in so much that I felt obliged to take his number and report him. I found the astronomer of the university gadding around after comets and other such odds and ends—tramps and derelicts of the skies. I told him prettly plainly that we couldn't have that. I told him it was no economy to go on piling up and piling up raw material in the way of new stars and comets and asteroids that we couldn't ever have any use for till we had worked off the old stock. I said if I caught him strawberrying around after any more asteroids, especially, I should have to fire him out. Privately, prejudice got the best of me there, I ought to confess it. At bottom I don't really mind comets so much, but somehow I have always been down on asteroids. There is nothing mature about them; I wouldn't sit up nights, the way that man does, if I could get a basketful of them. He said it was the best line of goods he had; he said he could trade them to Rochester for comets, and trade the comets to Harvard for nebulæ, and trade the nebulæ to the Smithsonian for flint hatchets. I felt obliged to stop this thing on the spot; I said we couldn't have the university turned into an astronomical junk shop.

And while I was at it I thought I might as well make the reform complete; the astronomer is extraordinarily mutinous; and so with your approval I will transfer him to the law department and put one of the law students in his place. A boy will be more biddable, more tractable, also cheaper. It is true he cannot be intrusted with important work at first, but he can comb the skies for nebulæ till he gets his hand in. I have other changes in mind, but, as they are in the nature of surprises, I judge it politic to leave them unspecified at this time.

WELCOME HOME

To a Baseball Team Returning From a World Tour by Way of the Sandwich Islands (1889)

THOUGH not a native, as intimated by the chairman, I visited, a great many years ago, the Sandwich Islands—that peaceful land, that beautiful land, that far-off home of profound repose, and soft indolence, and dreamy solitude, where life is one long slumberous Sabbath, the climate one long delicious summer day, and the good that die experience no change, for they but fall asleep in one heaven and wake up in another. And these boys have played baseball *there!*—baseball, which is the very symbol, the outward and visible expression, of the drive and push and rush and struggle of the raging, tearing, booming nineteenth century! One cannot realize it, the place and the fact are so incongruous; it's like interrupting a funeral with a circus. Why, there's no legitimate point of contact, no possible kinship between baseball and the Sandwich Islands! Baseball is all fact; the islands all sentiment. In baseball you've got to do everything just right, or you don't get there; in the islands you've got to do everything just wrong, or you can't stay there. You do it wrong to get it right, for if you do it right you get it wrong; there isn't any way to get it right *but* to do it wrong, and the wronger you do it the righter it is. The natives illustrate this every day. They never mount a horse from the larboard side, they always mount him from the starboard; on the other hand, they never milk a cow on the starboard side, they always milk her on the larboard; it's why you see so many short people there—they've got their heads kicked off. When they meet on the road, they don't turn out to the right, they turn out to the left. And so, from always doing everything wrong end first, that way, it makes them left handed —left handed and cross eyed; they are all so. When a child is born, the mother goes right along with her ordinary work, without losing half a day; it's the father that knocks off and goes to bed till he gets over the circumstances. And those natives don't trace descent through the male line, but through the female; they say they always know who a child's mother was. Well, that odd system is well enough there, because there a woman often has as many as six or seven husbands, all at the same time and all properly married to her, and no blemish about the matter anywhere. Yet there is no fussing, no trouble. When a child is born the husbands all meet together in convention, in a perfectly orderly way, and elect the father. And the whole thing is perfectly fair; at least as fair as it would be anywhere. Of course, you can't keep politics out—you couldn't do that in any country; and so, if three of the husbands are Republicans and four are Democrats, it doesn't make any difference how strong a Republican aspect the baby has got, that election is going Democratic every time. And in the matter of that election those poor people stand at the proud altitude of the very highest Christian civilization; for they know, as well as we, that all women are ignorant, and so they don't allow that mother to vote. In those islands the cats haven't any tails and the snakes haven't any teeth; and what is still more irregular, the man that loses a game gets the pot. And as to dress; the native women all wear a single garment—but the men don't. No, the men don't wear anything at all; they hate display. When they even wear a smile they think they are overdressed. Speaking of birds, the only bird there that has ornamental feathers has only two—just barely enough to squeeze through with—and they are under its wings instead of on top of its head, where, of course, they ought to be to do any good. The native language is soft and liquid and flexible, and in every way efficient and satisfactory—till you get mad; then there you are; there isn't anything in it to swear with. Good judges all say it is the best Sunday language there is; but then all the other six days in the week it just hangs idle on your hands; it isn't any good for business and you can't work a telephone with it. Many a time the attention of the missionaries has been called to this defect, and they are always promising they are going to fix it; but, no, they go fooling along and fooling along and nothing is done. Speaking of education, everybody there is educated, from the highest to the lowest; in fact, it is the only country in the world where education is actually universal. And yet every now and then you run across instances of ignorance that are simply revolting—simply degrading to the human race. Think of it—there, the ten takes the ace! But let us not dwell on such things; they make a person ashamed. Well, the missionaries are always going to fix that, but they put it off, and put it off, and put it off, and so that nation is going to keep on going down and down and down, till some day you will see a pair of jacks beat a straight flush.

Well, it is refreshment to the jaded, water to the thirsty, to look upon men who have so lately breathed the soft airs of those isles of the blest and had before their eyes the inextinguishable vision of their beauty. No alien land in all the world has any deep, strong charm for me but that one, no other land could so longingly and so beseechingly haunt me, sleeping and waking, through half a lifetime, as that one has done. Other things leave me, but it abides; other things change, but it remains the same. For me its balmy airs are always blowing, its summer seas flashing in the sun, the pulsing of its surf-beat is in my ear; I can see its garlanded crags, its leaping cascades, its plumy palms drowsing by the shore, its remote summits floating like islands above the cloud rack; I can feel the spirit of its woodland solitudes, I can hear the splash of its brooks; in my nostrils still lives the breath of flowers that perished twenty years ago. And these world wanderers who sit before us here have lately looked upon these things!—and with eyes of flesh, not the unsatisfying vision of the spirit. I envy them that!

Yes, and I would envy them somewhat of the glories they have achieved in their illustrious march about the mighty circumference of the earth, if it were fair; but, no, it was an earned run, and envy would be out of place. I will rather applaud—add my hail and welcome to the vast shout now going up, from Maine to the Gulf, from the Florida Keys to frozen Alaska, out of the throats of the other sixty-five millions of their countrymen. They have carried the American name to the uttermost parts of the earth—and covered it with glory every time. That is a service to sentiment; but they did the general world a large practical service, also—a service to the great science of geography. Ah, think of that! We don't talk enough about that—don't give it its full value. Why, when these boys started out you couldn't see the equator at all; you could walk right over it and never know it was there. That is the kind of equator it was. Such an equator as that isn't any use to anybody; as for me, I would rather not have any equator at all than a dim thing like that, that you can't see. But that is all fixed now: you can see it now, you can't run over it now and not know it's there; and so I drink long life to the boys who ploughed a new equator round the globe stealing bases on their bellies!

ON FOREIGN CRITICS

After-dinner Speech (About 1889)

IF I look harried and worn, it is not from an ill conscience. It is from sitting up nights to worry about the foreign critic. He won't concede that we have a civilization—a "real" civilization. Five years ago, he said we had never contributed anything to the betterment of the world. And now comes Sir Lepel Griffin, whom I had not suspected of being in the world at all, and says, "There is no country calling itself civilized where one would not rather live than in America, except Russia." That settles it. That is, it settles it for Europe; but it doesn't make me any more comfortable than I was before.

What is "real" civilization? Nobody can answer that conundrum. They have all tried. Then suppose we try to get at what it is not, and then subtract the what it is not from the general sum, and call the remainder "real" civilization—so as to have a place to stand on while we throw bricks at these people. Let us say, then, in broad terms, that any system which has in it any one of these things—to wit, human slavery, despotic government, inequality, numerous and brutal punishments for crime, superstition almost universal, ignorance almost universal, and dirt and poverty almost universal—is not a real civilization, and any system which has none of them is. If you grant these terms, one may then consider this conundrum: How old is real civilization? The answer is easy and unassailable. A century ago it had not appeared anywhere in the world during a single instant since the world was made. If you grant these terms—and I don't see why it shouldn't be fair, since civilization must surely be fair, since civilization must surely mean the humanizing of a people, not a class—there is to-day but one real civilization in the world, and it is not yet thirty years old. We made the trip and hoisted its flag when we disposed of our slavery.

However, there are some partial civilizations scattered around over Europe—pretty lofty civilizations they are, too—but who begot them? What is the seed from which they sprang? Liberty and intelligence. What planted that seed? There are dates and statistics which suggest that it was the American Revolution that planted it. When that revolution began, monarchy had been on trial some thousands of years, over there, and was a distinct and convicted failure, every time. It had never produced anything but a vast, a nearly universal savagery, with a thin skim of civilization on top, and the main part of that was nickel plate and tinsel. The French, imbruted and impoverished by centuries of oppression and official robbery, were a starving nation clothed in rags, slaves of an aristocracy and smirking dandies clad in unearned silks and velvet. It makes one's cheek burn to read of the laws of the time and realize that they were for human beings; realize that they originated in this world and not in hell. Germany was unspeakable. In the Scotch lowlands the people lived in sties and were human swine; in the highlands drunkenness was general and it hardly smirched a young girl to have a family of her own. In England there was a sham liberty, and not much of that; crime was general; ignorance the same; poverty and misery were widespread; London fed a tenth of her population by charity; the law awarded the death penalty to almost every conceivable offense; what was called medical science by courtesy stood where it had stood for two thousand years; Tom Jones and Squire Western were gentlemen.

The printer's art had been known in Germany and France three and a quarter centuries, and in England three. In all that time there had not been a newspaper in Europe that was worthy the name. Monarchies had no use for that sort of dynamite. When we hoisted the banner of revolution and raised the first genuine shout for human liberty that had ever been heard, this was a newspaperless globe. Eight years later there were six daily journals in London to proclaim to all the nations the greatest birth this world had ever seen. Who woke that printing press out of its trance of three hundred years? Let us be permitted to consider that we did it. Who summoned the French slaves to rise and set the nation free? We did it. What resulted in England and on the Continent? Crippled liberty took up its bed and walked. From that day to this its march has not halted, and please God it never will. We are called the nation of inventors. And we are. We could still claim that title and wear its loftiest honors if we had stopped with the first thing we ever invented—which was human liberty. Out of that invention has come the Christian world's great civilization. Without it it was impossible—as the history of all the centuries has proved. Well, then, who invented civilization? Even Sir Lepel Griffin ought to be able to answer that question. It looks easy enough. *We* have contributed *nothing!* Nothing hurts me like ingratitude.

MISTAKEN IDENTITY

ADDRESS AT THE ANNUAL "LADIES' DAY," PAPYRUS CLUB, BOSTON

LADIES AND GENTLEMEN,—I am prefectly astonished—a-s-t-o-n-i-s-h-e-d—ladies and gentlemen—astonished at the way history repeats itself. I find myself situated at this moment exactly and precisely as I was once before, years ago, to a jot, to a tittle—to a very hair. There isn't a shade of difference. It is the most astonishing coincidence that ever—but wait. I will tell you the former instance, and then you will see it for yourself. Years ago I arrived one day at Salamanca, New York, eastward bound; must change cars there and take the sleeper train. There were crowds of people there, and they were swarming into the long sleeper train and packing it full, and it was a perfect purgatory of dust and confusion and gritting of teeth and soft, sweet, and low profanity. I asked the young man in the ticket office if I could have a sleeping-section, and he answered "No," with a snarl that shrivelled me up like burned leather. I went off, smarting under this insult to my dignity, and asked another local official, supplicatingly, if I couldn't have some poor little corner somewhere in a sleeping car; but he cut me short with a venomous "No, you can't; every corner is full. Now, don't bother me any more"; and he turned his back and walked off. My dignity was in a state now which cannot be described. I was so ruffled that—well, I said to my companion, "If these people knew who I am they—" But my companion cut me short there—"Don't talk such folly," he said; "if they did know who you are, do you suppose it would help your high-mightiness to a vacancy in a train which has no vacancies in it?"

This did not improve my condition any to speak of, but just then I observed that the colored porter of a sleeping car had his eye on me. I saw his dark countenance light up. He whispered to the uniformed conductor, punctuating with nods and jerks toward me, and straightway this conductor came forward, oozing politeness from every pore.

"Can I be of any service to you?" he asked. "Will you have a place in the sleeper?"

"Yes," I said, "and much oblige me, too. Give me anything—anything will answer."

"We have nothing left but the big family stateroom," he continued, "with two berths and a couple of armchairs in it, but it is entirely at your disposal. Here, Tom, take these satchels aboard!"

Then he touched his hat and we and the colored Tom moved along. I was bursting to drop just one little remark to my companion, but I held in and waited. Tom made us comfortable in that sumptuous great apartment, and then said, with many bows and a perfect affluence of smiles:

"Now, is dey anything you want, sah? Case you kin have jes' anything you wants. It don't make no difference what it is."

"Can I have some hot water and a tumbler at nine to-night—blazing hot?" I asked. "You know about the right temperature for a hot Scotch punch?"

"Yes, sah, dat you kin; you kin pen on it; I'll get it myself."

"Good! Now, that lamp is hung too high. Can I have a big coach candle fixed up just at the head of my bed, so that I can read comfortably?"

"Yes, sah, you kin; I'll fix her up myself, an' I'll fix her so she'll burn all night. Yes, sah; an' you can jes' call for anything you want, and dish yer whole railroad 'll be turned wrong end up an' inside out for to get it for you. Dat's so." And he disappeared.

Well, I tilted my head back, hooked my thumbs in my armholes, smiled a smile on my companion, and said, gently:

"Well, what do you say now?"

My companion was not in the humor to respond, and didn't. The next moment that smiling black face was thrust in at the crack of the door, and this speech followed:

"Laws bless you, sah, I knowed you in a minute. I told de conductah so. Laws! I knowed you de minute I sot eyes on you."

"Is that so, my boy?" (Handing him a quadruple fee.) "Who am I?"

"Jenuel McClellan," and he disappeared again.

My companion said, vinegarishly, "Well, well! what do you say now?" Right there comes in the marvelous coincidence I mentioned a while ago—*viz.*, I was speechless, and that is my condition now. Perceive it?

DALY THEATRE

ADDRESS AT A DINNER AFTER THE ONE HUNDREDTH PERFORMANCE OF "THE TAMING OF THE SHREW"

Mr. Clemens told the following story, which he incorporated afterward in Following the Equator.

I AM glad to be here. This is the hardest theatre in New York to get into, even at the front door. I never got in without hard work. I am glad we have got so far in at last. Two or three years ago I had an appointment to meet Mr. Daly on the stage of this theatre at eight o'clock in the evening. Well, I got on a train at Hartford to come to New York and keep the appointment. All I had to do was to come to the back door of the theatre on Sixth Avenue. I did not believe that; I did not believe it could be on Sixth Avenue, but that is what Daly's note said—come to that door, walk right in, and keep the appointment. It looked very easy. It looked easy enough, but I had not much confidence in the Sixth Avenue door.

Well, I was kind of bored on the train, and I bought some newspapers—New Haven newspapers—and there was not much news in them, so I read the advertisements. There was one advertisement of a bench show. I had heard of bench shows, and I often wondered what there was about them to interest people. I had seen bench shows—lectured to bench shows, in fact—but I didn't want to advertise them or to brag about them. Well, I read on a little, and learned that a bench show was not a bench show—but dogs, not benches at all—only dogs. I began to be interested, and as there was nothing else to do I read every bit of the advertisement, and learned that the biggest thing in this show was a St. Bernard dog that weighed one hundred and forty-five pounds. Before I got to New York I was so interested in the bench shows that I made up my mind to go to one the first chance I got. Down on Sixth Avenue, near where that back door might be, I began to take things leisurely. I did not like to be in too much of a hurry. There was not anything in sight that looked like a back door. The nearest approach to it was a cigar store. So I went in and bought a cigar, not too expensive, but it cost enough to pay for any information I might get and leave the dealer a fair profit. Well, I did not like to be too abrupt, to make the man think me crazy, by asking him if that was the way to Daly's Theatre, so I started gradually to lead up to the subject, asking him first if that was the way to Castle Garden. When I got to the real question, and he said he would show me the way, I was astonished. He sent me through a long hallway, and I found myself in a back yard. Then I went through a long passageway and into a little room, and there before my eyes was a big St. Bernard dog lying on a bench. There was another door beyond and I went there, and was met by a big, fierce man with a fur cap on and coat off, who remarked, "Phwat do yez want?" I told him I wanted to see Mr. Daly. "Yez can't see Mr. Daly this time of night," he responded. I urged that I had an appointment with Mr. Daly, and gave him my card, which did not seem to impress him much. "Yez can't get in and yez can't shmoke here. Throw away that cigar. If yez want to see Mr. Daly, yez'll have to be after going to the front door and buy a ticket, and then if yez have luck and he's around that way yez may see him." I was getting discouraged, but I had one resource left that had been of good service in similar emergencies. Firmly but kindly I told him my name was Mark Twain, and I awaited results. There was none. He was not fazed a bit. "Phwere's your order to see Mr. Daly?" he asked. I handed him the note, and he examined it intently. "My friend," I remarked, "you can read that better if you hold it the other side up." But he took no notice of the suggestion, and finally asked: "Where's Mr. Daly's name?" "There it is," I told him, "on the top of the page." "That's all right," he said, "that's where he always puts it; but I don't see the 'W' in his name," and he eyed me distrustfully. Finally he asked, "Phwat do yez want to see Mr. Daly for?" "Business." "Business?" "Yes." It was my only hope. "Phwat kind—theatres?" That was too much. "No." "What kind of shows, then?" "Bench shows." It was risky, but I was desperate. "Bench shows, is it—where?" The big man's face changed, and he began to look interested. "New Haven." "New Haven, it is? Ah, that's going to be a fine show. I'm glad to see you. Did you see a big dog in the other room?"

"Yes." "How much do you think that dog weighs?" "One hundred and forty-five pounds." "Look at that, now! He's a good judge of dogs, and no mistake. He weighs all of one hundred and thirty-eight. Sit down and shmoke—go on and shmoke your cigar, I'll tell Mr. Daly you are here." In a few minutes I was on the stage shaking hands with Mr. Daly, and the big man standing around glowing with satisfaction. "Come around in front," said Mr. Daly, "and see the performance. I will put you into my own box." And as I moved away I heard my honest friend mutter, "Well, he desarves it."

LOTOS CLUB DINNER IN HONOR OF MARK TWAIN

Address at the First Formal Dinner in the New Club-house, November 11, 1893

In introducing the guest of the eve`ning, Mr. Lawrence said:

"To-night the old faces appear once more amid new surroundings. The place where last we met about the table has vanished, and to-night we have our first Lotos dinner in a home that is all our own. It is peculiarly fitting that the board should now be spread in honor of one who has been a member of the club for full a score of years, and it is a happy augury for the future that our fellow-member whom we assemble to greet should be the bearer of a most distinguished name in the world of letters; for the Lotos Club is ever at its best when paying homage to genius in literature or in art. Is there a civilized being who has not heard the name of Mark Twain? We knew him long years ago, before he came out of the boundless West, brimful of wit and eloquence, with no reverence for anything, and went abroad to educate the untutored European in the subtleties of the American joke. The world has looked on and applauded while he has broken many images. He has led us in imagination all over the globe. With him as our guide we have traversed alike the Mississippi and the Sea of Galilee. At his bidding we have laughed at a thousand absurdities. By a laborious process of reasoning he has convinced us that the Egyptian mummies are actually dead. He has held us spellbound upon the plain at the foot of the great Sphinx, and we have joined him in weeping bitter tears at the tomb of Adam. To-night we greet him in the flesh. What name is there in literature that can be likened to his? Perhaps some of the distinguished gentlemen about this table can tell us, but I know of none. Himself his only parallel!"

MR. PRESIDENT, GENTLEMEN, AND FELLOW-MEMBERS OF THE LOTOS CLUB,—I have seldom in my lifetime listened to compliments so felicitously phrased or so well deserved. I return thanks for them from a full heart and an appreciative spirit, and I will say this in self-defense: While I am charged with having no reverence for anything, I wish to say that I have reverence for the man who can utter such truths, and I also have a deep reverence and a sincere one for a club that can do such justice to me. To be the chief guest of such a club is something to be envied, and if I read your countenances rightly I am envied. I am glad to see this club in such palatial quarters. I remember it twenty years ago when it was housed in a stable.

Now when I was studying for the ministry there were two or three things that struck my attention particularly. At the first banquet mentioned in history that other prodigal son who came back from his travels was invited to stand up and have his say. They were all there, his brethern, David and Goliath, and—er, and if he had had such experience as I have had he would have waited until those other people got through talking. He got up and testified to all his failings. Now if he had waited before telling all about his riotous living until the others had spoken he might not have given himself away as he did, and I think that I would give myself away if I should go on. I think I'd better wait until the others hand in their testimony; then if it is necessary for me to make an explanation, I will get up and explain, and if I cannot do that, I'll deny it happened.

LOTUS CLUB DINNER

Later in the evening Mr. Clemens made another speech, replying to a fire of short speeches by Charles Dudley Warner, Charles A. Dana, Seth Low, General Porter, and many others, each welcoming the guest of honor.

I don't see that I have a great deal to explain. I got off very well, considering the opportunities that these other fellows had. I don't see that Mr. Low said anything against me, and neither did Mr. Dana. However, I will say that I never heard so many lies told in one evening as were told by Mr. McKelway—and I consider myself very capable; but even in his case, when he got through, I was gratified by finding how much he hadn't found out. By accident he missed the very things that I didn't want to have said, and now, gentlemen, about Americanism.

I have been on the continent of Europe for two and a half years. I have met many Americans there, some sojourning for a short time only, others making protracted stays, and it has been very gratifying to me to find that nearly all preserved their Americanism. I have found they all like to see the Flag fly, and that their hearts rise when they see the Stars and Stripes. I met only one lady who had forgotten the land of her birth and glorified monarchical institutions.

I think it is a great thing to say that in two and a half years I met only one person who had fallen a victim to the shams—I think we may call them shams—of nobilities and of heredities. She was entirely lost in them. After I had listened to her for a long time, I said to her: "At least you must admit that we have one merit. We are not like the Chinese, who refuse to allow their citizens who are tired of the country to leave it. Thank God, we don't!"

AN UNDELIVERED SPEECH

The steamship St. Paul *was to have been launched from Cramp's shipyard in Philadelphia on March 25, 1895. A luncheon had been planned at which Mr. Clemens was to make a speech. Just before the final word was given a reporter asked Mr. Clemens for a copy of his speech to be deliverd at the luncheon. To facilitate the work of the reporter he loaned him a typewritten copy of the speech. It happened, however, that when the blocks were knocked away the big ship refused to budge, and no amount of labor could move her an inch. She had stuck fast upon the ways. As a result, the launching was postponed for a week or two; but in the meantime Mr. Clemens had gone to Europe. Years after a reporter called on Mr. Clemens and submitted the manuscript of the speech, which was as follows:*

DAY after to-morrow I sail for England in a ship of this line, the *Paris*. It will be my fourteenth crossing in three years and a half. Therefore, my presence here, as you see, is quite natural, quite commercial. I am interested in ships. They interest me more now than hotels do. When a new ship is launched I feel a desire to go and see if she will be good quarters for me to live in, particularly if she belongs to this line, for it is by this line that I have done most of my ferrying.

People wonder why I go so much. Well, I go partly for my health, partly to familiarize myself with the road. I have gone over the same road so many times now that I know all the whales that belong along the route, and latterly it is an embarrassment to me to meet them, for they do not look glad to see me, but annoyed, and they seem to say: "Here is this old derelict again."

Earlier in life this would have pained me and made me ashamed, but I am older now, and when I am behaving myself, and doing right, I do not care for a whale's opinion about me. When we are young we generally estimate an opinion by the size of the person that holds it, but later we find that that is an uncertain rule, for we realize that there are times when a hornet's opinion disturbs us more than an emperor's.

I do not mean that I care nothing at all for a whale's opinion, for that would be going to too great a length. Of course, it is better to have the good opinion of a whale than his disapproval; but my position is that if you cannot have a whale's good opinion, except at some sacrifice of principle or personal dignity, it is better to try to live without it. That is my idea about whales.

Yes, I have gone over that same route so often that I know my way without a compass, just by the waves. I know all the large waves and a good many of the small ones. Also the sunsets. I know every sunset and where it belongs just by its color. Necessarily, then, I do not make the passage now for scenery. That is all gone by.

What I prize most is safety, and in the second place swift transit and handiness. These are best furnished by the American line, whose water-tight compartments have no passage through them, no doors to be left open, and consequently no way for water to get from one of them to another in time of collision. If you nullify the peril which collisions threaten you with, you nullify the only very serious peril which attends voyages in the great liners of our day, and makes voyaging safer than staying at home.

When the *Paris* was half-torn to pieces some years ago, enough of the Atlantic ebbed and flowed through one end of her, during her long agony, to sink the fleets of the world if distributed among them; but she floated in perfect safety, and no life was lost. In time of collision the rock of Gibraltar is not safer than the *Paris* and other great ships of this line. This seems to be the only great line in the world that takes a passenger from metropolis to metropolis without the intervention of tugs and barges or bridges—takes him through without breaking bulk, so to speak.

On the English side he lands at a dock; on the dock a special train is waiting; in an hour and three-quarters he is in London. Nothing could be handier. If your journey were from a sandpit on our side to a lighthouse on the other, you could make it quicker by other lines, but that is not the case. The journey is from the city of New York to the city of London, and no line can do that journey quicker than this one, nor anywhere near as conveniently and handily. And when the passenger lands on our side he lands on the American side of the river, not in the provinces. As a very learned man said on the last voyage (he is head quartermaster of the New York and garboard streak of the middle watch): "When we land a passenger on the American side there's nothing betwixt him and his hotel but hell and the hackman."

I am glad, with you and the nation, to welcome the new ship. She is another pride, another consolation, for a great country whose mighty fleets have all vanished, and which has almost forgotten what it is to fly its flag to sea. I am not sure as to which St. Paul she is named for. Some think it is the one that is on the upper Mississippi, but the head quartermaster told me it was the one that killed Goliath. But it is not important. No matter which it is, let us give her hearty welcome and godspeed.

DIE SCHRECKEN DER DEUTSCHEN SPRACHE

ADDRESS TO THE VIENNA PRESS CLUB, NOVEMBER 21, 1897, AS DELIVERED IN GERMAN

ES hat mich tief gerührt, meine Herren, hier so gastfreundlich empfangen zu werden, von Kollegen aus meinem eigenen Berufe, in diesem von meiner eigenen Hiemath so weit entferntem Lande. Mein Herz ist voller Daknbarkeit, aber meine Armuth an deutschen Worten zwingt mich zu groszer Sparzamkeit des Ausdruckes. Entschuldigen Sie, meine Herren, dasz ich verlese, was ich Ihnen sagen will. (Er las aber nicht, Anm, d. Ref.) Die deutsche Sprache spreche ich nicht gut, doch haben mehrere Sächverständige mich versichert, dasz ich sie schreibe wie ein Engel. Mag sein—Mag sein—ich weisz nicht. Habe bis jetzt keine Behanntschaften mit Engeln gehabt. Das kommt später—wenn's dem lieben Gott gefällt—es hat heine Eile.

Seit lange, meine Herren, habe ich die leidenschaftliche Sehnsucht gehegt, eine Rede auf Deutsch zu halten, aber man hat mir's nie relauben wollen. Leute, die kein Gefühl für die Kunst hatten, legten mir immer Hindernissse in den Weg und vereitelten meinen Wunsch—zuweilen durch Vorwände, häufig durch Gewalt. Immer sagten diese Leute zu mir: "Schweigen Sie, Ew. Hochwohlgeborne! Ruhe, um

THE HORRORS OF THE GERMAN LANGUAGE

ADDRESS TO THE VIENNA PRESS CLUB, NOVEMBER 21, 1897

[A LITERAL TRANSLATION]

IT has me deeply touched, my gentlemen, here so hospitably received to be. From colleagues out of my own profession, in this from my own home so far distant land. My heart is full of gratitude, but my poverty of German words forces me to greater economy of expression. Excuse you, my gentlemen, that I read off, what I you say will. [But he didn't read].

The German language speak I not good, but have numerous connoisseurs me assured that I her write like an angel. Maybe—maybe—I know not. Have till now no acquaintance with the angels had. That comes later—when it the dear God please—it has no hurry.

Since long, my gentlemen, have I the passionate longing nursed a speech on German to hold, but one has me not permitted. Men, who no feeling for the art had, laid me ever hindrance in the way and made naught my desire—sometimes by excuses, often by force. Always said these men to me: "Keep you still, your Highness! Silence! For God's sake seek

Gotteswillen! Suche eine andere Art und Weise, Dich lästig zu machen."

Im jetzinger Fall, wie gewöhnlich, ist es mir schwierig geworden, mir die Erlaubniz zu verschaffen. Das Comite bedauerte sehr, aber es konnte mir die Erlaubnisz nicht bewilligen wegen eines Gesetzes, das von der Concoria verlangt, sie soll die deutsche Sprache schützen. Du liebe Zeit! Wieso hätte man mir das sagen können—mögen—dürfen—sollen? Ich bin ja der treueste Freund der deutschen Sprache—und nicht nur jetzt, sondern von lange her—ja vor zwanzig Jahren schon. Und nie habe ich das Verlangen gehabt, der edlen Sprache zu schaden; im Gegentheil, nur gewünscht, sie zu verbessern; ich wollte sie blos reformiren. Es ist der Traum meinen Lebens gewesen. Ich habe schon Besuche bei den verschiedenen deutschen Regierungen abgestattet und um Kontrakte gebeten. Ich bin jetzt nach Oesterreich in demselben Auftrag gekommen. Ich wurde nur einige Aenderungen anstrebun. Ich wurde blos die Sprachmethode—die uppige, weitschweifige Konstruktion—zusammernuchen; die ewig Parenthese unterdrücken, abschaffen, vernichten; dic Einführung von mehr als driezehn Subjekten in einen Satz verbieten; das Zeitwort so weit nach vorne rücken, bis man es ohne Fernrohr entdechen kann. Mit einem Wort, meine Herren, ich möchte Ihre geliebte Sprache vereinfachen, auf dasz, meine Herren, wenn Sie sie zum Gebet brauchen, nam sie dort oben versteht.

Ich flehe Sie an, von mir sich berathen zu lassen, führen Sie diese erwähnten Reformen aus. Dann another way and means yourself obnoxious to make."

In the present case, as usual it is me difficult become, for me the permission to obtain. The committee sorrowed deeply, but could me the permission not grant on account of a law which from the Concordia demands she shall the German language protect. Du liebe Zeit! How so had one to me this say could—might—dared—should. I am indeed the truest friend of the German language—and not only now, but from long since—yes, before twenty years already. And never have I the desire had the noble language to hurt; to the contrary, only wished she to improve—I would her only reform. It is the dream of my life been. I have already visits by the various German governments paid and for contracts prayed. I am now to Austria in the same task come. I would only some changes effect. I would only the language method—the luxurious, elaborate construction compress, the eternal parenthesis suppress, do away with, annihilate; the introduction of more than thirteen subjects in one sentence forbid; the verb so far to the front pull that one it without a telescope discover can. With one word, my gentlemen, I would your beloved language simplify so that, my gentlemen, when you her for prayer need, One her yonder-up understands.

I beseech you, from me yourself counsel to let, execute these mentioned reforms. Then will you an elegant language possess, and afterward, when you

ken. Herr Pötzl hat das Publikum glauben machen wollen, dasz ich nach Wien gekommen bin, um die Brücken zu verstopfen und den Verkehr zu hindern, während ich Beobachtungen sammle und aufziechne. Lassen Sie sich aber nicht von ihm anführen. Meine häufige Anwesenheit auf den Brücken hat einen ganz unschuldigen Grund. Dort geibt's den nöthigen Raum. Dort kann man einen edlen, langen, deutschen Satz ausdehnen, die Brückengeländer entlang, und seinen ganzen Inhalt mit einen Blick ubersehen. Auf das eine Ende des Geländers klebe ich das erste Glied eines trennbaren Zeitwortes und das Schluszglied klebe ich an's andere Ende—dann breite ich den Lieb des Satzes dazwischen aus. Gewöhnlich sing für meinen Zweck die Brücken der Stadt lang genug: wenn ich aber Pötzl's Schriften studiren will, fahe ich hinaus und benutze die herrliche unendliche Reichsbrücke. Aber das ist eine Verleumdung. Pötzl schreibt das schönste Deutsch. Vielleicht nicht so biegsam wie das meinige, aber in manchen Kleinigkeiten viel besser. Entschuldigen Sie diese Schmeicheleien. Die sind wohl verdient.

Nun bringe ich meine Rede um—nein—ich wollte sagen, ich bringe sie zum Schlusz. Ich bin ein Fremder—aber hier, uter Ihnen, habe ich es ganz vergessen. Und so, wieder, und noch wieder—biete ich Ihnen meinen herzlichsten Dank!

come am in order the bridges to clog up and the traffic to hinder, while I observations gather and note. Allow you yourselves but not from him deceived. My frequent presence on the bridges has an entirely innocent ground. Yonder gives it the necessary space, yonder can one a noble long German sentence elaborate, the bridge-railing along, and his whole contents with one glance overlook. On the one end of the railing pasted I the first member of a separable verb and the final member cleave I to the other end—then spread the body of the sentences between it out! Usually are for my purposes the bridges of the city long enough; when I but Pötzl's writings study will I ride out and use the glorious endless imperial bridge. But this is a calumny; Potzl writes the prettiest German. Perhaps not so pliable as the mine, but in many details much better. Excuse you these flatteries. These are well deserved.

Now I my speech execute—no, I would say I bring her to the close. I am a foreigner—but here, under you, have I it entirely forgotten. And so again and yet again proffer I you my heartiest thanks."

GERMAN FOR THE HUNGARIANS

ADDRESS AT THE JUBILEE CELEBRATION OF THE EMANCIPATION OF THE HUNGARIAN PRESS, MARCH 26, 1899

The Ministry and members of Parliament were present. The subject was the "Ausgleich"—i. e., *the arrangement for the apportionment of the taxes between Hungary and Austria. Paragraph* 14 *of the ausgleich fixes the proportion each country must pay to the support of the army. It is the paragraph which caused the trouble and prevented renewal of the arrangement.*

NOW that we are all here together, I think it will be a good idea to arrange the ausgleich. If you will act for Hungary I shall be quite willing to act for Austria, and this is the very time for it. There couldn't be a better, for we are all feeling friendly, fair-minded, and hospitable now, and full of admiration for each other, full of confidence in each other, full of the spirit of welcome, full of the grace of forgiveness, and the disposition to let bygones be bygones.

Let us not waste this golden, this beneficent, this providential opportunity. I am willing to make any concession you want, just so we get it settled. I am not only willing to let grain come in free, I am willing to pay the freight on it, and you may send delegates to the Reichsrath if you like. All I require is that they shall be quiet, peaceable people like your own deputies, and not disturb our proceedings.

If you want the Gegenseitigengeldbeitragendenverhältnismässigkeiten rearranged and readjusted I am ready for that. I will let you off at twenty-eight per cent—twenty-seven—even twenty-five if you insist, for there is nothing illiberal about me when I am out on a diplomatic debauch.

Now, in return for these concessions, I am willing to take anything in reason, and I think we may consider the business settled and the ausgleich ausgegloschen at last for ten solid years, and we will sign the papers in blank, and do it here and now.

Well, I am unspeakably glad to have that ausgleich off my hands. It has kept me awake nights for anderthalbjahr.

But I never could settle it before, because always when I called at the Foreign Office in Vienna to talk about it, there wasn't anybody at home, and that is not a place where you can go in and see for yourself whether it is a mistake or not, because the person who takes care of the front door there is of a size that discourages liberty of action and the free spirit of investigation. To think the ausgleich is abgemacht at last! It is a grand and beautiful consummation, and I am glad I came.

The way I feel now I do honestly believe I would rather be just my own humble self at this moment than paragraph 14.

TO THE WHITEFRIARS

ADDRESS AT THE DINNER GIVEN BY THE WHITEFRIARS' CLUB IN HONOR OF MR. CLEMENS, LONDON, JUNE 20, 1899

The Whitefriars' Club was founded by Dr. Samuel Johnson, and Mr. Clemens was made an honorary member in 1874. The members are representative of literary and journalistic London. The toast of "Our Guest" was proposed by Louis F. Austin, of the Illustrated London News, *and in the course of some humorous remarks he referred to the vow and to the imaginary woes of the "Friars," as the members of the club style themselves.*

MR. CHAIRMAN AND BRETHREN OF THE VOW—in whatever the vow is; for although I have been a member of this club for five-and-twenty years, I don't know any more about what that vow is than Mr. Austin seems to. But whatever the vow is, I don't care what it is. I have made a thousand vows.

There is no pleasure comparable to making a vow in the presence of one who appreciates that vow, in the presence of men who honor and appreciate you for making the vow, and men who admire you for making the vow.

There is only one pleasure higher than that, and that is to get outside and break the vow. A vow is always a pledge of some kind or other for the protection of your own morals and principles or somebody else's, and generally by the irony of fate, it is for the protection of your own morals.

Hence we have pledges that make us eschew tobacco or wine, and while you are taking the pledge there is a holy influence about that makes you feel you are reformed, and that you can never be so happy again in this world until—you get outside and take a drink.

I had forgotten that I was a member of this club—it is so long ago. But now I remember that I was here five-and-twenty years ago, and that I was then at a dinner of the Whitefriars' Club, and it was in those old days when you had just made two great finds. All London was talking about nothing else than that they had found Livingstone, and that the lost Sir Roger Tichborne had been found—and they were trying him for it.

And at the dinner, Chairman —— (I do not know who he was)—failed to come to time. The gentleman who had been appointed to pay me the customary compliments and to introduce me forgot the compliments, and did not know what they were.

And George Augustus Sala came in at the last moment, just when I was about to go without compliments altogether. And that man was a gifted man. They just called on him instantaneously, while he was going to sit down, to introduce the stranger, and Sala made one of those marvellous speeches which he was capable of making. I think no man talked so fast as Sala did. One did not need wine while he was making a speech. The rapidity of his utterance made a man drunk in a minute. An incomparable speech was that, an impromptu speech, and an impromptu speech is a seldom thing, and he did it so well.

He went into the whole history of the United States, and made it entirely new to me. He filled it with episodes and incidents that Washington never heard of, and he did it so convincingly that although I knew none of it had happened, from that day to this I do not know any history but Sala's.

I do not know anything so sad as a dinner where you are going to get up and say something by-and-by, and you do not know what it is. You sit and wonder and wonder what the gentleman is going to say who is going to introduce you. You know that if he says something severe, that if he will deride you, or traduce you, or do anything of that kind, he will furnish you with a text, because anybody can get up and talk against that.

Anybody can get up and straighten out his character. But when a gentleman gets up and merely tells the truth about you, what can you do?

Mr. Austin has done well. He has supplied so many texts that I will have to drop out a lot of them, and that is about as difficult as when you do not have any text at all. Now, he made a beautiful and smooth speech without any difficulty at all, and I could have done that if I had gone on with the schooling with which I began. I see here a gentleman on my left who was my master in the art of oratory more than twenty-five years ago.

When I look upon the inspiring face of Mr. Depew, it carries me a long way back. An old and valued friend of mine is he, and I saw his career as it came along, and it has reached pretty well up to now, when he, by another miscarriage of justice, is a

United States Senator. But those were delightful days when I was taking lessons in oratory.

My other master—the Ambassador—is not here yet. Under those two gentlemen I learned to make after-dinner speeches, and it was charming.

You know the New England dinner is the great occasion on the other side of the water. It is held every year to celebrate the landing of the Pilgrims. Those Pilgrims were a lot of people who were not needed in England, and you know they had great rivalry, and they were persuaded to go elsewhere, and they chartered a ship called *Mayflower* and set sail, and I have heard it said that they pumped the Atlantic Ocean through that ship sixteen times.

They fell in over there with the Dutch from Rotterdam, Amsterdam, and a lot of other places with profane names, and it is from that gang that Mr. Depew is descended.

On the other hand, Mr. Choate is descended from those Puritans who landed on a bitter night in December. Every year those people used to meet at a great banquet in New York, and those masters of mind in oratory had to make speeches. It was Doctor Depew's business to get up there and apologize for the Dutch, and Mr. Choate had to get up later and explain the crimes of the Puritans, and grand, beautiful times we used to have.

It is curious that after that long lapse of time I meet the Whitefriars again, some looking as young and fresh as in the old days, others showing a certain amount of wear and tear, and here, after all this time, I find one of the masters of oratory and the other named in the list.

And here we three meet again as exiles on one pretext or another, and you will notice that while we are absent there is a pleasing tranquillity in America—a building up of public confidence. We are doing the best we can for our country. I think we have spent our lives in serving our country, and we never serve it to greater advantage than when we get out of it.

But impromptu speaking—that is what I was trying to learn. That is a difficult thing. I used to do it in this way. I used to begin about a week ahead, and write out my impromptu speech and get it by heart. Then I brought it to the New England dinner printed on a piece of paper in my pocket, so that I could pass it to the reporters all cut and dried, and in order to do an impromptu speech as it should be done you have to indicate the places for pauses and hesitations. I put them all in it. And then you want the applause in the right places.

When I got to the place where it should come in, if it did not come in I did not care, but I had it marked in the paper. And these masters of mind used to wonder why it was my speech came out in the morning in the first person, while theirs went through the butchery of synopsis.

I do that kind of speech (I mean an offhand speech), and do it well, and make no mistake, in such a way to deceive the audience completely and make that audience believe it is an impromptu speech—that is art.

I was frightened out of it at last by an experience of Doctor Hayes. He was a sort of Nansen of that day. He had been to the North Pole, and it made him celebrated. He had even seen the polar bear climb the pole.

He had made one of those magnificent voyages such as Nansen made, and in those days when a man did anything which greatly distinguished him for the moment he had to come on to the lecture platform and tell all about it.

Doctor Hayes was a great, magnificent creature like Nansen, superbly built. He was to appear in Boston. He wrote his lecture out, and it was his purpose to read it from manuscript; but in an evil hour he concluded that it would be a good thing to preface it with something rather handsome, poetical, and beautiful that he could get off by heart and deliver as if it were the thought of the moment.

He had not had my experience, and could not do that. He came on the platform, held his manuscript down, and began with a beautiful piece of oratory. He spoke something like this:

"When a lonely human being, a pigmy in the midst of the architecture of nature, stands solitary on those icy waters and looks abroad to the horizon and sees mighty castles and temples of eternal ice raising up their pinnacles tipped by the pencil of the departing sun—"

Here a man came across the platform and touched him on the shoulder, and said: "One minute." And then to the audience:

"Is Mrs. John Smith in the house? Her husband has slipped on the ice and broken his leg."

And you could see the Mrs. John Smiths get up

everywhere and drift out of the house, and it made great gaps everywhere. Then Doctor Hayes began again: "When a lonely man, a pigmy in the architecture—" The janitor came in again and shouted: "It is not Mrs. John Smith! It is Mrs. John Jones!"

Then all the Mrs. Joneses got up and left. Once more the speaker started, and was in the midst of the sentence when he was interrupted again, and the result was that the lecture was not delivered. But the lecturer interviewed the janitor afterward in a private room, and of the fragments of that janitor they took "twelve basketsful."

Now, I don't want to sit down just in this way. I have been talking with so much levity that I have said no serious thing, and you are really no better or wiser, although Robert Buchanan has suggested that I am a person who deals in wisdom. I have said nothing which would make you better than when you came here.

I should be sorry to sit down without having said one serious word which you can carry home and relate to your children and the old people who are not able to get away.

And this is just a little maxim which has saved me from many a difficulty and many a disaster, and in times of tribulation and uncertainty has come to my rescue, as it shall to yours if you observe it as I do day and night.

I always use it in an emergency, and you can take it home as a legacy from me, and it is: "When in doubt, tell the truth."

AUTHORS' CLUB

Address at the Dinner Given in Honor of Mr. Clemens, London, June, 1899

Mr. Clemens was introduced by Sir Walter Besant.

IT does not embarrass me to hear my books praised so much. It only pleases and delights me. I have not gone beyond the age when embarrassment is possible, but I have reached the age when I know how to conceal it. It is such a satisfaction to me to hear Sir Walter Besant, who is much more capable than I to judge of my work, deliver a judgment which is such a contentment to my spirit.

Well, I have thought well of the books myself, but I think more of them now. It charms me also to hear Sir Spencer Walpole deliver a similar judgment, and I shall treasure his remarks also. I shall not discount the praises in any possible way. When I report them to my family they shall lose nothing. There are, however, certain hereditities which come down to us which our writings of the present day may be traced to. I, for instance, read the *Walpole Letters* when I was a boy. I absorbed them, gathered in their grace, wit, and humor, and put them away to be used by-and-by. One does that so unconsciously with things one really likes. I am reminded now of what use those letters have been to me.

do with it. It comes of habit, which accounts for many things.

Yesterday, for example, I was at a luncheon party. At the end of the party a great dignitary of the English Established Church went away half an hour before anybody else and carried off my hat. Now, that was an innocent act on his part. He went out first, and, of course, had the choice of hats. As a rule I try to get out first myself. But I hold that it was an innocent, unconscious act, due, perhaps, to heredity. He was thinking about ecclesiastical matters, and when a man is in that condition of mind he will take anybody's hat. The result was that the whole afternoon I was under the influence of his clerical hat and could not tell a lie. Of course, he was hard at it.

It is a compliment to both of us. His hat fitted me exactly; my hat fitted him exactly. So I judge I was born to rise to high dignity in the Church some how or other, but I do not know what he was born for. That is an illustration of the influence of habit, and it is perceptible here when they say "an" hospital, "an" European, "an" historical.

The business aspect of the Fourth of July is not perfect as it stands. See what it costs us every year with loss of life, the crippling of thousands with its fireworks, and the burning down of property. It is not only sacred to patriotism and universal freedom, but to the surgeon, the undertaker, the insurance offices—and they are working it for all it is worth.

I am pleased to see that we have a cessation of war for the time. This coming from me, a soldier, you will appreciate. I was a soldier in the Southern war for two weeks, and when gentlemen get up to speak of the great deeds our army and navy have recently done, why, it goes all through me and fires up the old war spirit. I had in my first engagement three horses shot under me. The next shots went over my head, the next hit me in the back. Then I retired to meet an engagement.

I thank you, gentlemen, for making even a slight reference to the war profession, in which I distinguished myself, short as my career was.

THEORETICAL AND PRACTICAL MORALS

The New Vagabonds Club, of London, made up of the leading younger literary men of the day, gave a dinner in honor of Mr. and Mrs. Clemens, July 8, 1899.

IT has always been difficult—leave that word difficult—not exceedingly difficult, but just difficult, nothing more than that, not the slightest shade to add to that—just difficult—to respond properly, in the right phraseology, when compliments are paid to me; but it is more than difficult when the compliments are paid to a better than I—my wife.

And while I am not here to testify against myself—I can't be expected to do so, a prisoner in your own country is not admitted to do so—as to which member of the family wrote my books, I could say in general that really I wrote the books myself. My wife puts the facts in, and they make it respectable. My modesty won't suffer while compliments are being paid to literature, and through literature to my family. I can't get enough of them.

I am curiously situated to-night. It so rarely happens that I am introduced by a humorist; I am generally introduced by a person of grave walk and carriage. That makes the proper background of gravity for brightness. I am going to alter to suit, and haply I may say some humorous things.

When you start with a blaze of sunshine and upburst of humor, when you begin with that, the proper office of humor is to reflect, to put you into that pensive mood of deep thought, to make you think of your sins, if you wish half an hour to fly. Humor makes me reflect now to-night, it sets the thinking machinery in motion. Always, when I am thinking, there comes suggestions of what I am, and what we all are, and what we are coming to. A sermon comes from my lips always when I listen to a humorous speech.

I seize the opportunity to throw away frivolities, to say something to plant the seed, and make all better than when I came. In Mr. Grossmith's remarks there was a subtle something suggesting my favorite theory of the difference between theoretical morals and practical morals. I try to instill practical morals in the place of theatrical—I mean theoretical; but as an addendum—an annex—something added to theoretical morals.

When your chairman said it was the first time he had ever taken the chair, he did not mean that he had not taken lots of other things; he attended my first lecture and took notes. This indicated the man's disposition. There was nothing else flying around, so he took notes; he would have taken anything he could get.

As by the fires of experience, so by commission of crime, you learn real morals. Commit all the crimes, familiarize yourself with all sins, take them in rotation (there are only two or three thousand of them), stick to it. commit two or three every day, and by-and-by you will be proof against them. When you are through you will be proof against all sins and morally perfect. You will be vaccinated against every possible commission of them. This is the only way.

I will read you a written statement upon the subject that I wrote three years ago to read to the Sabbath schools. [Here the lecturer turned his pockets out, but without success.] No! I have left it home. Still, it was a mere statement of facts, illustrating the value of practical morals produced by the commission of crime.

I was at a great school yesterday (St. Paul's), where for four hundred years they have been busy with brains, and building up England by producing Pepys, Miltons, and Marlboroughs. Six hundred boys left to nothing in the world but theoretical morality. I wanted to become the professor of practical morality, but the high master was away, so I suppose I shall have to go on making my living the same old way—by adding practical to theoretical morality.

What are the glory that was Greece, the grandeur that was Rome, compared to the glory and grandeur and majesty of a perfected morality such as you see before you?

The New Vagabonds are old vagabonds (undergoing the old sort of reform). You drank my health; I hope I have not been unuseful. Take this system of morality to your hearts. Take it home to your neighbors and your graves, and I hope that it will be a long time before you arrive there.

HENRY IRVING

The Dramatic and Literary Society of London gave a welcome-home dinner to Sir Henry Irving at the Savoy Hotel, London, June 9, 1900. In proposing the toast of "The Drama" Mr. Clemens said:

I FIND my task a very easy one. I have been a dramatist for thirty years. I have had an ambition in all that time to overdo the work of the Spaniard who said he left behind him four hundred dramas when he died. I leave behind me four hundred and fifteen, and am not yet dead.

The greatest of all the arts is to write a drama. It is a most difficult thing. It requires the highest talent possible and the rarest gifts. No, there is another talent that ranks with it—for anybody can write a drama—I had four hundred of them—but to get one accepted requires real ability. And I have never had that felicity yet.

But human nature is so constructed, we are so persistent, that when we know that we are born to a thing we do not care what the world thinks about it. We go on exploiting that talent year after year, as I have done. I shall go on writing dramas, and some day the impossible may happen, but I am not looking for it.

In writing plays the chief thing is novelty. The world grows tired of solid forms in all the arts. I struck a new idea myself years ago. I was not surprised at it. I was always expecting it would happen. A person who has suffered disappointment for many years loses confidence, and I thought I had better make inquiries before I exploited my new idea of doing a drama in the form of a dream, so I wrote to a great authority on knowledge of all kinds, and asked him whether it was new.

I could depend upon him. He lived in my dear home in America—that dear home, dearer to me through taxes. He sent me a list of plays in which that old device had been used, and he said that there was also a modern lot. He travelled back to China and to a play dated two thousand six hundred years before the Christian era. He said he would follow it up with a list of the previous plays of the kind, and in his innocence would have carried them back to the Flood.

That is the most discouraging thing that has ever happened to me in my dramatic career. I have done a world of good in a silent and private way, and have furnished Sir Henry Irving with plays and plays and plays. What has he achieved through that influence? See where he stands now—on the summit of his art in two worlds—and it was I who put him there—that partly put him there.

I need not enlarge upon the influence the drama has exerted upon civilization. It has made good morals entertaining. I am to be followed by Mr. Pinero. I conceive that we stand at the head of the profession. He has not written as many plays as I have, but he has had that God-given talent, which I lack, of working them off on the manager. I couple his name with this toast, and add the hope that his influence will be supported in exercising his masterly handicraft in that great gift, and that he will long live to continue his fine work.

LATER SPEECHES

WELCOME HOME

Address at the Dinner in His Honor at the Lotos Club, November 10, 1900

In August, 1895, *just before sailing for Australia, Mr. Clemens issued the following statement:*

"It has been reported that I sacrificed, for the benefit of the creditors, the property of the publishing firm whose financial backer I was, and that I am now lecturing for my own benefit.

"This is an error. I intend the lectures, as well as the property, for the creditors. The law recognizes no mortgage on a man's brains, and a merchant who has given up all he has may take advantage of the laws of insolvency and may start free again for himself. But I am not a business man, and honor is a harder master than the law. It cannot compromise for less than one hundred cents on a dollar, and its debts are never outlawed.

"I had a two-thirds interest in the publishing firm whose capital I furnished. If the firm had prospered I would have expected to collect two-thirds of the profits. As it is, I expect to pay all the debts. My partner has no resources, and I do not look for assistance to my wife, whose contributions in cash from her own means have nearly equaled the claims of all creditors combined. She has taken nothing; on the contrary, she has helped and intends to help me to satisfy the obligations due to the rest of the creditors.

"It is my intention to ask my creditors to accept that as a legal discharge, and trust to my honor to pay the other fifty per cent as fast as I can earn it. From my reception thus far on my lecturing tour, I am confident that if I live I can pay off the last debt within four years.

"After which, at the age of sixty-four, I can make a fresh and unincumbered start in life. I am going to Australia, India, and South Africa, and next year I hope to make a tour of the great cities of the United States."

I THANK you all, out of my heart for this fraternal welcome, and it seems almost too fine, almost too magnificent, for a humble Missourian such as I am, far from his native haunts on the banks of the Mississippi; yet my modesty is in a degree fortified by observing that I am not the only Missourian who has been honored here to-night, for I see at this very table—here is a Missourian [indicating Mr. McKelway], and there is a Missourian [indicating Mr. Depew], and there is another Missourian—and Hendrix and Clemens; and last but not least, the greatest Missourian of them all—here he sits—Tom Reed, who has always concealed his birth till now. And since I have been away I know what has been happening in his case: he has deserted politics, and now is leading a creditable life. He has reformed, and God prosper him; and I judge, by a remark which he made upstairs awhile ago, that he had found a new business that is utterly suited to his make and constitution, and all he is doing now is that he is around raising the average of personal beauty.

But I am grateful to the president for the kind words which he has said of me, and it is not for me to say whether these praises were deserved or not. I prefer to accept them just as they stand, without concerning myself with the statistics upon which they have been built, but only with that large matter, that essential matter, the good-fellowship, the kindliness, the magnanimity, and generosity that prompted their utterance. Well, many things have happened since I sat here before, and now that I think of it, the president's reference to the debts which were left by the bankrupt firm of Charles L. Webster & Co. gives me an opportunity to say a word which I very much wish to say, not for myself, but for ninety-five men and women whom I shall always hold in high esteem and in pleasant remembrance—the creditors of that firm. They treated me well; they treated me handsomely. There were ninety-six of them, and by not a finger's weight did ninety-five of them add to the burden of that time for me. Ninety-five out of the ninety-six—they didn't indicate by any word or sign that they were anxious about their money. They treated me well, and I shall not forget it; I could not forget it if I wanted to. Many of them said, "Don't you worry, don't you hurry"; that's what they said. Why, if I could have that kind of creditors always, and that experience, I would recognize it as a personal loss to be out of debt. I owe those ninety-five creditors a debt of homage, and I pay it now in such measures as one may pay so fine a debt in mere words. Yes, they said that very thing. I was not personally acquainted with ten of them, and yet they said, "Don't you worry, and don't you hurry." I know that phrase by heart, and if all the other music should perish out of the world it would still sing to me. I appreciate that; I am glad to say this word; people say so much about me, and they forget those creditors. They were handsomer than I was—or Tom Reed.

Oh, you have been doing many things in this time that I have been absent; you have done lots of things, some that are well worth remembering, too.

Now, we have fought a righteous war since I have gone, and that is rare in history—a righteous war is so rare that it is almost unknown in history; but by the grace of that war we set Cuba free, and we joined her to those three or four nations that exist on this earth; and we started out to set those poor Filipinos free, too, and why, why, why that most righteous purpose of ours has apparently miscarried I suppose I never shall know.

But we have made a most creditable record in China in these days—our sound and level-headed administration has made a most creditable record over there, and there are some of the Powers that cannot say that by any means. The Yellow Terror is threatening this world to-day. It is looming vast and ominous on that distant horizon. I do not know what is going to be the result of that Yellow Terror, but our government has had no hand in evoking it, and let's be happy in that and proud of it.

We have nursed free silver, we watched by its cradle; we have done the best we could to raise that child, but those pestiferous Republicans have—well, they keep giving it the measles every chance they get, and we never shall raise that child. Well, that's no matter—there's plenty of other things to do, and we must think of something else. Well, we have tried a President four years, criticised him and found fault with him the whole time, and turned around a day or two ago with votes enough to spare to elect another. O consistency! consistency! thy name—I don't know what thy name is—Thompson will do—any name will do—but you see there is the fact, there is the consistency. Then we have tried for governor an illustrious Rough Rider, and we liked him so much in that great office that now we have made him Vice-President—not in order that that office shall give him distinction, but that he may confer distinction upon that office. And it's needed, too—it's needed. And now, for a while anyway, we shall not be stammering and embarrassed when a stranger asks us, "What is the name of the Vice-President?" This one is known; this one is pretty well known, pretty widely known, and in some quarters favorably. I am not accustomed to dealing in these fulsome compliments, and I am probably overdoing it a little; but—well, my old affectionate admiration for Governor Roosevelt has probably betrayed me into the complimentary excess; but I know him, and you know him; and if you give him rope enough—I mean if—oh yes, he will justify that compliment; leave it just as it is. And now we have put in his place Mr. Odell, another Rough Rider, I suppose; all the fat things go to that profession now. Why, I could have been a Rough Rider myself if I had known that this political Klondike was going to open up, and I would have been a Rough Rider if I could have gone to war on an automobile—but not on a horse! No, I know the horse too well; I have known the horse in war and in peace, and there is no place where a horse is comfortable. The horse has too many caprices, and he is too much given to initiative. He invents too many new ideas. No, I don't want anything to do with a horse.

And then we have taken Chauncey Depew out of

a useful and active life and made him a Senator—embalmed him, corked him up. And I am not grieving. That man has said many a true thing about me in his time, and I always said something would happen to him. Look at that [pointing to Mr. Depew] gilded mummy! He has made my life a sorrow to me at many a banquet on both sides of the ocean, and now he has got it. Perish the hand that pulls that cork!

All these things have happened, all these things have come to pass, while I have been away, and it just shows how little a Mugwump can be missed in a cold, unfeeling world, even when he is the last one that is left—a GRAND OLD PARTY all by himself. And there is another thing that has happened, perhaps the most imposing event of them all: the institution called the Daughters of the Crown—the Daughters of the Royal Crown—has established itself and gone into business. Now, there's an American idea for you; there's an idea born of God knows what kind of specialized insanity, but not softening of the brain—you cannot soften a thing that doesn't exist—the Daughters of the Royal Crown! Nobody eligible but American descendants of Charles II. Dear me, how the fancy product of that old harem still holds out!

Well, I am truly glad to foregather with you again, and partake of the bread and salt of this hospitable house once more. Seven years ago, when I was your guest here, when I was old and despondent, you gave me the grip and the word that lift a man up and make him glad to be alive; and now I come back from my exile young again, fresh and alive, and ready to begin life once more, and your welcome puts the finishing touch upon my restored youth and makes it real to me, and not a gracious dream that must vanish with the morning. I thank you.

GALVESTON ORPHAN BAZAAR

ADDRESS AT A FAIR HELD AT THE WALDORF-ASTORIA, NEW YORK, IN OCTOBER, 1900, IN AID OF THE ORPHANS AT GALVESTON

I EXPECTED that the Governor of Texas would occupy this place first and would speak to you, and in the course of his remarks would drop a text for me to talk from; but with the proverbial obstinacy that is proverbial with governors, they go back on their duties, and he has not come here, and has not furnished me with a text, and I am here without a text. I have no text except what you furnish me with your handsome faces, and—but I won't continue that, for I could go on forever about attractive faces, beautiful dresses, and other things. But, after all, compliments should be in order in a place like this.

I have been in New York two or three days, and have been in a condition of strict diligence night and day, the object of this diligence being to regulate the moral and political situation on this planet—put it on a sound basis—and when you are regulating the conditions of a planet it requires a great deal of talk in a great many kinds of ways, and when you have talked a lot the emptier you get. When I am situated like that, with nothing to say, I feel as though I were a sort of fraud; I seem to be playing a part, and please consider I am playing a part for want of something better, and this is not unfamiliar to me; I have often done this before.

When I was here about eight years ago I was coming up in a car of the elevated road. Very few people were in that car, and on one end of it there was no one, except on the opposite seat, where sat a man about fifty years old, with a most winning face and an elegant eye—a beautiful eye; and I took him from his dress to be a master mechanic, a man who had a vocation. He had with him a very fine little child of about four or five years. I was watching the affection which existed between those two. I judged he was the grandfather, perhaps. It was really a pretty child, and I was admiring her, and as soon as he saw I was admiring her he began to notice me.

I could see his admiration of me in his eye, and I did what everybody else would do—admired the child four times as much, knowing I would get four times as much of his admiration. Things went on very pleasantly. I was making my way into his heart.

By-and-by, when he almost reached the station where he was to get off, he got up, crossed over, and he said: "Now I am going to say something to you which I hope you will regard as a compliment." And then he went on to say: "I have never seen Mark Twain, but I have seen a portrait of him, and any friend of mine will tell you that when I have once seen a portrait of a man I place it in my eye and store it away in my memory, and I can tell you now that you look enough like Mark Twain to be his brother. Now," he said, "I hope you take this as a compliment."

I said: "I will be frank with you. In my desire to look like that excellent character I have dressed for the character; I have been playing a part."

He said: "That is all right, that is all right; you look very well on the outside, but when it comes to to the inside you are probably not in it with the original."

So when I come to a place like this with nothing valuable to say I always play a part. But I will say before I sit down that when it comes to saying anything here I will express myself in this way: I am heartily in sympathy with you in your efforts to help those who were sufferers in this calamity, and in your desire to help those who were rendered homeless, and in saying this I wish to impress on you the fact that I am not playing a part.

LITERATURE

ADDRESS AT THE ROYAL LITERARY FUND BANQUET, LONDON, MAY 4, 1900

Anthony Hope introduced Mr. Clemens to make the response to the toast "Literature."

MR. HOPE has been able to deal adequately with this toast without assistance from me. Still, I was born generous. If he had advanced any theories that needed refutation or correction I would have attended to them, and if he had made any statements stronger than those which he is in the habit of making I would have dealt with them.

In fact, I was surprised at the mildness of his statements. I could not have made such statements if I had preferred to, because to exaggerate is the only way I can approximate to the truth. You cannot have a theory without principles. Principles is another name for prejudices. I have no prejudices in politics, religion, literature, or anything else.

I am now on my way to my own country to run for the presidency because there are not yet enough candidates in the field, and those who have entered are too much hampered by their own principles, which are prejudices.

I propose to go there to purify the political atmosphere. I am in favor of everything everybody is in favor of. What you should do is to satisfy the whole nation, not half of it, for then you would only be half a President.

There could not be a broader platform than mine. I am in favor of anything and everything—of temperance and intemperance, morality and qualified immorality, gold standard and free silver.

I have tried all sorts of things, and that is why I want to try the great position of ruler of a country. I have been in turn reporter, editor, publisher, author, lawyer, burglar, I have worked my way up, and wish to continue to do so.

I read to-day in a magazine article that Christendom issued last year fifty-five thousand new books. Consider what that means! Fifty-five thousand new books meant fifty-four thousand new authors. We are going to have them all on our hands to take care of sooner or later. Therefore, double your subscriptions to the literary fund!

DISAPPEARANCE OF LITERATURE

ADDRESS AT THE DINNER OF THE NINETEENTH CENTURY CLUB, AT SHERRY'S, NEW YORK, NOVEMBER 20, 1900

Mr. Clemens spoke to the toast "The Disappearance of Literature." Doctor Gould presided, and in introducing Mr. Clemens said that he (the speaker), when in Germany, had to do a lot of apologizing for a certain literary man who was taking what the Germans thought undue liberties with their language.

IT wasn't necessary for your chairman to apologize for me in Germany. It wasn't necessary at all. Instead of that he ought to have impressed upon those poor benighted Teutons the service I rendered them. Their language had needed untangling for a good many years. Nobody else seemed to want to take the job, and so I took it, and I flatter myself that I made a pretty good job of it. The Germans have an inhuman way of cutting up their verbs. Now a verb has a hard time enough of it in this world when it's all together. It's downright inhuman to split it up. But that's just what those Germans do. They take part of a verb and put it down here, like a stake, and they take the other part of it and put it away over yonder like another stake, and between these two limits they just shovel in German. I maintain that there is no necessity for apologizing for a man who helped in a small way to stop such mutilation.

We have heard a discussion to-night on the disappearance of literature. That's no new thing. That's what certain kinds of literature have been doing for several years. The fact is, my friend, that the fashion in literature changes, and the literary tailors have to change their cuts or go out of business. Professor Winchester here, if I remember fairly correctly what he said, remarked that few, if any, of the novels produced to-day would live as long as the novels of Walter Scott. That may be his notion. Maybe he is right; but so far as I am concerned, I don't care if they don't.

Professor Winchester also said something about there being no modern epics like *Paradise Lost*. I guess he's right. He talked as if he was pretty familiar with that piece of literary work, and nobody would suppose that he never had read it. I don't believe any of you have ever read *Paradise Lost*, and you don't want to. That's something that you just want to take on trust. It's a classic, just as Professor Winchester says, and it meets his definition of a classic—something that everybody wants to have read and nobody wants to read.

Professor Trent also had a good deal to say about the disappearance of literature. He said that Scott would outlive all his critics. I guess that's true. The fact of the business is, you've got to be one of two ages to appreciate Scott. When you're eighteen you can read *Ivanhoe*, and you want to wait until you are ninety to read some of the rest. It takes a pretty well-regulated abstemious critic to live ninety years.

PUBLIC EDUCATION ASSOCIATION

ADDRESS AT A MEETING OF THE BERKELEY LYCEUM, NEW YORK, NOVEMBER 23, 1900

I DON'T suppose that I am called here as an expert on education, for that would show a lack of foresight on your part and a deliberate intention to remind me of my shortcomings.

As I sat here looking around for an idea it struck me that I was called for two reasons. One was to do good to me, a poor unfortunate traveller on the world's wide ocean, by giving me a knowledge of the nature and scope of your society and letting me know that others beside myself have been of some use in the world. The other reason that I can see is that you have called me to show by way of contrast what education can accomplish if administered in the right sort of doses.

Your worthy president said that the school pictures, which have received the admiration of the world at the Paris Exposition, have been sent to Russia, and this was a compliment from that Government—which is very surprising to me. Why, it is only an hour since I read a cablegram in the newspapers beginning "Russia Proposes to Retrench." I was not expecting such a thunderbolt, and I thought what a happy thing it will be for Russians when the retrenchment will bring home the thirty thousand

Russian troops now in Manchuria, to live in peaceful pursuits. I thought this was what Germany should do also without delay, and that France and all the other nations in China should follow suit.

Why should not China be free from the foreigners, who are only making trouble on her soil? If they would only go home, what a pleasant place China would be for the Chinese! We do not allow Chinamen to come here, and I say in all seriousness that it would be a graceful thing to let China decide who shall go there.

China never wanted foreigners any more than foreigners wanted Chinamen, and on this question I am with the Boxers every time. The Boxer is a patriot. He loves his country better than he does the countries of other people. I wish him success. The Boxer believes in driving us out of his country. I am a Boxer, too, for I believe in driving him out of our country.

When I read the Russian despatch further my dream of world peace vanished. It said that the vast expense of maintaining the army had made it necessary to retrench, and so the Government had decided that to support the army it would be necessary to withdraw the appropriation from the public schools. This is a monstrous idea to us. We believe that out of the public school grows the greatness of a nation.

It is curious to reflect how history repeats itself the world over. Why, I remember the same thing was done when I was a boy on the Mississippi River. There was a proposition in a township there to discontinue public schools because they were too expensive. An old farmer spoke up and said if they stopped the schools they would not save anything, because every time a school was closed a jail had to be built.

It's like feeding a dog on his own tail. He'll never get fat. I believe it is better to support schools than jails.

The work of your association is better and shows more wisdom than the Czar of Russia and all his people. This is not much of a compliment, but it's the best I've got in stock.

MUNICIPAL GOVERNMENT

ADDRESS AT THE ANNUAL DINNER OF THE ST. NICHOLAS SOCIETY, NEW YORK, DECEMBER 6, 1900

Doctor Mackay, in his response to the toast "St. Nicholas," referred to Mr. Clemens, saying: "Mark Twain is as true a preacher of true righteousness as any bishop, priest, or minister of any church to-day, because he moves men to forget their faults by cheerful well doing instead of making them sour and morbid by everlasting bending their attention to the seamy and sober side of life."

MR. CHAIRMAN AND GENTLEMEN OF THE ST. NICHOLAS SOCIETY,—These are, indeed, prosperous days for me. Night before last, in a speech, the Bishop of the Diocese of New York complimented me for my contribution to theology, and to-night the Reverend Doctor Mackay has elected me to the ministry. I thanked Bishop Potter then for his compliment, and I thank Doctor Mackay now for that promotion. I think that both have discerned in me what I long ago discerned, but what I was afraid the world would never learn to recognize.

In this absence of nine years I find a great improvement in the city of New York. I am glad to speak on that as a toast—"The City of New York." Some say it has improved because I have been away. Others, and I agree with them, say it has improved because I have come back. We must judge of a city, as of a man, by its external appearances and by its inward character. In externals the foreigner coming to these shores is more impressed at first by our skyscrapers. They are new to him. He has not done anything of the sort since he built the tower of Babel. The foreigner is shocked by them.

In the daylight they are ugly. They are—well, too chimneyfied and too snaggy—like a mouth that needs attention from a dentist; like a cemetery that is all monuments and no gravestones. But at night, seen from the river where they are columns towering against the sky, all sparkling with light, they are fairylike; they are beauty more satisfactory to the soul and more enchanting than anything that man has dreamed of since the Arabian nights. We can't always have the beautiful aspect of things. Let us make the most of our sights that are beautiful and let the others go. When your foreigner makes disagreeable comments on New York by daylight, float him down the river at night.

What has made these skyscrapers possible is the elevator. The cigar box which the European calls a "lift" needs but to be compared with our elevators to be appreciated. The lift stops to reflect between floors. That is all right in a hearse, but not in elevators. The American elevator acts like the man's patent purge—it worked. As the inventor said, "This purge doesn't waste any time fooling around; it attends strictly to business."

That New Yorkers have the cleanest, quickest, and most admirable system of street railways in the world has been forced upon you by the abnormal appreciation you have of your hackman. We ought always to be grateful to him for that service. Nobody else would have brought such a system into existence for us. We ought to build him a monument. We owe him one as much as we owe one to anybody. Let it be a tall one. Nothing permanent, of course; build it of plaster, say. Then gaze at it and realize how grateful we are—for the time being—and then pull it down and throw it on the ash heap. That's the way to honor your public heroes.

As to our streets, I find them cleaner than they used to be. I miss those dear old landmarks, the symmetrical mountain ranges of dust and dirt that used to be piled up along the streets for the wind and rain to tear down at their pleasure. Yes, New York is cleaner than Bombay. I realize that I have been in Bombay, that I now am in New York; that it is not my duty to flatter Bombay, but rather to flatter New York.

Compared with the wretched attempts of London to light that city, New York may fairly be said to be a well-lighted city. Why, London's attempt at good lighting is almost as bad as London's attempt at rapid transit. There is just one good system of rapid transit in London—the "Tube," and that, of course, had been put in by Americans. Perhaps, after a while, those Americans will come back and give New York also a good underground system. Perhaps they have already begun. I have been so busy since I came back that I haven't had time as yet to go down cellar.

But it is by the laws of the city, it is by the manners

of the city, it is by the ideals of the city, it is by the customs of the city and by the municipal government which all these elements correct, support, and foster, by which the foreigner judges the city. It is by these that he realizes that New York may, indeed, hold her head high among the cities of the world. It is by these standards that he knows whether to class the city higher or lower than the other municipalities of the world.

Gentlemen, you have the best municipal government in the world—the purest and the most fragrant. The very angels envy you, and wish they could establish a government like it in heaven. You got it by a noble fidelity to civic duty. You got it by stern and ever-watchful exertion of the great powers with which you are charged by the rights which were handed down to you by your forefathers, by your manly refusal to let base men invade the high places of your government, and by instant retaliation when any public officer has insulted you in the city's name by swerving in the slightest from the upright and full performance of his duty. It is you who have made this city the envy of the cities of the world. God will bless you for it—God will bless you for it. Why, when you approach the final resting-place the angels of heaven will gather at the gates and cry out:

"Here they come! Show them to the archangel's box, and turn the limelight on them!"

MUNICIPAL CORRUPTION

ADDRESS AT THE CITY CLUB DINNER, JANUARY 4, 1901

Bishop Potter told how an alleged representative of Tammany Hall asked him in effect if he would cease his warfare upon the Police Department if a certain captain and inspector were dismissed. He replied that he would never be satisfied until the "man at the top" and the "system" which permitted evils in the Police Department were crushed.

THE Bishop has just spoken of a condition of things which none of us can deny, and which ought not to exist; that is, the lust of gain—a lust which does not stop short of the penitentiary or the jail to accomplish its ends. But we may be sure of one thing, and that is that this sort of thing is not universal. If it were, this country would not be. You may put this down as a fact: that out of every fifty men, forty-nine are clean. Then why is it, you may ask, that the forty-nine don't have things the way they want them? I'll tell you why it is. A good deal has been said here to-night about what is to be accomplished by organization. That's just the thing. It's because the fiftieth fellow and his pals are organized and the other forty-nine are not that the dirty one rubs it into the clean fellows every time.

You may say organize, organize, organize; but there may be so much organization that it will interfere with the work to be done. The Bishop here had an experience of that sort, and told all about it downtown the other night. He was painting a barn—it was his own barn—and yet he was informed that his work must stop; he was a nonunion painter, and couldn't continue at that sort of job.

Now, all these conditions of which you complain should be remedied, and I am here to tell you just how to do it. I've been a statesman without salary for many years, and I have accomplished great and widespread good. I don't know that it has benefited anybody very much, even if it was good; but I do know that it hasn't harmed me very much, and it hasn't made me any richer.

We hold the balance of power. Put up your best men for office, and we shall support the better one. With the election of the best man for Mayor would follow the selection of the best man for Police Commissioner and Chief of Police.

My first lesson in the craft of statesmanship was taken at an early age. Fifty-one years ago I was fourteen years old, and we had a society in the town I lived in, patterned after the Freemasons, or the Ancient Order of United Farmers, or some such thing—just what it was patterned after doesn't matter. It had an inside guard and an outside guard, and a past grand warden, and a lot of such things, so as to give dignity to the organization and offices to the members.

Generally speaking it was a pretty good sort of organization, and some of the very best boys in the village, including—but I mustn't get personal on an occasion like this—and the society would have got along pretty well had it not been for the fact that there were a certain number of the members who could be bought. They got to be an infernal nuisance. Every time we had an election the candidates had to go around and see the purchasable members. The price per vote was paid in doughnuts, and it depended somewhat on the appetites of the individuals as to the price of the votes.

This thing ran along until some of us, the really very best boys in the organization, decided that these corrupt practices must stop, and for the purpose of stopping them we organized a third party. We had a name, but we were never known by that name. Those who didn't like us called us the Anti-Doughnut party, but we didn't mind that.

We said: "Call us what you please; the name doesn't matter. We are organized for a principle." By-and-by the election came around, and we made a big mistake. We were triumphantly beaten. That taught us a lesson. Then and there we decided never again to nominate anybody for anything. We decided simply to force the other two parties in the society to nominate their very best men. Although we were organized for a principle, we didn't care much about that. Principles aren't of much account anyway, except at election time. After that you hang them up to let them season.

The next time we had an election we told both the other parties that we'd beat any candidates put up by any one of them of whom we didn't approve. In that election we did business. We got the man we wanted. I suppose they called us the Anti-

Doughnut party because they couldn't buy us with their doughnuts. They didn't have enough of them. Most reformers arrive at their price sooner or later, and I suppose we would have had our price; but our opponents weren't offering anything but doughnuts, and those we spurned.

Now it seems to me that an Anti-Doughnut party is just what is wanted in the present emergency. I would have the Anti-Doughnuts felt in every city and hamlet and school district in this State and in the United States. I was an Anti-Doughnut in my boyhood, and I'm an Anti-Doughnut still. The modern designation is Mugwump. There used to be quite a number of us Mugwumps, but I think I'm the only one left. I had a vote this fall, and I began to make some inquiries as to what I had better do with it.

I don't know anything about finance, and I never did, and I know some pretty shrewd financiers, and they told me that Mr. Bryan wasn't safe on any financial question. I said to myself, then, that it wouldn't do for me to vote for Bryan, and I rather thought—I know now—that McKinley wasn't just right on this Philippine question, and so I just didn't vote for anybody. I've got that vote yet, and I've kept it clean, ready to deposit at some other election. It wasn't cast for any wildcat financial theories, and it wasn't cast to support the man who sends our boys as volunteers out into the Philippines to get shot down under a polluted flag.

VOTES FOR WOMEN

At the Annual Meeting of the Hebrew Technical School for Girls, Held in the Temple Emmanuel, January 20, 1901

Mr. Clemens was introduced by President Meyer, who said: "In one of Mr. Clemens's works he expressed his opinion of men, saying he had no choice between Hebrew and Gentile, black men or white; to him all men were alike. But I never could find that he expressed his opinion of women; perhaps that opinion was so exalted that he could not express it. We shall now be called to hear what he thinks of women."

LADIES AND GENTLEMEN,—It is a small help that I can afford, but it is just such help that one can give as coming from the heart through the mouth. The report of Mr. Meyer was admirable, and I was as interested in it as you have been. Why, I'm twice as old as he, and I've had so much experience that I would say to him, when he makes his appeal for help: "Don't make it for to-day or to-morrow, but collect the money on the spot."

We are all creatures of sudden impulse. We must be worked up by steam, as it were. Get them to write their wills now, or it may be too late by-and-by. Fifteen or twenty years ago I had an experience I shall never forget. I got into a church which was crowded by a sweltering and panting multitude. The city missionary of our town—Hartford—made a telling appeal for help. He told of personal experiences among the poor in cellars and top lofts requiring instances of devotion and help. The poor are always good to the poor. When a person with his millions gives a hundred thousand dollars it makes a great noise in the world, but he does not miss it; it's the widow's mite that makes no noise but does the best work.

I remembered on that occasion in the Hartford church the collection was being taken up. The appeal had so stirred me that I could hardly wait for the hat or plate to come my way. I had four hundred dollars in my pocket, and I was anxious to drop it in the plate and wanted to borrow more. But the plate was so long in coming my way that the fever-heat of beneficence was going down lower and lower—going down at the rate of a hundred dollars a minute. The plate was passed too late. When it finally came to me, my enthusiasm had gone down so much that I kept my four hundred dollars—and stole a dime from the plate. So, you see, time sometimes leads to crime.

Oh, many a time have I thought of that and regretted it, and I adjure you all to give while the fever is on you.

Referring to woman's sphere in life, I'll say that woman is always right. For twenty-five years I've been a woman's rights man. I have always believed, long before my mother died, that, with her gray hairs and admirable intellect, perhaps she knew as much as I did. Perhaps she knew as much about voting as I.

I should like to see the time come when women shall help to make the laws. I should like to see that whip-lash, the ballot, in the hands of women. As for this city's government, I don't want to say much, except that it is a shame—a shame; but if I should live twenty-five years longer—and there is no reason why I shouldn't—I think I'll see women handle the ballot. If women had the ballot to-day, the state of things in this town would not exist.

If all the women in this town had a vote to-day they would elect a mayor at the next election, and they would rise in their might and change the awful state of things now existing here.

UNIVERSITY SETTLEMENT SOCIETY

After the serious addresses were made, Seth Low introduced Mr. Clemens at the Settlement House, February 2, 1901.

THE older we grow the greater becomes our wonder at how much ignorance one can contain without bursting one's clothes. Ten days ago I did not know anything about the University Settlement except what I'd read in the pamphlets sent me. Now, after being here and hearing Mrs. Hewitt and Mrs. Thomas, it seems to me I know of nothing like it at all. It's a charity that carries no humiliation with it. Marvellous it is, to think of schools where you don't have to drive the children in but drive them out. It was not so in my day.

Down-stairs just now I saw a dancing lesson going on. You must pay a cent for a lesson. You can't get it for nothing. That's the reason I never learned to dance.

But it was the pawnbroker's shop you have here that interested me mightily. I've known something about pawnbrokers' shops in my time, but here you have a wonderful plan. The ordinary pawnbroker charges thirty-six per cent a year for a loan, and I've paid more myself, but here a man or woman in distress can obtain a loan for one per cent a month! It's wonderful!

I've been interested in all I've heard to-day, especially in the romance recounted by Mrs. Thomas, which reminds me that I have a romance of my own in my autobiography, which I am building for the instruction of the world.

In San Francisco, many years ago, when I was a newspaper reporter (perhaps I should say I had been and was willing to be), a pawnbroker was taking care of what property I had. There was a friend of mine, a poet, out of a job, and he was having a hard time of it, too.

Well, my friend the poet thought his life was a failure, and I told him I thought it was, and then he said he thought he ought to commit suicide, and I said "all right," which was disinterested advice to a friend in trouble; but, like all such advice, there was just a little bit of self-interest back of it, for if I could get a "scoop" on the other newspapers I could get a job.

The poet could be spared, and so, largely for his own good and partly for mine, I kept the thing in his mind, which was necessary, as would-be suicides are very changeable and hard to hold to their purpose. He had a preference for a pistol, which was an extravagance, for we hadn't enough between us to hire a pistol. A fork would have been easier.

And so he concluded to drown himself, and I said it was an excellent idea—the only trouble being that he was so good a swimmer. So we went down to the beach. I went along to see that the thing was done right. Then something most romantic happened. There came in on the sea something that had been on its way for three years. It rolled in across the broad Pacific with a message that was full of meaning to that poor poet and cast itself at his feet. It was a life preserver! This was a complication. And then I had an idea—he never had any, especially when he was going to write poetry; I suggested that we pawn the life preserver and get a revolver.

The pawnbroker gave us an old derringer with a bullet as big as a hickory nut. When he heard that it was only a poet that was going to kill himself he did not quibble. Well, we succeeded in sending a bullet right through his head. It was a terrible moment when he placed that pistol against his forehead and stood for an instant. I said, "Oh, pull the trigger!" and he did, and cleaned out all the gray matter in his brains. It carried the poetic faculty away, and now he's a useful member of society.

Now, therefore, I realize that there's no more beneficent institution than this penny fund of yours, and I want all the poets to know this. I did think about writing you a check, but now I think I'll send you a few copies of what one of your little members called *Strawberry Finn.*

ON LINCOLN'S BIRTHDAY

Introducing Col. Watterson at the celebration of Abraham Lincoln's 92d Birthday Anniversary, Carnegie Hall, February 11, 1901, *to raise funds for the Lincoln Memorial University at Cumberland Gap, Tennessee.*

LADIES AND GENTLEMEN,—The remainder of my duties as presiding chairman here this evening are but two—only two. One of them is easy, and the other difficult. That is to say, I must introduce the orator, and then keep still and give him a chance. The name of Henry Watterson carries with it its own explanation. It is like an electric light on top of Madison Square Garden; you touch the button and the light flashes up out of the darkness. You mention the name of Henry Watterson, and your minds are at once illuminated with the splendid radiance of his fame and achievements. A journalist, a soldier, an orator, a statesman, a rebel. Yes, he was a rebel; and, better still, now he is a reconstructed rebel.

It is a curious circumstance that without collusion of any kind, but merely in obedience to a strange and pleasant and dramatic freak of destiny, he and I, kinsmen by blood,[1] for we are that—and one-time rebels—for we were that—chosen out of a million surviving quondam rebels to come here and

[1] Colonel Watterson's forbears had intermarried with the Lamptons, Mark Twain's maternal ancestors.

bare our heads in reverence and love of that noble soul whom forty years ago we tried with all our hearts and all our strength to defeat and dispossess—Abraham Lincoln! Is the Rebellion ended and forgotten? Are the Blue and the Gray one to-day? By authority of this sign we may answer yes; there was a Rebellion—that incident is closed.

I was born and reared in a slave state; my father was a slave owner; and in the Civil War I was a second lieutenant in the Confederate service. For a while. This second cousin of mine, Colonel Watterson, the orator of this present occasion, was born and reared in a slave state, was a colonel in the Confederate service, and rendered me such assistance as he could in my self-appointed task of annihilating the Federal armies and breaking up the Union. I laid my plans with wisdom and foresight, and if Colonel Watterson had obeyed my orders I should have succeeded in my giant undertaking. It was my intention to drive General Grant into the Pacific—if I could get transportation—and I told Colonel Watterson to surround the Eastern armies and wait till I came. But he was insubordinate and stood upon a punctilio of military etiquette; he refused to take orders from a second lieutenant—and the Union was saved. This is the first time this secret has been revealed. Until now no one outside the family has known the facts. But there they stand—Watterson saved the Union. Yet to this day that man gets no pension. Those were great days, splendid days. What an uprising it was! For the hearts of the whole nation, North and South, were in the war. We of the South were not ashamed; for, like the men of the North, we were fighting for flags we loved; and when men fight for these things, and under these convictions, with nothing sordid to tarnish their cause, that cause is holy, the blood spilled for it is sacred, the life that is laid down for it is consecrated. To-day we no longer regret the result, to-day we are glad that it came out as it did, but we are not ashamed that we did our endeavor; we did our bravest best, against despairing odds, for the cause which was precious to us and which our conscience approved; and we are proud—and you are proud—the kindred blood in your veins answers when I say it—you are proud of the record we made in those mighty collisions in the fields.

What an uprising it was! We did not have to supplicate for soldiers on either side. "We are coming, Father Abraham, three hundred thousand strong!" That was the music North and South. The very choicest young blood and brawn and brain rose up from Maine to the Gulf and flocked to the standards—just as men always do when in their eyes their cause is great and fine and their hearts are in it; just as men flocked to the Crusades, sacrificing all they possessed to the cause, and entering cheerfully upon hardships which we cannot even imagine in this age, and upon toilsome and wasting journeys which in our time would be the equivalent of circumnavigating the globe five times over.

North and South we put our hearts into that colossal struggle, and out of it came the blessed fulfilment of the prophecy of the immortal Gettysburg speech which said: "We here highly resolve that these dead shall not have died in vain; that this nation, under God, shall have a new birth of freedom; and that a government of the people, by the people, for the people, shall not perish from the earth."

We are here to honor the birthday of the greatest citizen, and the noblest and the best, after Washington, that this land or any other has yet produced. The old wounds are healed; you and we are brothers again; you testify by honoring two of us, once soldiers of the Lost Cause and foes of your great and good leader—with the privilege of assisting here; and we testify it by laying our honest homage at the feet of Abraham Lincoln and in forgetting that you of the North and we of the South were ever enemies, and remembering only that we are now indistinguishably fused together and namable by one common great name—Americans.

OSTEOPATHY

On February 27, 1901, Mr. Clemens appeared before the Assembly Committee in Albany, New York, in favor of the Seymour bill legalizing the practice of osteopathy.

MR. CHAIRMAN AND GENTLEMEN,—Dr. Van Fleet is the gentleman who gave me the character. I have heard my character discussed a thousand times before you were born, sir, and shown the iniquities in it, and you did not get more than half of them.

I was touched and distressed when they brought that part of a child in here, and proved—I don't exactly know what, unless it was that you should not take a child to pieces in that way. What remarkable names those diseases have! It makes me envious of the man that has them all. I have had many diseases, and am thankful for all I have had.

One of the gentlemen spoke of the knowledge of something else found in Sweden, a treatment which I took. It is, I suppose, a kindred thing. There is apparently no great difference between them. I was a year and a half in London and Sweden, in the hands of that grand old man, Mr. Kellgren.

I cannot call him a doctor, for he has not the authority to give a certificate if a patient should die, but fortunately they don't.

The State stands as a mighty Gibraltar clothed with power. It stands between me and my body, and tells me what kind of a doctor I must employ. When my soul is sick unlimited spiritual liberty is given me by the State. Now then, it doesn't seem logical that the State shall depart from this great policy, the health of the soul, and change about and take the other position in the matter of smaller consequences—the health of the body.

The Bell bill limitations would drive the osteopaths out of the State. Oh, dear me! when you drive somebody out of the State you create the same condition as prevailed in the Garden of Eden. You want the thing that you can't have. I didn't care much about the osteopaths, but as soon as I found they were going to drive them out I got in a state of uneasiness, and I can't sleep nights now.

I know how Adam felt in the Garden of Eden about the prohibited apple. Adam didn't want the apple till he found out he couldn't have it, just as he would have wanted osteopathy if he couldn't have it.

Whose property is my body? Probably mine. I so regard it. If I experiment with it, who must be answerable? I, not the State. If I choose injudiciously, does the State die? Oh, no.

I was the subject of my mother's experiment. She was wise. She made experiments cautiously. She didn't pick out just any child in the flock. No, she chose judiciously. She chose one she could spare, and she couldn't spare the others. I was the choice child of the flock, so I had to take all of the experiments.

In 1844 Kneipp filled the world with the wonder of the water cure. Mother wanted to try it, but on sober second thought she put me through. A bucket of ice water was poured over to see the effect. Then I was rubbed down with flannels, a sheet was dipped in the water, and I was put to bed. I perspired so much that mother put a life preserver to bed with me.

But this had nothing but a spiritual effect on me, and I didn't care for that. When they took off the sheet it was yellow from the output of my conscience, the exudation of sin. It purified me spiritually, and it remains until this day.

I have experimented with osteopathy and allopathy. I took a chance at the latter for old times' sake, for, three times, when a boy, mother's new methods got me so near death's door she had to call in the family physician to pull me out.

The physicians think they are moved by regard for the best interest of the public. Isn't there a little touch of self-interest back of it all? It seems to me there is, and I don't claim to have all the virtues—only nine or ten of them.

I was born in the "Banner State," and by "Banner State" I mean Missouri. Osteopathy was born in the same State, and both of us are getting along reasonably well. At a time during my younger days my attention was attracted to a picture of a house which bore the inscription, "Christ Disputing With the Doctors."

I could attach no other meaning to it than that Christ was actually quarrelling with the doctors. So I asked an old slave, who was a sort of a herb doctor in a small way—unlicensed, of course—what the meaning of the picture was. "What has he done?" I asked. And the colored man replied: "Humph, he ain't got no license."

BUSINESS

The alumni of Eastman College gave their annual banquet, March 30, 1901, at the Y. M. C. A. Building. Mr. James G. Cannon, of the Fourth National Bank, made the first speech of the evening, after which Mr. Clemens was introduced by Mr. Bailey as the personal friend of Tom Sawyer, who was one of the types of successful business men.

MR. CANNON has furnished me with texts enough to last as slow a speaker as myself all the rest of the night. I took exception to the introducing of Mr. Cannon as a great financier, as if he were the only great financier present. I am a financier. But my methods are not the same as Mr. Cannon's.

I cannot say that I have turned out the great business man that I thought I was when I began life. But I am comparatively young yet, and may learn. I am rather inclined to believe that what troubled me was that I got the big-head early in the game. I want to explain to you a few points of difference between the principles of business as I see them and those that Mr. Cannon believes in.

He says that the primary rule of business success is loyalty to your employer. That's all right—as a theory. What is the matter with loyalty to yourself? As nearly as I can understand Mr. Cannon's methods, there is one great drawback to them. He wants you to work a great deal. Diligence is a good thing, but taking things easy is much more—restful. My idea is that the employer should be the busy man, and the employee the idle one. The employer should be the worried man, and the employee the happy one. And why not? He gets the salary. My plan is to get another man to do the work for me. In that there's more repose. What I want is repose first, last, and all the time.

Mr. Cannon says that there are three cardinal rules of business success; they are diligence, honesty, and truthfulness. Well, diligence is all right. Let it go as a theory. Honesty is the best policy—when there is money in it. But truthfulness is one of the most dangerous—why, this man is misleading you.

I had an experience to-day with my wife which illustrates this. I was acknowledging a belated invitation to another dinner for this evening, which seemed to have been sent about ten days ago. It only reached me this morning. I was mortified at the discourtesy into which I had been brought by this delay, and wondered what was being thought of me by my hosts. As I had accepted your invitation, of course I had to send regrets to my other friends.

When I started to write this note my wife came up and stood looking over my shoulder. Women always want to know what is going on. Said she: "Should not that read in the third person?" I conceded that it should, put aside what I was writing, and commenced over again. That seemed to satisfy her, and so she sat down and let me proceed. I then —finished my first note—and so sent what I intended.

I never could have done this if I had let my wife know the truth about it. Here is what I wrote:

To the Ohio Society,—I have at this moment received a most kind invitation (eleven days old) from Mr. Southard, president; and a like one (ten days old) from Mr. Bryant, president of the Press Club. I thank the society cordially for the compliment of these invitations, although I am booked elsewhere and cannot come.

But, oh, I should like to know the name of the Lightning Express by which they were forwarded; for I owe a friend a dozen chickens, and I believe it will be cheaper to send eggs instead, and let them develop on the road.

Sincerely yours,

Mark Twain.

I want to tell you of some of my experiences in business, and then I will be in a position to lay down one general rule for the guidance of those who want to succeed in business. My first effort was about twenty-five years ago. I took hold of an invention—I don't know now what it was all about, but some one came to me and told me it was a good thing, and that there was lots of money in it. He persuaded me to invest $15,000, and I lived up to my beliefs by engaging a man to develop it. To make a long story short, I sunk $40,000 in it.

Then I took up the publication of a book. I called in a publisher and said to him: "I want you to publish this book along lines which I shall lay down. I am the employer, and you are the employee. I am going to show them some new kinks in the publishing business. And I want you to draw on me for money as you go along," which he did. He drew on me for $56,000. Then I asked him to take the book and call it off. But he refused to do that.

My next venture was with a machine for doing something or other. I knew less about that than I did about the invention. But I sunk $170,000 in the business, and I can't for the life of me recollect what it was the machine was to do.

I was still undismayed. You see, one of the strong points about my business life was that I never gave up. I undertook to publish General Grant's book, and made $140,000 in six months. My axiom is, to succeed in business: avoid my example.

DINNER TO HAMILTON W. MABIE

ADDRESS DELIVERED APRIL 29, 1901

In introducing Mr. Clemens, Doctor Van Dyke said:

"The longer the speaking goes on to-night the more I wonder how I got this job, and the only explanation I can give for it is that it is the same kind of compensation for the number of articles I have sent to *The Outlook*, to be rejected by Hamilton W. Mabie. There is one man here to-night that has a job cut out for him that none of you would have had—a man whose humor has put a girdle of light around the globe, and whose sense of humor has been an example for all five continents. He is going to speak to you. Gentlemen, you know him best as Mark Twain."

MR. CHAIRMAN AND GENTLEMEN,—This man knows now how it feels to be the chief guest, and if he has enjoyed it he is the first man I have ever seen in that position that did enjoy it. And I know, by side remarks which he made to me before his ordeal came upon him, that he was feeling as some of the rest of us have felt under the same circumstances. He was afraid that he would not do himself justice; but he did—to my surprise. It is a most serious thing to be a chief guest on an occasion like this, and it is admirable, it is fine. It is a great compliment to a man that he shall come out of it so gloriously as Mr. Mabie came out of it to-night—to my surprise. He did it well.

He appears to be editor of *The Outlook*, and notwithstanding that, I have every admiration, because when everything is said concerning *The Outlook*, after all one must admit that it is frank in its delinquencies, that is it outspoken in its departures from facts, that it is vigorous in its mistaken criticism of men like me. I have lived in this world a long, long time, and I know you must judge a man by the editorials that he puts in his paper. A man is always better than his printed opinions. A man always reserves to himself on the inside a purity and an honesty and a justice that are a credit to him, whereas the things that he prints are just the reverse.

Oh yes, you must not judge a man by what he writes in his paper. Even in an ordinary secular paper a man must observe some care about it; he must be better than the principles which he puts in print. And that is the case with Mr. Mabie. Why, to see what he writes about me and the missionaries you would think he did not have any principles.[1] But that is Mr. Mabie in his public capacity. Mr. Mabie in his private capacity is just as clean a man as I am.

In this very room, a month or two ago, some people admired that portrait; some admired this, but the great majority fastened on that, and said, "There is a portrait that is a beautiful piece of art." When that portrait is a hundred years old it will suggest what were the manners and customs in our time. Just as they talk about Mr. Mabie to-night, in that enthusiastic way, pointing out the

[1] Reference to the drastic articles written by Mark Twain on the missionaries in China. These articles had stirred up all the religious papers—including the *Outlook*.

various virtues of the man and the grace of his spirit, and all that, so was that portrait talked about. They were enthusiastic, just as we men have been over the character and the work of Mr. Mabie. And when they were through they said that portrait, fine as it is, that work, beautiful as it is, that piece of humanity on that canvas, gracious and fine as it is, does not rise to those perfections that exist in the man himself. Come up, Mr. Alexander. [The reference was to James W. Alexander, who happened to be sitting beneath the portrait of himself on the wall.] Now, I should come up and show myself. But he cannot do it, he cannot do it. He was born that way, he was reared in that way. Let his modesty be an example, and I wish some of you had it, too. But that is just what I have been saying—that portrait, fine as it is, is not as fine as the man represents, and all the things that have been said about Mr. Mabie, and certainly they have been very nobly worded and beautiful, still fall short of the real Mabie.

THE DINNER TO MR. CHOATE

AT A DINNER GIVEN IN HONOR OF AMBASSADOR JOSEPH H. CHOATE AT THE LOTOS CLUB, NOVEMBER 24, 1901

The speakers, among others, were: Senator Depew, William Henry White, Speaker Thomas Reed, and Mr. Choate. Mr. Clemens spoke, in part, as follows:

THE greatness of this country rests on two anecdotes. The first one is that of Washington and his hatchet, representing the foundation of true speaking, which is the characteristic of our people. The second one is an old one, and I've been waiting to hear it to-night; but as nobody has told it yet, I will tell it.

You've heard it before, and you'll hear it many, many times more. It is an anecdote of our guest, of the time when he was engaged as a young man with a gentle Hebrew, in the process of skinning the client. The main part in that business is the collection of the bill for services in skinning the man. "Services" is the term used in that craft for the operation of that kind—diplomatic in its nature.

Choate's—co-respondent—made out a bill for five hundred dollars for his services, so called. But Choate told him he better leave the matter to him, and the next day he collected the bill for the services and handed the Hebrew five thousand dollars, saying, "That's your half of the loot," and inducing that memorable response: "Almost thou persuadest me to become a Christian."

The deep-thinkers didn't merely laugh when that happened. They stopped to think, and said: "There's a rising man. He must be rescued from the law and consecrated to diplomacy. The commercial advantages of a great nation lie there in the man's keeping. We no longer require a man to take care of our moral character before the world. Washington and his anecdote have done that. We require a man to take care of our commercial prosperity."

Mr. Choate has carried that trait with him, and, as Mr. Carnegie has said, he has worked like a mole underground.

We see the result when American railroad iron is sold so cheap in England that the poorest family can have it. He has so beguiled that Cabinet of England.

He has been spreading the commerce of this nation, and has depressed English commerce in the same ratio. This was the principle underlying that anecdote, and the wise men saw it; the principle of give and take—give one and take ten—the principle of diplomacy.

SIXTY-SEVENTH BIRTHDAY

AT THE METROPOLITAN CLUB, NEW YORK, NOVEMBER 28, 1902

Address at a dinner given in honor of Mr. Clemens by Colonel Harvey. President of Harper & Brothers.

I THINK I ought to be allowed to talk as long as I want to, for the reason that I have cancelled all my winter's engagements of every kind, for good and sufficient reasons, and am making no new engagements for this winter, and, therefore, this is the only chance I shall have to disembowel my skull for a year—close the mouth in that portrait for a year. I want to offer thanks and homage to the chairman for this innovation which he has introduced here, which is an improvement, as I consider it, on the old-fashioned style of conducting occasions like this. That was bad—that was a bad, bad, bad arrangement. Under that old custom when the chairman got up and made a speech, he introduced the prisoner at the bar, and covered him all over with compliments, nothing but compliments, not a thing but compliments, never a slur, and sat down and left that man to get up and talk without a text. You cannot talk on compliments; that is not a text. No modest person, and I was born one, can talk on compliments. A man gets up and is filled to the eyes with happy emotions, but his tongue is tied; he has nothing to say; he is in the condition of Doctor Rice's friend who came home drunk and explained it to his wife, and his wife said to him, "John, when you have drunk all the whiskey you want, you ought to ask for sarsaparilla." He said, "Yes, but when I have drunk all the whiskey I want I can't say sarsaparilla." And so I think it is much better to leave a man unmolested until the testimony and pleadings are all in. Otherwise he is dumb—he is at the sarsaparilla stage.

Before I get to the higgledy-piggledy point, as Mr. Howells suggested I do, I want to thank you, gentlemen, for this very high honor you are doing me, and I am quite competent to estimate it at its value. I see around me captains of all the illustrious industries, most distinguished men; there are more than fifty here, and I believe I know thirty-nine of them well. I could probably borrow money from—from the others, anyway. It is a proud thing to me, indeed, to see such a distinguished company gather here on such an occasion as this, when there is no foreign prince to be fêted—when you have come here not to do honor to hereditary privilege and ancient lineage, but to do reverence to mere moral excellence and elemental veracity—and, dear me, how old it seems to make me! I look around me and I see three or four persons I have known so many, many years. I have known Mr. Secretary Hay—John Hay, as the nation and the rest of his friends love to call him—I have known John Hay and Tom Reed and the Reverend Twichell close upon thirty-six years. Close upon thirty-six years I have known those venerable men. I have known Mr. Howells nearly thirty-four years, and I knew Chauncey Depew before he could walk straight, and before he learned to tell the truth. Twenty-seven years ago I heard him make the most noble, eloquent and beautiful speech that has ever fallen from even his capable lips. Tom Reed said that my principle defect was inaccuracy of statement. Well, suppose that that is true. What's the use of telling the truth all the time? I never tell the truth about Tom Reed—but that is his defect, truth; he speaks the truth always. Tom Reed has a good heart, and he has a good intellect, but he hasn't any judgment. Why, when Tom Reed was invited to lecture to the Ladies' Society for the Procreation or Procrastination, or something, of morals, I don't know what it was—advancement, I suppose, of pure morals—he had the immoral indiscretion to begin by saying that some of us can't be optimists, but by judiciously utilizing the opportunities that Providence puts in our way we can all be bigamists. You perceive his limitations. Anything he has in his mind he states, if he thinks it is true. Well, that was true, but that was no place to say it—so they fired him out.

A lot of accounts have been settled here to-night for me; I have held grudges against some of these people, but they have all been wiped out by the very handsome compliments that have been paid me. Even Wayne MacVeagh—I have had a grudge against him many years. The first time I saw Wayne MacVeagh was at a private dinner party at Charles A. Dana's, and when I got there he was clattering along, and I tried to get a word in here and there; but you know what Wayne MacVeagh is when he is started, and I could not get in five words to his one—or one word to his five. I struggled along and struggled along, and—well, I wanted to tell and I was trying to tell a dream I had had the night before, and it was a remarkable dream, a dream worth people's while to listen to, a dream recounting Sam Jones the revivalist's reception in heaven. I was on a train, and was approaching the celestial way station—I had a through ticket—and I noticed a man sitting alongside of me asleep, and he had his ticket in his hat. He was the remains of the Archbishop of Canterbury; I recognized him by his photograph. I had nothing against him, so I took his ticket and let him have mine. He didn't object—he wasn't in a condition to object—and presently when the train stopped at the heavenly station—well, I got off, and he went on by request—but there they all were, the angels, you know, millions of them, every one with a torch; they had arranged for a torch-light procession; they were expecting the Archbishop, and when I got off they started to raise a shout, but it didn't materialize. I don't know whether they were disappointed. I suppose they had a lot of superstitious ideas about the Archbishop and what he should look like, and I didn't fill the bill, and I was trying to explain to Saint Peter, and was doing it in the German tongue, because I didn't want to be too explicit. Well, I found it was no use, I couldn't get along, for Wayne MacVeagh was occupying the whole place, and I said to Mr. Dana,

"What is the matter with that man? Who is that man with the long tongue? What's the trouble with him, that long, lank cadaver, old oil-derrick out of a job—who is that?" "Well, now," Mr. Dana said, "you don't want to meddle with him; you had better keep quiet; because that's a bad man. Talk! He was born to talk. Don't let him get out with you; he'll skin you." I said, "I have been skinned, skinned, and skinned for years, there is nothing left." He said, "Oh, you'll find there is; that man is the very seed and inspiration of that proverb which says, 'No matter how close you skin an onion, a clever man can always peel it again.'" Well, I reflected and I quieted down. That would never occur to Tom Reed. He's got no discretion. Well, MacVeagh is just the same man; he hasn't changed a bit in all those years; he has been peeling Mr. Mitchell lately. That's the kind of man he is.

Mr. Howells—that poem of his is admirable; that's the way to treat a person. Howells has a peculiar gift for seeing the merits of people, and he has always exhibited them in my favor. Howells has never written anything about me that I couldn't read six or seven times a day; he is always just and always fair; he has written more appreciatively of me than anyone in this world, and published it in the *North American Review*. He did me the justice to say that my intentions—he italicized that—that my intentions were always good, that I wounded people's conventions rather than their convictions. Now, I wouldn't want anything handsomer than that said of me. I would rather wait, with anything harsh I might have to say, till the convictions become conventions. Bangs has traced me all the way down. He can't find that honest man, but I will look for him in the looking-glass when I get home. It was intimated by the Colonel that it is New England that makes New York and builds up this country and makes it great, overlooking the fact that there's a lot of people here who came from elsewhere, like John Hay from away out West, and Howells from Ohio, and St. Clair McKelway and me from Missouri, and we are doing what we can to build up New York a little—elevate it. Why, when I was living in that village of Hannibal, Missouri, on the banks of the Mississippi, and Hay up in the town of Warsaw, also on the banks of the Mississippi River—it is an emotional bit of the Mississippi, and when it is low water you have to climb up to it on a ladder, and when it floods you have to hunt for it with a deep-sea lead—but it is a great and beautiful country. In that old time it was a paradise for simplicity—it was a simple, simple life, cheap but comfortable, and full of sweetness, and there was nothing of this rage of modern civilization there at all. It was a delectable land. I went out there last June, and I met in that town of Hannibal a schoolmate of mine, John Briggs, whom I had not seen for more than fifty years. I tell you, that was a meeting! That pal whom I had known as a little boy long ago, and knew now as a stately man three or four inches over six feet and browned by exposure to many climes, he was back there to see that old place again. We spent a whole afternoon going about here and there and yonder, and hunting up the scenes and talking of the crimes which we had committed so long ago. It was a heartbreaking delight, full of pathos, laughter, and tears, all mixed together; and we called the roll of the boys and girls that we picnicked and sweethearted with so many years ago, and there were hardly half a dozen of them left; the rest were in their graves; and we went up there on the summit of that hill, a treasured place in my memory, the summit of Holiday's Hill, and looked out again over that magnificent panorama of the Mississippi River, sweeping along league after league, a level green paradise on one side, and retreating capes and promontories as far as you could see on the other, fading away in the soft, rich lights of the remote distance. I recognized then that I was seeing now the most enchanting river view the planet could furnish. I never knew it when I was a boy; it took an educated eye that had travelled over the globe to know and appreciate it; and John said, "Can you point out the place where Bear Creek used to be before the railroad came?" I said, "Yes, it ran along yonder." "And can you point out the swimming hole?" "Yes, out there." And he said, "Can you point out the place where we stole the skiff?" Well, I didn't know which one he meant. Such a wilderness of events had intervened since that day, more than fifty years ago, it took me more than five minutes to call back that little incident, and then I did call it back; it was a white skiff, and we painted it red to allay suspicion. And the saddest, saddest man came along—a stranger he was—and he looked that red skiff over so pathetically, and he said: "Well, if it weren't for its complexion I'd know whose skiff that was." He said it in that pleading way, you know, that appeals for sympathy and suggestion; we were full of sympathy for him, but we weren't in any condition to offer suggestions. I can see him yet as he turned away with that same sad look on his face and vanished out of history forever. I wonder what became of that man. I know what became of the skiff. Well, it was a beautiful life, a lovely life. There was no crime. Merely little things like pillaging orchards and watermelon patches and breaking the Sabbath—we didn't break the Sabbath often enough to signify—once a week perhaps. But we were good boys, good Presbyterian boys, all Presbyterian boys, and loyal and all that; anyway, we were good Presbyterian boys when the weather was doubtful; when it was fair, we did wander a little from the fold.

Look at John Hay and me. There we were in obscurity, and look where we are now. Consider the ladder which he has climbed, the illustrious vocations he has served—and vocations is the right word; he has in all those vocations acquitted himself with high credit and honor to his country and to the mother that bore him. Scholar, soldier, diplomat, poet, historian—now, see where we are. He is Secretary of State and I am a gentleman. It could not happen in any other country. Our institutions give men the positions that of right belong to them through merit; all you men have won your places, not by heredities, and not by family influences or extraneous help, but only by the natural gifts God gave you at your birth, made effective by your own energies; this is the country to live in.

Now, there is one invisible guest here. A part of me is present; the larger part, the better part, is yonder at her home; that is my wife, and she has a good many personal friends here, and I think it won't distress any one of them to know that, although she is going to be confined to that bed for many months to come from that nervous prostration, there is not any danger and she is coming along very well—and I think it quite appropriate that I should speak of her. I knew her for the first time just in the same year that I first knew John Hay and Tom Reed and Mr. Twichell—thirty-six years ago—and she has been the best friend I have ever had, and that is saying a good deal; she has reared me—she and Twichell together—and what I am I owe to them. Twichell—why, it is such a pleasure to look upon Twichell's face! For five-and-twenty years I was under the Rev. Mr. Twichell's tuition, I was in his pastorate, occupying a pew in his church, and held him in due reverence. That man is full of all the graces that go to make a person companionable and beloved; and wherever Twichell goes to start a church the people flock there to buy the land; they find real estate goes up all around the spot, and the envious and the thoughtful always try to get Twichell to move to their neighborhood and start a church; and wherever you see him go you can go and buy land there with confidence, feeling sure that there will be a double price for you before very long. I am not saying this to flatter Mr. Twichell; it is the fact. Many and many a time I have attended the annual sale in his church, and bought up all the pews on a margin—and it would have been better for me spiritually and financially if I had stayed under his wing.

I have tried to do good in this world, and it is marvellous in how many different ways I have done good, and it is comfortable to reflect—now, there's Mr. Rogers—just out of the affection I bear that man many a time I have given him points in finance that he had never thought of—and if he could lay aside envy, prejudice, and superstition, and utilize those ideas in his business, it would make a difference in his bank account.

Well, I like the poetry. I like all the speeches and the poetry, too. I like Doctor Van Dyke's poem. I wish I could return thanks in proper measure to you, gentlemen, who have spoken and violated your feelings to pay me compliments; some were merited and some you overlooked, it is true; and Colonel Harvey did slander every one of you, and put things into my mouth that I never said, never thought of at all.

And now, my wife and I, out of our single heart, return you our deepest and most grateful thanks, and—yesterday was her birthday.

SEVENTIETH BIRTHDAY

ADDRESS AT A DINNER GIVEN BY COLONEL GEORGE HARVEY AT DELMONICO'S, DECEMBER 5, 1905, TO CELEBRATE THE SEVENTIETH ANNIVERSARY OF MR. CLEMENS'S BIRTH

Mr. Howells introduced Mr. Clemens:

"Now, ladies and gentlemen, and Colonel Harvey, I will try to be greedy on your behalf in wishing the health of our honored and, in view of his great age, our revered guest. I will not say, 'O King, live forever!' but 'O King, live as long as you like!'" [Amid great applause and waving of napkins all rose and drank to Mark Twain.]

WELL, if I had made that joke, it would be the best one I ever made, and in the prettiest language, too. I never can get quite to that height. But I appreciate that joke, and I shall remember it—and I shall use it when occasion requires.

I have had a great many birthdays in my time. I remember the first one very well, and I always think of it with indignation; everything was so crude, unæsthetic, primeval. Nothing like this at all. No proper appreciative preparation made; nothing really ready. Now, for a person born with high and delicate instincts—why, even the cradle wasn't whitewashed—nothing ready at all. I hadn't any hair, I hadn't any teeth, I hadn't any clothes, I had to go to my first banquet just like that. Well, everybody came swarming in. It was the merest little bit of a village

Seventieth Birthday Dinner Group, at Delmonico's, December 5, 1905: Left to Right: Kate Douglas Riggs; Mark Twain; Rev. Joseph H. Twichell; Bliss Carman; Ruth McEnery Stuart; Mary E. Wilkins Freeman; Henry Mills Alden; Henry H. Rogers

—hardly that, just a little hamlet, in the backwoods of Missouri, where nothing ever happened, and the people were all interested, and they all came; they looked me over to see if there was anything fresh in my line. Why, nothing ever happened in that village—I—why, I was the only thing that had really happened there for months and months and months; and although I say it myself that shouldn't, I came the nearest to being a real event that had happened in that village in more than two years. Well, those people came, they came with that curiosity which is so provincial, with that frankness which also is so provincial, and they examined me all around and gave their opinion. Nobody asked them, and I shouldn't have minded if anybody had paid me a compliment, but nobody did. Their opinions were all just green with prejudice, and I feel those opinions to this day. Well, I stood that as long as—you know I was courteous, and I stood it to the limit. I stood it an hour, and then the worm turned. I was the worm; it was my turn to turn, and I turned. I knew very well the strength of my position; I knew that I was the only spotlessly pure and innocent person in that whole town, and I came out and said so. And they could not say a word. It was so true. They blushed; they were embarrassed. Well, that was the first after-dinner speech I ever made. I think it was after dinner.

It's a long stretch between that first birthday speech and this one. That was my cradle song, and this is my swan song, I suppose. I am used to swan songs; I have sung them several times.

This is my seventieth birthday, and I wonder if you all rise to the size of that proposition, realizing all the significance of that phrase, seventieth birthday.

The seventieth birthday! It is the time of life when you arrive at a new and awful dignity; when you may throw aside the decent reserves which have oppressed you for a generation and stand unafraid and unabashed upon your seven-terraced summit and look down and teach—unrebuked. You can tell the world how you got there. It is what they all do. You shall never get tired of telling by what delicate arts and deep moralities you climb up to that great place. You will explain the process and dwell on the particulars with senile rapture. I have been anxious to explain my own system this long time, and now at last I have the right.

I have achieved my seventy years in the usual way: by sticking strictly to a scheme of life which would kill anybody else. It sounds like an exaggeration, but that is really the common rule for attaining old age. When we examine the programme of any of these garrulous old people we always find that the habits which have preserved them would have decayed us; that the way of life which enabled them to live upon the property of their heirs so long, as Mr. Choate says, would have put us out of commission ahead of time. I will offer here, as a sound maxim, this: That we can't reach old age by another man's road.

I will now teach, offering my way of life to whomsoever desires to commit suicide by the scheme which has enabled me to beat the doctor and the hangman for seventy years. Some of the details may sound untrue, but they are not. I am not here to deceive; I am here to teach.

We have no permanent habits until we are forty. Then they begin to harden, presently they petrify, then business begins. Since forty I have been regular about going to bed and getting up—and that is one of the main things. I have made it a rule to go to bed when there wasn't anybody left to sit up with; and I have made it a rule to get up when I had to. This has resulted in an unswerving regularity of irregularity. It has saved me sound, but it would injure another person.

In the matter of diet—which is another main thing—I have been persistently strict in sticking to the things which didn't agree with me until one or the other of us got the best of it. Until lately I got the best of it myself. But last spring I stopped frolicking with mince pie after midnight; up to then I had always believed it wasn't loaded. For thirty years I have taken coffee and bread at eight in the morning, and no bite nor sup until seven-thirty in the evening. Eleven hours. That is all right for me, and is wholesome, because I have never had a headache in my life, but headachy people would not reach seventy comfortably by that road, and they would be foolish to try it. And I wish to urge upon you this—which I think is wisdom—that if you find you can't make seventy by any but an uncomfortable road, don't you go. When they take off the Pullman and retire you to the rancid smoker, put on your things, count your checks, and get out at the first way station where there's a cemetery.

I have made it a rule never to smoke more than one cigar at a time. I have no other restriction as regards smoking. I do not know just when I began to smoke, I only know that it was in my father's lifetime, and that I was discreet. He passed from this life early in 1847, when I was a shade past eleven; ever since than I have smoked publicly. As an example to others, and not that I care for moderation myself, it has always been my rule never to smoke when asleep, and never to refrain when awake. It is a good rule. I mean, for me; but some of you know quite well that it wouldn't answer for everybody that's trying to get to be seventy.

I smoke in bed until I have to go to sleep; I wake up in the night, sometimes once, sometimes twice, sometimes three times, and I never waste any of these opportunities to smoke. This habit is so old and dear and precious to me that I would feel as you, sir, would feel if you should lose the only moral you've got—meaning the chairman—if you've got one: I am making no charges. I will grant, here, that I have stopped smoking now and then, for a few months at a time, but it was not on principle, it was only to show off; it was to pulverize those critics who said I was a slave to my habits and couldn't break my bonds.

To-day it is all of sixty years since I began to smoke the limit. I have never bought cigars with life belts around them. I early found that those were too expensive for me. I have always bought

Steamship "Quaker City" and the Author of "Innocents Abroad"

RUSSIAN SUFFERERS

On December 18, 1905, *an entertainment was given at the Casino for the benefit of the Russian sufferers. After the performance Mr. Clemens spoke.*

LADIES AND GENTLEMEN,—It seems a sort of cruelty to inflict upon an audience like this our rude English tongue, after we have heard that divine speech flowing in that lucid Gallic tongue.

It has always been a marvel to me—that French language; it has always been a puzzle to me. How beautiful that language is. How expressive it seems to be. How full of grace it is.

And when it comes from lips like those, how eloquent and how liquid it is. And, oh, I am always deceived—I always think I am going to understand it.

Oh, it is such a delight to me, such a delight to me, to meet Madame Bernhardt, and laugh hand to hand and heart to heart with her.

I have seen her play, as we all have, and oh, that is divine; but I have always wanted to know Madame Bernhardt herself—her fiery self. I have wanted to know that beautiful character.

Why, she is the youngest person I ever saw, except myself—for I always feel young when I come in the presence of young people.

I have a pleasant recollection of an incident so many years ago—when Madame Bernhardt came to

Hartford, where I lived, and she was going to play and the tickets were three dollars, and there were two lovely women—a widow and her daughter—neighbors of ours, highly cultivated ladies they were; their tastes were fine and elevated, but they were very poor, and they said: "Well, we must not spend six dollars on a pleasure of the mind, a pleasure of intellect; we must spend it, if it must go at all, to furnish to somebody bread to eat."

And so they sorrowed over the fact that they had to give up that great pleasure of seeing Madame Bernhardt, but there were two neighbors equally highly cultivated and who could not afford bread, and those good-hearted Joneses sent that six dollars—deprived themselves of it—and sent it to those poor Smiths to buy bread with. And those Smiths took it and bought tickets with it to see Madame Bernhardt.

Oh yes, some people have tastes and intelligence also.

Now, I was going to make a speech—I supposed I was, but I am not. It is late, late; and so I am going to tell a story; and there is this advantage about a story, anyway, that whatever moral or valuable thing you put into a speech, why, it gets diffused among those involuted sentences and possibly your audience goes away without finding out what that valuable thing was that you were trying to confer upon it; but, dear me, you put the same jewel into a story and it becomes the keystone of that story, and you are bound to get it—it flashes, it flames, it is the jewel in the toad's head—you don't overlook that.

Now, if I am going to talk on such a subject as, for instance, the lost opportunity—oh, the lost opportunity. Anybody in this house who has reached the turn of life—sixty, or seventy, or even fifty, or along there—when he goes back along his history, there he finds it mile-stoned all the way with the lost opportunity, and you know how pathetic that is.

You younger ones cannot know the full pathos that lies in those words—the lost opportunity; but anybody who is old, who has really lived and felt this life, he knows the pathos of the lost opportunity.

Now, I will tell you a story whose moral is that, whose lesson is that, whose lament is that.

I was in a village which is a suburb of New Bedford several years ago—well, New Bedford is a suburb of Fair Haven, or perhaps it is the other way; in any case, it took both of those towns to make a great center of the great whaling industry of the first half of the nineteenth century, and I was up there at Fair Haven some years ago with a friend of mine.

There was a dedication of a great town hall, a public building, and we were there in the afternoon. This great building was filled, like this great theatre, with rejoicing villagers, and my friend and I started down the centre aisle. He saw a man standing in that aisle, and he said: "Now, look at that bronzed veteran—at that mahogany-faced man. Now, tell me, do you see anything about that man's face that is emotional? Do you see anything about it that suggests that inside that man anywhere there are fires that can be started? Would you ever imagine that that is a human volcano?"

"Why, no," I said, "I would not. He looks like a wooden Indian in front of a cigar store."

"Very well," said my friend, "I will show you that there is emotion even in that unpromising place. I will just go to that man and I will just mention in the most casual way an incident in his life. That man is getting along toward ninety years old. He is past eighty. I will mention an incident of fifty or sixty years ago. Now, just watch the effect, and it will be so casual that if you don't watch you won't know when I do say that thing—but you just watch the effect."

He went on down there and accosted this antiquity, and made a remark or two. I could not catch up. They were so casual I could not recognize which one it was that touched that bottom, for in an instant that old man was literally in eruption and was filling the whole place with profanity of the most exquisite kind. You never heard such accomplished profanity. I never heard it also delivered with such eloquence.

I never enjoyed profanity as I enjoyed it then—more than if I had been uttering it myself. There is nothing like listening to an artist—all his passions passing away in lava, smoke, thunder, lightning, and earthquake.

Then this friend said to me: "Now, I will tell you about that. About sixty years ago that man was a young fellow of twenty-three, and had just come home from a three years' whaling voyage. He came into that village of his, happy and proud because now, instead of being chief mate, he was going to be master of a whale ship, and he was proud and happy about it.

"Then he found that there had been a kind of a cold frost come upon that town and the whole region roundabout; for while he had been away the Father Mathew temperance excitement had come upon the whole region. Therefore, everybody had taken the pledge; there wasn't anybody for miles and miles around that had not taken the pledge.

"So you can see what a solitude it was to this young man, who was fond of his grog. And he was just an outcast, because when they found he would not join Father Mathew's Society they ostracized him, and he went about that town three weeks, day and night, in utter loneliness—the only human being in the whole place who ever took grog, and he had to take it privately.

"If you don't know what it is to be ostracized, to be shunned by your fellow-man, may you never know it. Then he recognized that there was something more valuable in this life than grog, and that is the fellowship of your fellow-man. And at last he gave it up, and at nine o'clock one night he went down to the Father Mathew Temperance Society, and with a broken heart he said: 'Put my name down for membership in this society.'

"And then he went away crying, and at earliest dawn the next morning they came for him and routed him out, and they said that new ship of his was ready to sail on a three years' voyage. In a minute he was on board that ship and gone.

"And he said—well, he was not out of sight of that town till he began to repent, but he had made up his mind that he would not take a drink, and so that whole voyage of three years was a three years' agony to that man because he saw all the time the mistake he had made.

"He felt it all through; he had constant reminders of it, because the crew would pass him with their grog, come out on the deck and take it, and there was the torturous smell of it.

"He went through the whole three years of suffering, and at last coming into port it was snowy, it was cold, he was stamping through the snow two feet deep on the deck and longing to get home, and there was his crew torturing him to the last minute with hot grog, but at last he had his reward. He really did get to shore at last, and jumped and ran and bought a jug and rushed to the society's office and said to the secretary:

"'Take my name off your membership books, and do it right away! I have got a three years' thirst on.'

"And the secretary said: 'It is not necessary. You were blackballed!'"

JOAN OF ARC

Address at the Dinner of the Society of Illustrators, Given at the Aldine Association Club, December 22, 1905

Just before Mr. Clemens made his speech, a young woman attired as Joan of Arc, with a page bearing her flag of battle, courtesied reverently and tendered Mr. Clemens a laurel wreath on a satin pillow. He tried to speak, but his voice failed from excess of emotion. "I thank you!" he finally exclaimed, and, pulling himself together, he began his speech.

NOW there is an illustration [pointing to the retreating Joan of Arc]. That is exactly what I wanted—precisely what I wanted—when I was describing to myself Joan of Arc, after studying her history and her character for twelve years diligently.

That was the product—not the conventional Joan of Arc. Wherever you find the conventional Joan of Arc in history she is an offence to anybody who knows the story of that wonderful girl.

Why, she was—she was almost supreme in several details. She had a marvellous intellect; she had a great heart, had a noble spirit, was absolutely pure in her character, her feeling, her language, her words, her everything—she was only eighteen years old.

Now put that heart into such a breast—eighteen years old—and give it that masterly intellect which showed in the face, and furnish it with that almost godlike spirit, and what are you going to have? The conventional Joan of Arc? Not by any means. That is impossible. I cannot comprehend any such thing as that.

You must have a creature like that young and fair and beautiful girl we just saw. And her spirit must look out of the eyes. The figure should be—the figure should be in harmony with all that, but, oh, what we get in the conventional picture, and it is always the conventional picture!

I hope you will allow me to say that your guild, when you take the conventional, you have got it at second hand. Certainly, if you had studied and studied, then you might have something else as a result, but when you have the common convention you stick to that.

You cannot prevail upon the artist to do it; he always gives you a Joan of Arc—the lovely creature that started a great career at thirteen, but whose greatness arrived when she was eighteen; and merely because she was a girl he cannot see the divinity in her, and so he paints a peasant, a coarse and lubberly figure—the figure of a cotton bale, and he clothes that in the coarsest raiment of the peasant region—just like a fish woman, her hair cropped like that of a Russian peasant, and that face of hers, which should be beautiful and which should radiate all the glories which are in the spirit and in her heart—that expression in that face is always just the fixed expression of a ham.

But now Mr. Beard has intimated a moment ago, and so has Sir Purdon-Clarke also, that the artist, the illustrator, does not often get the idea of the man whose book he is illustrating. Here is a very remarkable instance of the other thing in Mr. Beard, who illustrated a book of mine. You may never have heard of it. I will tell you about it now—*A Yankee in King Arthur's Court.*

Now, Beard got everything that I put into that book and a little more besides. Those pictures of Beard's in that book—oh, from the first page to the last is one vast sardonic laugh at the trivialities, the servilities of our poor human race, and also at the professions and the insolence of priestcraft and king-craft—those creatures that make slaves of themselves and have not the manliness to shake it off. Beard put it all in that book. I meant it to be there. I put a lot of it there and Beard put the rest.

That publisher of mine in Hartford had an eye for the pennies, and he saved them. He did not waste any on the illustrations. He had a very good artist—Williams—who had never taken a lesson in drawing. Everything he did was original. The publisher hired the cheapest wood-engraver he could find, and in my early books you can see a trace of that. You can see that if Williams had had a chance he would have made some very good pictures. He had a good heart and good intentions.

I had a character in the first book he illustrated—*The Innocents Abroad*. That was a boy seventeen or eighteen years old—Jack Van Nostrand—a New York boy, who, to my mind, was a very remarkable creature. I tried to get Williams to understand that boy, and make a picture of Jack that would be worthy of Jack.

Jack was a most singular combination. He was born and reared in New York here. He was as delicate in his feelings, as clean and pure and refined in his feelings as any lovely girl that ever was, but whenever he expressed a feeling he did it in Bowery slang, and it was a most curious combination—that delicacy of his and that apparent coarseness. There was no coarseness inside of Jack at all, and Jack, in the course of seventeen or eighteen years, had acquired a capital of ignorance that was marvellous—ignorance of various things, not of all things. For instance, he did not know anything about the Bible. He had never been in Sunday-school. Jack got more out of the Holy Land than anybody else, because the others knew what they were expecting, but it was a land of surprise to him.

I said in the book that we found him watching a turtle on a log, stoning that turtle, and he was stoning that turtle because he had read that "The song of the turtle was heard in the land," and this turtle wouldn't sing. It sounded absurd, but it was charged on Jack as a fact, and as he went along through that country he had a proper foil in an old rebel colonel, who was superintendent and head engineer in a large Sunday-school in Wheeling, West Virginia. That man was full of enthusiasm wherever he went, and would stand and deliver himself of speeches, and Jack would listen to those speeches of the colonel and wonder.

Jack had made a trip as a child almost across this continent in the first overland stage-coach. That man's name who ran that line of stages—well, I declare that name is gone. Well, names will go.

Halliday—ah, that's the name—Ben Halliday, your uncle [turning to Mr. Carnegie]. That was the fellow—Ben Halliday—and Jack was full of admiration at the prodigious speed that that line of stages made—and it was good speed—one hundred and twenty-five miles a day, going day and night, and it was the event of Jack's life, and there at the Fords of the Jordan the colonel was inspired to a speech (he was always making a speech), so he called us up to him. He called up five sinners and three saints. It has been only lately that Mr. Carnegie beatified me. And he said: "Here are the Fords of the Jordan —a monumental place. At this very point, when Moses brought the children of Israel through—he brought the children of Israel from Egypt through the desert you see there—he guarded them through that desert patiently, patiently during forty years, and brought them to this spot safe and sound. There you see—there is the scene of what Moses did."

And Jack said: "Moses who?"

"Oh," he says, "Jack, you ought not to ask that! Moses, the great lawgiver! Moses, the great patriot! Moses, the great warrior! Moses, the great guide, who, as I tell you, brought these people through these three hundred miles of sand in forty years, and landed them safe and sound."

Jack said: "There's nothin' in that! Three hundred miles in forty years! Ben Halliday would have snaked 'em through in thirty-six hours."

Well, I was speaking of Jack's innocence, and it was beautiful. Jack was not ignorant on all subjects. That boy was a deep student in the history of Anglo-

Saxon liberty, and he was a patriot all the way through to the marrow. There was a subject that interested him all the time. Other subjects were of no concern to Jack, but that quaint, inscrutable innocence of his I could not get Williams to put into the picture.

Yes, Williams wanted to do it. He said: "I will make him as innocent as a virgin." He thought a moment, and then said, "I will make him as innocent as an unborn virgin," which covered the ground.

I was reminded of Jack because I came across a letter to-day which is over thirty years old that Jack wrote. Jack was doomed to consumption. He was very long and slim, poor creature, and in a year or two after he got back from that excursion to the Holy Land he went on a ride on horseback through Colorado, and he did not last but a year or two.

He wrote this letter, not to me, but to a friend of mine, and he said: "I have ridden horseback"—this was three years after—"I have ridden horseback four hundred miles through a desert country where you never see anything but cattle now and then, and now and then a cattle station—ten miles apart, twenty miles apart. Now you tell Clemens that in all that stretch of four hundred miles I have seen only two books—the Bible and *Innocents Abroad*—the Bible in good repair.

I say that he had studied, and he had, the real Saxon liberty, the acquirement of our liberty, and Jack used to repeat some verses—I don't know where they came from, but I thought of them to-day when

I saw this letter—that that boy could have been talking of himself in those quoted lines from that unknown poet:

> "For he had sat at Sidney's feet
> And walked with him in plain apart,
> And through the centuries heard the beat
> Of Freedom's march through Cromwell's heart."

And he was that kind of a boy. He should have lived, and yet he should not have lived, because he died at that early age—he couldn't have been more than twenty—he had seen all there was to see in the world that was worth the trouble of living in it; he had seen all of this world that is valuable; he had seen all of this world that was illusion, and illusion is the only valuable thing in it. He had arrived at the point where presently the illusions would cease and he would have entered upon the realities of life, and God help the man that has arrived at that point.

TAXES AND MORALS

ADDRESS AT CARNEGIE HALL, NEW YORK, JANUARY 22, 1906

At the twenty-fifth anniversary of the founding of Tuskegee Institute by Booker Washington, Mr. Choate presided, and in introducing Mr. Clemens declared that he made play his work, and that when he worked hardest he did so lying in bed.

I CAME here in the responsible capacity of policeman to watch Mr. Choate. This is an occasion of grave and serious importance, and it seems necessary for me to be present, so that if he tried to work off any statement that required correction, reduction, refutation, or exposure, there would be a tried friend of the public to protect the house. He has not made one statement whose veracity fails to tally exactly with my own standard. I have never seen a person improve so. This makes me thankful and proud of a country that can produce such men—two such men. And all in the same country. We can't be with you always; we are passing away, and then—well, everything will have to stop, I reckon. It is a sad thought. But in spirit I shall still be with you. Choate, too—if he can.

Every born American among the eighty millions, let his creed or destitution of creed be what it may, is indisputably a Christian to this degree—that his moral constitution is Christian.

There are two kinds of Christian morals, one pri-

vate and the other public. These two are so distinct, so unrelated, that they are no more akin to each other than are archangels and politicians. During three hundred and sixty-three days in the year the American citizen is true to his Christian private morals, and keeps undefiled the nation's character at its best and highest; then in the other two days of the year he leaves his Christian private morals at home and carries his Christian public morals to the tax office and the polls, and does the best he can to damage and undo his whole year's faithful and righteous work. Without a blush he will vote for an unclean boss if that boss is his party's Moses, without compunction he will vote against the best man in the whole land if he is on the other ticket. Every year in a number of cities and States he helps put corrupt men in office, whereas if he would but throw away his Christian public morals, and carry his Christian private morals to the polls, he could promptly purify the public service and make the possession of office a high and honorable distinction.

Once a year he lays aside his Christian private morals and hires a ferry-boat and piles up his bonds in a warehouse in New Jersey for three days, and gets out his Christian public morals and goes to the tax office and holds up his hands and swears he wishes he may never-never if he's got a cent in the world, so help him. The next day the list appears in the papers—a column and a quarter of names, in fine print, and every man in the list a billionaire and member of a couple of churches. I know all those people. I have friendly, social, and criminal rela-

tions with the whole lot of them. They never miss a sermon when they are so's to be around, and they never miss swearing-off day, whether they are so's to be around or not.

I used to be an honest man. I am crumbling. No—I have crumbled. When they assessed me at $75,000 a fortnight ago I went out and tried to borrow the money, and couldn't; then when I found they were letting a whole crop of millionaires live in New York at a third of the price they were charging me I was hurt, I was indignant, and said: "This is the last feather. I am not going to run this town all by myself." In that moment—in that memorable moment—I began to crumble. In fifteen minutes the disintegration was complete. In fifteen minutes I had become just a mere moral sand pile; and I lifted up my hand along with those seasoned and experienced deacons and swore off every rag of personal property I've got in the world, clear down to cork leg, glass eye, and what is left of my wig.

Those tax officers were moved; they were profoundly moved. They had long been accustomed to seeing hardened old grafters act like that, and they could endure the spectacle; but they were expecting better things of me, a chartered, professional moralist, and they were saddened.

I fell visibly in their respect and esteem, and I should have fallen in my own, except that I had already struck bottom, and there wasn't any place to fall to.

At Tuskegee they will jump to misleading conclusions from insufficient evidence, along with Doctor

Parkhurst, and they will deceive the student with the superstition that no gentleman ever swears.

Look at those good millionaires; aren't they gentlemen? Well, they swear. Only once in a year, maybe, but there's enough bulk to it to make up for the lost time. And do they lose anything by it? No, they don't; they save enough in three minutes to support the family seven years. When they swear, do we shudder? No—unless they say "damn!" Then we do. It shrivels us all up. Yet we ought not to feel so about it, because we all swear—everybody. Including the ladies. Including Doctor Parkhurst, that strong and brave and excellent citizen, but superficially educated.

For it is not the word that is the sin, it is the spirit back of the word. When an irritated lady says "oh!" the spirit back of it is "damn!" and that is the way it is going to be recorded against her. It always makes me so sorry when I hear a lady swear like that. But if she says "damn," and says it in an amiable, nice way, it isn't going to be recorded at all.

The idea that no gentleman ever swears is all wrong; he can swear and still be a gentleman if he does it in a nice and benevolent and affectionate way. The historian, John Fiske, whom I knew well and loved, was a spotless and most noble and upright Christian gentleman, and yet he swore once. Not exactly that, maybe; still, he—but I will tell you about it.

One day, when he was deeply immersed in his work, his wife came in, much moved and profoundly

distressed, and said: "I am sorry to disturb you, John, but I must, for this is a serious matter, and needs to be attended to at once."

Then, lamenting, she brought a grave accusation against their little son. She said: "He has been saying his Aunt Mary is a fool and his Aunt Martha is a damned fool." Mr. Fiske reflected upon the matter a minute, then said: "Oh, well, it's about the distinction I should make between them myself."

Mr. Washington, I beg you to convey these teachings to your great and prosperous and most beneficent education institution, and add them to the prodigal mental and moral riches wherewith you equip your fortunate protégés for the struggle of life.

LAYMAN'S SERMON

The Young Men's Christian Association asked Mr. Clemens to deliver a lay sermon at the Majestic Theatre, New York, March 4, 1906. More than five thousand young men tried to get into the theatre, and in a short time traffic was practically stopped in the adjacent streets. The police reserves had to be called out to thin the crowd. Doctor Fagnani had said something before about the police episode, and Mr. Clemens took it up.

I HAVE been listening to what was said here, and there is in it a lesson of citizenship. You created the police, and you are responsible for them. One must pause, therefore, before criticising them too harshly. They are citizens, just as we are. A little of citizenship ought to be taught at the mother's knee and in the nursery. Citizenship is what makes a republic; monarchies can get along without it. What keeps a republic on its legs is good citizenship.

Organization is necessary in all things. It is even necessary in reform. I was an organization myself once—for twelve hours. I was in Chicago a few years ago about to depart for New York. There were with me Mr. Osgood, a publisher, and a stenographer. I picked out a stateroom on a train, the principal feature of which was that it contained the privilege of smoking. The train had started but a short time when the conductor came in and said that there had been a mistake made, and asked that we vacate the apartment. I refused, but when I went

out on the platform Osgood and the stenographer agreed to accept a section. They were too modest.

Now, I am not modest. I was born modest, but it didn't last. I asserted myself, insisted upon my rights, and finally the Pullman conductor and the train conductor capitulated, and I was left in possession.

I went into the dining car the next morning for breakfast. Ordinarily I only care for coffee and rolls, but this particular morning I espied an important-looking man on the other side of the car eating broiled chicken. I asked for broiled chicken, and I was told by the waiter and later by the dining-car conductor that there was no broiled chicken. There must have been an argument, for the Pullman conductor came in and remarked: "If he wants broiled chicken, give it to him. If you haven't got it on the train, stop somewhere. It will be better for all concerned!" I got the chicken.

It is from experiences such as these that you get your education of life, and you string them into jewels or into tinware, as you may choose. I have received recently several letters asking my counsel or advice. The principal request is for some incident that may prove helpful to the young. There were a lot of incidents in my career to help me long—sometimes they helped me along faster than I wanted to go.

Here is such a request. It is a telegram from Joplin, Missouri, and it reads: "In what one of your works can we find the definition of a gentleman?"

I have not answered that telegram, either; I

couldn't. I don't remember that I ever defined a gentleman, but it seems to me that if any man has just merciful and kindly instincts he would be a gentleman, for he would need nothing else in the world.

I received the other day a letter from my old friend, William Dean Howells—Howells, the head of American literature. No one is able to stand with him. He is an old, old friend of mine, and he writes me, "To-morrow I shall be sixty-nine years old." Why, I am surprised at Howells writing that! I have known him longer than that. I'm sorry to see a man trying to appear so young. Let's see. Howells says now, "I see you have been burying Patrick. I suppose he was old, too."

No, he was never old—Patrick. He came to us thirty-six years ago. He was my coachman on the morning that I drove my young bride to our new home. He was a young Irishman, slender, tall, lithe, honest, truthful, and he never changed in all his life. He really was with us but twenty-five years, for he did not go with us to Europe, but he never regarded that as separation. As the children grew up he was their guide. He was all honor, honesty, and affection. He was with us in New Hampshire, with us last summer, and his hair was just as black, his eyes were just as blue, his form just as straight, and his heart just as good as on the day we first met. In all the long years Patrick never made a mistake. He never needed an order, he never received a command. He knew. I have been asked for my idea of an ideal gentleman, and I give it to you—Patrick McAleer.

MORALS AND MEMORY

Mr. Clemens was the guest of honor at a reception held at Barnard College (Columbia University), March 7, 1906, by the Barnard Union. One of the young ladies presented Mr. Clemens, and thanked him for his amiability in coming to make them an address. She closed with the expression of the great joy it gave her fellow-collegians, "because we all love you."

IF any one here loves me, she has my sincere thanks. Nay, if any one here is so good as to love me—why, I'll be a brother to her. She shall have my sincere, warm, unsullied affection. When I was coming up in the car with the very kind young lady who was delegated to show me the way, she asked me what I was going to talk about. And I said I wasn't sure. I said I had some illustrations, and I was going to bring them in. I said I was certain to give those illustrations, but that I hadn't the faintest notion what they were going to illustrate.

Now, I've been thinking it over in this forest glade [indicating the woods of Arcady on the scene setting], and I've decided to work them in with something about morals and the caprices of memory. That seems to me to be a pretty good subject. You see, everybody has a memory and it's pretty sure to have caprices. And, of course, everybody has morals.

It's my opinion that every one I know has morals, though I wouldn't like to ask. I know I have. But I'd rather teach them than practice them any day.

"Give them to others"—that's my motto. Then you never have any use for them when you're left without. Now, speaking of the caprices of memory in general, and of mine in particular, it's strange to think of all the tricks this little mental process plays on us. Here we're endowed with a faculty of mind that ought to be more supremely serviceable to us than them all. And what happens? This memory of ours stores up a perfect record of the most useless facts and anecdotes and experiences. And all the things that we ought to know—that we need to know—that we'd profit by knowing—it casts aside with the careless indifference of a girl refusing her true lover. It's terrible to think of this phenomenon. I tremble in all my members when I consider all the really valuable things that I've forgotten in seventy years—when I meditate upon the caprices of my memory.

There's a bird out in California that is one perfect symbol of the human memory. I've forgotten the bird's name (just because it would be valuable for me to know it—to recall it to your own minds, perhaps).

But this fool of a creature goes around collecting the most ridiculous things you can imagine and storing them up. He never selects a thing that could ever prove of the slightest help to him; but he goes about gathering iron forks, and spoons, and tin cans, and broken mouse-traps—all sorts of rubbish that is difficult for him to carry and yet be any use when he gets it. Why, that bird will go by a gold watch to bring back one of those patent cake-pans.

Now, my mind is just like that, and my mind isn't very different from yours—and so our minds are just like that bird. We pass by what would be of inestimable value to us, and pack our memories with the most trivial odds and ends that never by any chance, under any circumstances whatsoever, could be of the slightest use to any one.

Now, things that I have remembered are constantly popping into my head. And I am repeatedly startled by the vividness with which they recur to me after the lapse of years and their utter uselessness in being remembered at all.

I was thinking over some on my way up here. They were illustrations I spoke about to the young lady on the way up. And I've come to the conclusion, curious though it is, that I can use every one of these freaks of memory to teach you all a lesson. I'm convinced that each one has its moral. And I think it's my duty to hand the moral on to you.

Now, I recall that when I was a boy I was a good boy—I was a very good boy. Why, I was the best boy in my school. I was the best boy in that little Mississippi town where I lived. The population was only about twenty million. You may not believe it, but I was the best boy in that State—and in the United States, for that matter.

But I don't know why I never heard any one say that but myself. I always recognized it. But even those nearest and dearest to me couldn't seem to see it. My mother, especially, seemed to think there was something wrong with that estimate. And she never got over that prejudice.

Now, when my mother got to be eighty-five years old her memory failed her. She forgot little threads that hold life's patches of meaning together. She was living out West then, and I went on to visit her.

I hadn't seen my mother in a year or so. And when I got there she knew my face; knew I was married; knew I had a family, and that I was living with them. But she couldn't, for the life of her, tell my name or who I was. So I told her I was her boy.

"But you don't live with me," she said.

"No," said I, "I'm living in Hartford."

"What are you doing there?"

"Going to school."

"Large school?"

"Very large."

"All boys?"

"All boys."

"And how do you stand?" said my mother.

"I'm the best boy in that school," I answered.

"Well," said my mother, with a return of her old fire, "I'd like to know what the other boys are like."

Now, one point in this story is the fact that my mother's mind went back to my school days, and remembered my little youthful self-prejudice when she'd forgotten everything else about me.

The other point is the moral. There's one there that you will find if you search for it.

Now, here's something else I remember. It's about the first time I ever stole a watermelon. "Stole" is a strong word. Stole? Stole? No, I don't mean that. It was the first time I ever withdrew a watermelon, retired it from circulation—the first time I

ever *extracted* a watermelon. That is exactly the word I want—"extracted." It is definite. It is precise. It perfectly conveys my idea. Its use in dentistry connotes the delicate shade of meaning I am looking for. You know we never extract our own teeth.

And it was not my watermelon that I extracted. I extracted that watermelon from a farmer's wagon while he was inside negotiating with another customer. I carried that watermelon to one of the secluded recesses of the lumber-yard, and there I broke it open.

It was a green watermelon.

Well, do you know when I saw that I began to feel sorry—sorry—sorry. It seemed to me that I had done wrong. I reflected deeply. I reflected that I was young—I think I was just eleven. But I knew that though immature I did not lack moral advancement. I knew what a boy ought to do who had extracted a watermelon—like that.

I considered George Washington, and what action he would have taken under similar circumstances. Then I knew there was just one thing to make me feel right inside, and that was—Restitution.

So I said to myself: "I will do that. I will take that green watermelon back where I got it from." And the minute I had said it I felt that great moral uplift that comes to you when you've made a noble resolution.

So I gathered up the biggest fragments, and I carried them back to the farmer's wagon, and I restored the watermelon—what was left of it. And I made him give me a good one in place of it, too.

And I told him he ought to be ashamed of himself going around working off his worthless, old, green watermelons on trusting purchasers who had to rely on him. How could they tell from the outside whether the melons were good or not? That was his business. And if he didn't reform, I told him I'd see that he didn't get any more of my trade—nor anybody else's I knew, if I could help it.

You know that man was as contrite as a revivalist's last convert. He said he was all broken up to think I'd gotten a green watermelon. He promised me he would never carry another green watermelon if he starved for it. And he drove off—a better man.

Now, do you see what I did for that man? He was on a downward path, and I rescued him. But all I got out of it was a watermelon.

Yet I'd rather have that memory—just that memory of the good I did for that depraved farmer—than all the material gain you can think of. Look at the lesson he got! I never got anything like that from it. But I ought to be satisfied. I was only eleven years old, but I secured everlasting benefit to other people.

The moral in this is perfectly clear, and I think there's one in the next memory I'm going to tell you about.

When I was seventeen I was very bashful, and a sixteen-year-old girl came to stay a week with us. She was a peach, and I was seized with a happiness not of this world.

One evening my mother suggested that, to enter-

tain her, I take her to the theatre. I didn't really like to, because I was seventeen and sensitive about appearing in the streets with a girl. I couldn't see my way to enjoying my delight in public. But we went.

I didn't feel very happy. I couldn't seem to keep my mind on the play. I became conscious, after a while, that that was due less to my lovely company than my boots. They were sweet to look upon, as smooth as skin, but fitted ten times as close. I got oblivious to the play and the girl and the other people and everything but my boots until—I hitched one partly off. The sensation was sensuously perfect. I couldn't help it. I had to get the other off, partly. Then I was obliged to get them off altogether, except that I kept my feet in the legs so they couldn't get away.

From that time I enjoyed the play. But the first thing I knew the curtain came down, like that, without my notice, and I hadn't any boots on. What's more, they wouldn't go on. I tugged strenuously. And the people in our row got up and fussed and said things until the peach and I simply had to move on.

We moved—the girl on one arm and the boots under the other.

We walked home that way, sixteen blocks, with a retinue a mile long. Every time we passed a lamp-post death gripped me at the throat. But we got home—and I had on white socks.

If I live to be nine hundred and ninety-nine years old I don't suppose I could ever forget that walk.

I trust that you will carry away some good thought from these lessons I have given you, and that the memory of them will inspire you to higher things, and elevate you to plans far above the old—and—and—

And I tell you one thing, young ladies: I've had a better time with you to-day than with that peach fifty-three years ago.

WHEN IN DOUBT, TELL THE TRUTH

Mark Twain's speech at the dinner of the "Freundschaft Society," March 9, 1906, had as a basis the words of introduction used by Toastmaster Frank, who, referring to Pudd'nhead Wilson, *used the phrase, "When in doubt, tell the truth."*

MR. CHAIRMAN, MR. PUTZEL, AND GENTLEMEN OF THE FREUNDSCHAFT,—That maxim I did invent, but never expected it to be applied to me. I meant to say, "When *you* are in doubt;" when I am in doubt myself I use more sagacity.

Mr. Grout suggested that if I have anything to say against Mr. Putzel, or any criticism of his career or his character, I am the last person to come out on account of that maxim and tell the truth. That is altogether a mistake.

I do think it is right for other people to be virtuous so that they can be happy hereafter, but if I knew every impropriety that even Mr. Putzel has committed in his life, I would not mention one of them. My judgment has been maturing for seventy years, and I have got to that point where I know better than that.

Mr. Putzel stands related to me in a very tender way (through the tax office), and it does not behoove me to say anything which could by any possibility militate against that condition of things.

Now, that word—taxes, taxes, taxes! I have heard

it to-night. I have heard it all night. I wish somebody would change that subject; that is a very sore subject to me.

I was so relieved when Judge Leventritt did find something that was not taxable—when he said that the commissioner could not tax your patience. And that comforted me. We've got so much taxation. I don't know of a single foreign product that enters this country untaxed except the answer to prayer.

On an occasion like this the proprieties require that you merely pay compliments to the guest of the occasion, and I am merely here to pay compliments to the guest of the occasion, not to criticise him in any way, and I can say only complimentary things to him.

When I went down to the tax office some time ago, for the first time in New York, I saw Mr. Putzel sitting in the "Seat of Perjury." I recognized him right away. I warmed to him on the spot. I didn't know that I had ever seen him before, but just as soon as I saw him I recognized him. I had met him twenty-five years before, and at that time had achieved a knowledge of his abilities and something more than that.

I thought: "Now, this is the man whom I saw twenty-five years ago." On that occasion I not only went free at his hands, but carried off something more than that. I hoped it would happen again.

It was twenty-five years ago when I saw him, a young clerk in Putnam's book store. I went in there and asked for George Haven Putnam, and handed him my card, and then the young man said Mr.

Putnam was busy and I couldn't see him. Well, I had merely called in a social way, and so it didn't matter.

I was going out when I saw a great big, fat, interesting-looking book lying there, and I took it up. It was an account of the invasion of England in the fourteenth century by the Preaching Friar, and it interested me.

I asked him the price of it, and he said four dollars.

"Well," I said, "what discount do you allow to publishers?"

He said: "Forty per cent off."

I said: "All right, I am a publisher."

He put down the figure, forty per cent off, on a card.

Then I said: "What discount do you allow to authors?"

He said: "Forty per cent off."

"Well," I said, "set me down as an author."

"Now," said I, "what discount do you allow to the clergy?"

He said: "Forty per cent off."

I said to him that I was only on the road, and that I was studying for the ministry. I asked him wouldn't he knock off twenty per cent for that. He set down the figure, and he never smiled once.

I was working off these humorous brilliancies on him and getting no return—not a scintillation in his eye, not a spark of recognition of what I was doing there. I was almost in despair.

I thought I might try him once more, so I said: "Now, I am also a member of the human race. Will you let me have the ten per cent off for that?" He set it down, and never smiled.

Well, I gave it up. I said: "There is my card with my address on it, but I have not any money with me. Will you please send the bill to Hartford?" I took up the book and was going away.

He said: "Wait a minute. There is forty cents coming to you."

When I met him in the tax office I thought maybe I could make something again, but I could not. But I had not any idea I could when I came, and as it turned out I did get off entirely free.

I put up my hand and made a statement. It gave me a good deal of pain to do that. I was not used to it. I was born and reared in the higher circles of Missouri, and there we don't do such things—didn't in my time, but we have got that little matter settled—got a sort of tax levied on me.

Then he touched me. Yes, he touched me this time, because he cried—cried! He was moved to tears to see that I, a virtuous person only a year before, after immersion for one year—during one year in the New York morals—had no more conscience than a millionaire.

INTRODUCING DOCTOR VAN DYKE
(1906)

I AM here, ostensibly, to introduce to you the lecturer of the occasion, the Reverend Doctor van Dyke, of Princeton University; not to tell you who he is—you know that already; not to praise his delicious books—they praise themselves better than any words of mine could do it for them. Then is there any real use or advantage in my being here at all? Yes; I am here to talk and put in the time while Doctor van Dyke reflects upon what he is going to say, and whether he had better say it or not.

Chance has furnished me a text—a text which offers me an opportunity to teach, an opportunity to be instructive; and if I have a passion for anything, it is for teaching. It is noble to teach oneself; it is still nobler to teach others—and less trouble. My text is a telegram from the *Daily Review*, an Illinois newspaper, which says, "In what book of yours will we find a definition of a gentleman?" This question has been asked me a number of times by mail in the past month or two, and I have not replied; but if it is now going to be taken up by telegraph, it is time for me to say something, and I think that this is the right time and place for it.

The source of these inquiries was an Associated Press telegram of a month or so ago, which said, in substance, that a citizen of Joplin, Missouri, who had just died, had left ten thousand dollars to be devoted to the dissemination among young men of Mark Twain's idea of the true gentleman. This was a puzzle to me, for I had never in my life uttered in print a definition of that word—a word which once had a concrete meaning, but has no clear and definite meaning now, either in America or elsewhere. In England, long ago, and in America in early times the term was compact and definite, and was restricted to a certain grade of birth, and it had nothing to do with character; a gentleman could commit all the crimes and bestialities known to the Newgate Calendar, and be shunned and despised by everybody, great and small, and no one could dispute it. But in our day how would you define that loose and shackly and shadowy and colorless word?—in case you had thirty-five years to do it in. None but a very self-complacent and elaborately incompetent person would ever try to define it; and then the result wouldn't be worth the violent mental strain it had cost.

The weeks drifted along, and I remained puzzled; but at last when this telegram came I suddenly remembered! Remembered that I had once defined the word? Not at all. What I remembered was this: In the first fortnight of March, four years ago, a New York lady defined the word in a published interview. The main feature of her definition was that no man is a gentleman who hasn't had a college education. Oh, dear me—Adam, for instance! And Arkwright—and Watt—and Stephenson—and Whitney—and Franklin—and Fulton—and Morse—and Elias Howe—and Edison—and Graham Bell—and Lincoln—and Washington—and—and me. What a project! to select and set apart a majestic and monumental class for the people's reverence and homage, then degrade it, belittle it, make it trivial, make it comical, make it grotesque, by leaving out of it the makers of history, the uplifters of man, the creators and preservers of civilizations! The idea of leaving *us* out! It was my privilege to laugh, if I did it privately. Very well, I did it privately. Considering the fact that the person who proposes to define that word must be equipped with almost limitless knowledge and daring and placid self-confidence, it seemed to me that the late Simon Hanks, of Cape Cod, had surely changed his sex and was come again. The poet says:

> 'The Lord knows all things, great and small;
> With doubt He's never vexed;
> Ah yes, the good Lord knows it all—
> But Simon Hanks comes next."

The matter seemed settled. But the New York papers have long known that no large question is ever really settled until I have been consulted; it is the way they feel about it, and they show it by always sending to me when they get uneasy; so the interviewers came up to Riverdale to get the verdict. I was in bed, trying to amuse the bronchitis, therefore I got myself excused. I said not a word upon the subject to any one. Yet there was a long and fictitious interview pretending to come from me, in one of the papers the next morning—the only instance in which a paper on either side of the Atlantic had treated me uncourteously and unfairly for many years. I was made to speak in the first person and to furnish my idea of what a gentleman is.

You will perceive that there is a sort of grotesque and degraded humor about that situation. All definers of the modern gentleman are agreed that among his qualities must be honesty, courtesy, and truthfulness. Very well, here is a journalist who sends to me a forger to represent him, then prints the forger's product and filches money with it from his deceived readers—yet if I should assert that he is not a gentleman his friends could quite properly require me to prove it, and I couldn't do it; for I don't know what a gentleman is—a gentleman on the indefinite modern plan. It's the fourth dimension to me, with the unsquared circle and the nebular theory added.

There is also another humorous detail or two about the situation. The forged interview deceived and beguiled that trusting and well-meaning citizen of Joplin before he died, and pillaged his heirs after he was in his grave. They can't get the bequeathed money, for it has to go to the dissemination of my definition of what a gentleman is. The proposed class in gentlemanliness can't get it, for my definition doesn't exist and has never existed. The money is tied up for good and all. I believe it is the most dismally and pathetically and sardonically humorous incident I have ever come across.

Now then, can't we define the American gentleman at all? As a whole—no. We can define the best part of him, the valuable part; it is as far as we can get. The rest of him is hazy, diffused, uncertain; it is this, that, and the other thing; it is everything and nothing, according to Tom, Dick, and Harry's undigested notion; and when you've got the jumble all jumbled together to suit you, if it still seems to lack something, whitewash it with a college education and call game.

What shall we say is the best part, the accepted part, the essential part, of the American gentleman? Let us say it is courtesy and a blemishless character. What is courtesy? Consideration for others. Is there a good deal of it in the American character? So far as I have observed, no. Is it an American characteristic? So far as I have observed, the most striking, the most prominent, the most American of all American characteristics is the poverty of it in the American character. Even the foreigner loses his kindly politeness as soon as we get him Americanized. When we have been abroad among either the naked savages or the clothed civilized, for even so brief a time as a year, the first thing we notice when we get back home is the wanton and unprovoked discourtesies that assail us at every turn. They begin at the customs pier and they follow us everywhere. Such of you as have been abroad will feel, with remembered pangs and cheek burnings, that I am speaking the truth; the rest of you will confess it some day when you come home from abroad. You will step into the trolley with your heart so full of thankfulness to be at home again that you can't speak; you are so glad, so happy, so grateful, that the tears blur everything, and you say to yourself, "Oh, *am* I really and truly at home once more?" Then the conductor bawls out "Come, step lively, will you!" and you realize that you are. You realize that in no country on the planet, savage or civilized, but your own could you hear your unoffending old father and mother and your gentle young sister assailed with that brutal insult; also, that no people on the planet but ours is meek enough to stand it. We allow our commonest rights to be trampled underfoot every day and everywhere; among us citizenship is an unknown virtue. We have never claimed to be the Uncourteous Nation, the Unpolite Nation, I don't know where, there being no competition. Is it because we are also the Too-Modest Nation? Probably. Is that why we still keep that old, quiet, courtly uninsolent, uncharacteristic *E pluribus Unum* for our national motto, instead of replacing it with an up-to-date one, full of national character, "Come, *step* lively!"

I am working hard, day and night, without salary or hope of applause, upon my high and self-appointed task of reforming our national manners, and I ask for your help. Am I polite, do you ask? Well . . . no. I'm an American myself. Why don't I begin by reforming my own manners? I have already explained that in the beginning. I said, it is noble to teach oneself, but still nobler to teach others—and less trouble.

Having now finished this extraneous and unofficial lecture, I invite the real lecturer to approach and deliver to you his message; but I do it courteously; you will never hear me say to Reverend Doctor van Dyke, whom I and the nation revere, "Come, *step* lively!"

BILLIARDS

Mr. Clemens attended a billiard tourney on the evening of April 24, 1906, and was called on to tell a story.

THE game of billiards has destroyed my naturally sweet disposition. Once, when I was an underpaid reporter in Virginia City, whenever I wished to play billiards I went out to look for an easy mark. One day a stranger came to town and opened a billiard parlor. I looked him over casually. When he proposed a game, I answered, "All right."

"Just knock the balls around a little so that I can get your gait," he said; and when I had done so, he remarked: "I will be perfectly fair with you. I'll play you left-handed." I felt hurt, for he was cross-eyed, freckled, and had red hair, and I determined to teach him a lesson. He won first shot, ran out, took my half dollar, and all I got was the opportunity to chalk my cue.

"If you can play like that with your left hand," I said, "I'd like to see you play with your right."

"Couldn't play at all," he said. "I'm left-handed."

"MARK TWAIN'S FIRST APPEARANCE"

On October 5, 1906, Mr. Clemens, following a musical recital by his daughter in Norfolk, Conn., addressed her audience on the subject of stage-fright. He thanked the people for making things as easy as possible for his daughter's American début as a contralto, and then told of his first experience before the public.

MY heart goes out in sympathy to any one who is making his first appearance before an audience of human beings. By a direct process of memory I go back forty years, less one month—for I'm older than I look.

I recall the occasion of my first appearance. San Francisco knew me then only as a reporter, and I was to make my bow to San Francisco as a lecturer. I knew that nothing short of compulsion would get me to the theatre. So I bound myself by a hard-and-fast contract so that I could not escape. I got to the theatre forty-five minutes before the hour set for the lecture. My knees were shaking so that I didn't know whether I could stand up. If there is an awful, horrible malady in the world, it is stage-fright—and seasickness. They are a pair. I had stage-fright then for the first and last time. I was only seasick once, too. It was on a little ship on which there were two hundred other passengers. I—was—sick. I was so sick that there wasn't any left for those other two hundred passengers.

It was dark and lonely behind the scenes in that

theatre, and I peeked through the little peek-holes they have in theatre curtains and looked into the big auditorium. That was dark and empty, too. By-and-by it lighted up, and the audience began to arrive.

I had got a number of friends of mine, stalwart men, to sprinkle themselves through the audience armed with big clubs. Every time I said anything they could possibly guess I intended to be funny they were to pound those clubs on the floor. Then there was a kind lady in a box up there, also a good friend of mine, the wife of the Governor. She was to watch me intently, and whenever I glanced toward her she was going to deliver a gubernatorial laugh that would lead the whole audience into applause.

At last I began. I had the manuscript tucked under a United States flag in front of me where I could get at it in case of need. But I managed to get started without it. I walked up and down—I was young in those days and needed the exercise—and talked and talked.

Right in the middle of the speech I had placed a gem. I had put in a moving, pathetic part which was to get at the hearts and souls of my hearers. When I delivered it they did just what I hoped and expected. They sat silent and awed. I had touched them. Then I happened to glance up at the box where the Governor's wife was—you know what happened.

Well, after the first agonizing five minutes, my stage-fright left me, never to return. I know if I was going to be hanged I could get up and make a good showing, and I intended to. But I shall never forget my feelings before the agony left me, and I got up here to thank you for her for helping my daughter, by your kindness, to live through her first appearance. And I want to thank you for your appreciation of her singing, which is, by-the-way, hereditary.

IN AID OF THE BLIND

ADDRESS AT A PUBLIC MEETING OF THE NEW YORK ASSOCIATION FOR PROMOTING THE INTERESTS OF THE BLIND, AT THE WALDORF-ASTORIA, MARCH 29, 1906

IF you detect any awkwardness in my movements and infelicities in my conduct I will offer the explanation that I never presided at a meeting of any kind before in my life, and that I do find it out of my line. I suppose I could do anything anybody else could, but I recognized that experience helps, and I do feel the lack of that experience. I don't feel as graceful and easy as I ought to be in order to impress an audience. I shall not pretend that I know how to umpire a meeting like this, and I shall just take the humble place of the Essex band.

There was a great gathering in a small New England town about twenty-five years ago. I remember that circumstance because there was something that happened at that time. It was a great occasion. They gathered in the milita and orators and everybody from all the towns around. It was an extraordinary occasion.

The little local paper threw itself into ecstasies of admiration and tried to do itself proud from beginning to end. It praised the orators, the militia, and all the bands that came from everywhere, and all this in honest country newspaper detail, but the writer ran out of adjectives toward the end. Having exhausted his whole magazine of praise and glorification, he found he still had one band left over. He had to say something about it, and he said: "The Essex band done the best it could."

I am an Essex band on this occasion, and I am going to get through as well as inexperience and good intentions will enable me. I have got all the documents here necessary to instruct you in the objects and intentions of this meeting and also of the association which has called the meeting. But they are too voluminous. I could not pack those statistics into my head, and I had to give it up. I shall have to just reduce all that mass of statistics to a few salient facts. There are too many statistics and figure for me. I never could do anything with figures, never had any talent for mathematics, never accomplished anything in my efforts at that rugged study, and to-day the only mathematics I know is multiplication, and the minute I get away up in that, as soon as I reach nine times seven——

[Mr. Clemens lapsed into deep thought for a moment. He was trying to figure out nine times seven, but it was a hopeless task, and he turned to St. Clair McKelway, who sat near him. Mr. McKelway whispered the answer, and the speaker resumed:]

I've got it now. It's eighty-four. Well, I can get that far all right with a little hesitation. After that I am uncertain, and I can't manage a statistic.

"This association for the"——

[Mr. Clemens was in another dilemma. Again he was obliged to turn to Mr. McKelway.]

Oh yes, for promoting the interests of the blind. It's a long name. If I could I would write it out for you and let you take it home and study it, but I don't know how to spell it. And Mr. Carnegie is down in Virginia somewhere. Well, anyway, the object of that association which has been recently organized, five months ago, in fact, is in the hands of very, very energetic, intelligent, and capable people, and they will push it to success very surely, and all the more surely if you will give them a little of your assistance out of your pockets.

The intention, the purpose, is to search out all the blind and find work for them to do so that they may earn their own bread. Now it is dismal enough to be blind—it is dreary, dreary life at best, but it can be largely ameliorated by finding something for these poor blind people to do with their hands. The time passes so heavily that it is never day or night with them, it is always night, and when they have to sit with folded hands and with nothing to do to amuse or entertain or employ their minds, it is drearier and drearier.

And then the knowledge they have that they must subsist on charity, and so often reluctant charity, it would renew their lives if they could have something to do with their hands and pass their time and at the same time earn their bread, and know the sweetness of the bread which is the result of the labor of one's own hands. They need that cheer and pleasure. It is the only way you can turn their night into day, to give them happy hearts, the only thing you can put in the place of the blessed sun. That you can do in the way I speak of.

Blind people generally who have seen the light know what it is to miss the light. Those who have gone blind since they were twenty years old—their lives are unendingly dreary. But they can be taught to use their hands and to employ themselves at a great many industries. That association from which this draws its birth in Cambridge, Massachusetts, has taught its blind to make many things. They make them better than most people, and more honest than people who have the use of their eyes. The goods they make are readily salable. People like them. And so they are supporting themselves, and it is a matter of cheer, cheer. They pass their time now not too irksomely as they formerly did.

What this association needs and wants is $15,000. The figures are set down, and what the money is for, and there is no graft in it or I would not be here. And they hope to beguile that out of your pockets, and you will find affixed to the program an opportunity, that little blank which you will fill out and promise so much money now or to-morrow or some time. Then, there is another opportunity which is still better, and that is that you shall subscribe an annual sum.

I have invented a good many useful things in my time, but never anything better than that of getting money out of people who don't want to part with it. It is always for good objects, of course. This is the plan: When you call upon a person to contribute to a great and good object, and you think he should furnish about one thousand dollars, he disappoints you as like as not. Much the best way to work him to supply that thousand dollars is to split it into parts and contribute, say a hundred dollars a year, or fifty, or whatever the sum may be. Let him contribute ten or twenty a year. He doesn't feel that, but he does feel it when you call upon him to contribute a large amount. When you get used to it you would rather contribute than borrow money.

I tried it in Helen Keller's case. Mr. Hutton wrote me in 1896 or 1897 when I was in London and said: "The gentleman who has been so liberal in taking care of Helen Keller has died without making provision for her in his will, and now they don't know what to do." They were proposing to raise a fund, and he thought $50,000 enough to furnish an income of $2,400 or $2,500 a year for the support of that wonderful girl and her wonderful teacher, Miss Sullivan, now Mrs. Macy. I wrote to Mr. Hutton and said: "Go on, get up your fund. It will be slow, but if you want quick work, I propose this system," the system I speak of, of asking people to contribute such and such a sum from year to year and drop out whenever they please, and he would find there wouldn't be any difficulty, people wouldn't feel the burden of it. And he wrote back saying he had raised the $2,400 a year indefinitely by that system in a single afternoon. We would like to do something just like that to-night. We will take as many checks as you care to give. You can leave your donations in the big room outside.

I knew once what it was to be blind. I shall never forget that experience. I have been as blind as anybody ever was for three or four hours, and the sufferings that I endured and the mishaps and the accidents that are burning in my memory make my sympathy rise when I feel for the blind and always shall feel. I once went to Heidelberg on an excursion. I took a clergyman along with me, the Rev. Joseph Twichell, of Hartford, who is still among the living despite that fact. I always travel with clergymen when I can. It is better for them, it is better for me. And any preacher who goes out with me in stormy weather and without a lightning rod is a good one. The Reverend Twichell is one of those people filled with patience and endurance, two good ingredients for a man travelling with me, so we got along very well together. In that old town they have not altered a house nor built one in 1,500 years. We went to the inn and they placed Twichell and me in a most colossal bedroom, the largest I ever saw or heard of. It was as big as this room.

I didn't take much notice of the place. I didn't really get my bearings. I noticed Twichell got a German bed about two feet wide, the kind in which you've got to lie on your edge, because there isn't room to lie on your back, and he was way down south in that big room, and I was way up north at the other end of it, with a regular Sahara in between.

We went to bed. Twichell went to sleep, but then he had his conscience loaded and it was easy for him to get to sleep. I couldn't get to sleep. It was one of those torturing kinds of lovely summer nights when you hear various kinds of noises now and then. A mouse away off in the southwest. You throw things at the mouse. That encourages the mouse.

But I couldn't stand it, and about two o'clock I got up and thought I would give it up and go out in the square where there was one of those tinkling fountains, and sit on its brink and dream, full of romance.

I got out of bed, and I ought to have lit a candle, but I didn't think of it until it was too late. It was the darkest place that ever was. There has never been darkness any thicker than that. It just lay in cakes.

I thought that before dressing I would accumulate my clothes. I pawed around in the dark and found everything packed together on the floor except one sock. I couldn't get on the track of that sock. It might have occurred to me that maybe it was in the wash. But I didn't think of that. I went excursioning on my hands and knees. Presently I thought, "I am never going to find it; I'll go back to bed again." That is what I tried to do during the next three hours. I had lost the bearings of that bed. I was going in the wrong direction all the time. By-and-by I came in collision with a chair and that encouraged me.

It seemed to me, as far as I could recollect, there was only a chair here and there and yonder, five or six of them scattered over this territory, and I thought maybe after I found that chair I might find the next one. Well, I did. And I found another and another and another. I kept going around on my hands and knees, having those sudden collisions, and finally when I banged into another chair I almost lost my temper. And I raised up, garbed as I was, not for public exhibition, right in front of a mirror fifteen or sixteen feet high. I hadn't noticed the mirror; didn't know it was there.

Then I got down on my hands and knees and went on another exploring expedition.

As far as I could remember there were six chairs in that Oklahoma, and one table, a great big heavy table, not a good table to hit with your head when rushing madly along. In the course of time I collided with thirty-five chairs and tables enough to stock that dining-room out there. It was a hospital for decayed furniture, and it was in a worse condition when I got through with it. I went on and on, and at last got to a place where I could feel my way up, and there was a shelf. I knew that wasn't in the middle of the room. Up to that time I was afraid I had gotten out of the city.

I was very careful and pawed along that shelf, and there was a pitcher of water about a foot high, and it was at the head of Twichell's bed, but I didn't know it. I felt that pitcher going and I grabbed at it, but it didn't help any and came right down on Twichell and nearly drowned him. But it woke him up. I was grateful to have company on any terms. He lit a match, and there I was, way down south when I ought to have been back up yonder. My bed was out of sight it was so far away. You needed a telescope to find it. Twichell comforted me and I scrubbed him off and we got sociable.

But that night wasn't wasted. I had my pedometer on my leg. Twichell and I were in a pedometer match. Twichell had longer legs than I. The only way I could keep up was to wear my pedometer to bed. I always walk in my sleep, and on this occasion I gained sixteen miles on him. After all, I never found that sock. I never have seen it from that day to this. But that adventure taught me what it is to be blind. That was one of the most serious occasions of my whole life, yet I never can speak of it without somebody thinking it isn't serious. You try it and see how serious it is to be as the blind are and I was that night.

[Mr. Clemens read several letters of regret. He then introduced Joseph H. Choate, saying:]

It is now my privilege to present to you Mr. Choate. I don't have to really introduce him. I don't have to praise him, or to flatter him. I could say truly that in the forty-seven years I have been familiarly acquainted with him he has always been the handsomest man America has ever produced. And I hope and believe he will hold the belt forty-five years more. He has served his country ably, faithfully, and brilliantly. He stands at the summit, at the very top in the esteem and regard of his countrymen, and if I could say one word which would lift him any higher in his countrymen's esteem and affection, I would say that word whether it was true or not.

SPELLING AND PICTURES

ADDRESS AT THE ANNUAL DINNER OF THE ASSOCIATED PRESS, AT THE WALDORF-ASTORIA, SEPTEMBER 18, 1906

I AM here to make an appeal to the nations in behalf of the simplified spelling. I have come here because they cannot all be reached except through you. There are only two forces that can carry light to all the corners of the globe—only two—the sun in the heavens and the Associated Press down here. I may seem to be flattering the sun, but I do not mean it so; I am meaning only to be just and fair all around. You speak with a million voices; no one can reach so many races, so many hearts and intellects, as you—except Rudyard Kipling, and he cannot do it without your help. If the Associated Press will adopt and use our simplified forms, and thus spread them to the ends of the earth, covering the whole spacious planet with them as with a garden of flowers, our difficulties are at an end.

Every day of the three hundred and sixty-five the only pages of the world's countless newspapers that are read by all the human beings and angels and devils that can read, are these pages that are built out of Associated Press despatches. And so I beg you, I beseech you—oh, I implore you to spell them in our simplified forms. Do this daily, constantly, persistently, for three months—only three months—

it is all I ask. The infallible result?—victory, victory all down the line. For by that time all eyes here and above and below will have become adjusted to the change and in love with it, and the present clumsy and ragged forms will be grotesque to the eye and revolting to the soul. And we shall be rid of phthisis and phthisic and pneumonia and pneumatics, and diphtheria and pterodactyl, and all those other insane words which no man addicted to the simple Christian life can try to spell and not lose some of the bloom of his piety in the demoralizing attempt. Do not doubt it. We are chameleons, and our partialities and prejudices change places with an easy and blessed facility, and we are soon wonted to the change and happy in it.

Do I seem to be seeking the good of the world? That is the idea. It is my public attitude; privately I am merely seeking my own profit. We all do it, but it is sound and it is virtuous, for no public interest is anything other or nobler than a massed accumulation of private interests. In 1883, when the simplified-spelling movement first tried to make a noise, I was indifferent to it; more—I even irreverently scoffed at it. What I needed was an object lesson, you see. It is the only way to teach some people. Very well, I got it. At that time I was scrambling along, earning the family's bread on magazine work at seven cents a word, compound words at single rates, just as it is in the dark present. I was the property of a magazine, a seven-cent slave under a boiler-iron contract. One day there came a note from the editor requiring me to write ten pages on this revolting text: "Considerations concerning the alleged subterranean holophotal extemporaneousness of the conchyliaceous superimbrication of the Ornithorhyncus, as foreshadowed by the unintelligibility of its plesiosaurian anisodactylous aspects."

Ten pages of that. Each and every word a seventeen-jointed vestibuled railroad train. Seven cents a word. I saw starvation staring the family in the face. I went to the editor, and I took a stenographer along so as to have the interview down in black and white, for no magazine editor can ever remember any part of a business talk except the part that's got graft in it for him and the magazine. I said, "Read that text, Jackson, and let it go on the record; read it out loud." He read it: "Considerations concerning the alleged subterranean holophotal extemporaneousness of the conchyliaceous superimbrication of the Ornithorhyncus, as foreshadowed by the unintelligibility of its plesiosaurian anisodactylous aspects."

I said, "You want ten pages of those rumbling, great, long, summer thunderpeals, and you expect to get them at seven cents a peal?"

He said, "A word's a word, and seven cents is the contract; what are you going to do about it?"

I said, "Jackson, this is cold-blooded oppression. What's an average English word?"

He said, "Six letters."

I said, "Nothing of the kind; that's French, and includes the spaces between the words; an average English word is four letters and a half. By hard, honest labor I've dug all the large words out of my vocabulary and shaved it down till the average is three letters and a half. I can put one thousand and two hundred words on your page, and there's not another man alive that can come within two hundred of it. My page is worth eighty-four dollars to me. It takes exactly as long to fill your magazine pages with long words as it does with short ones—four hours. Now, then, look at the criminal injustice of this requirement of yours. I am careful, I am economical of my time and labor. For the family's sake I've got to be so. So I never write 'metropolis' for seven cents, because I can get the same money for 'city.' I never write 'policeman,' because I can get the same price for 'cop.' And so on and so on. I never write 'valetudinarian' at all, for not even hunger and wretchedness can humble me to the point where I will do a word like that for seven cents; I wouldn't do it for fifteen. Examine your obscene text, please; count the words."

He counted and said it was twenty-four. I asked him to count the letters. He made it two hundred and three.

I said, "Now, I hope you see the whole size of your crime. With my vocabulary I would make sixty words out of those two hundred and five letters, and get four dollars and twenty cents for it; whereas for your inhuman twenty-four I would get only one dollar and sixty-eight cents. The pages of these sky-scrapers of yours would pay me only about three hundred dollars; in my simplified vocabulary the same space and the same labor would pay me eight hundred and forty dollars. I do not wish to work upon this scandalous job by the piece. I want to be hired by the year." He coldly refused. I said:

"Then for the sake of the family, if you have no feeling for me, you ought at least to allow me over-time on that word extemporaneousness." Again he coldly refused. I seldom say a harsh word to any one, but I was not master of myself then, and I spoke right out and called him an anisodactylous plesiosaurian conchyliaceous Ornithorhyncus, and rotten to the heart with holophotal subterranean extemporaneousness. God forgive me for that wanton crime; he lived only two hours.

From that day to this I have been a devoted and hard-working member of the heaven-born institution, the International Association for the Prevention of Cruelty to Authors, and now I am laboring with Carnegie's Simplified Committee, and with my heart in the work. . . .

Now then, let us look at this mighty question reasonably, rationally, sanely—yes, and calmly, not excitedly. What is the real function, the essential function, the supreme function, of language? Isn't it merely to convey ideas and emotions? Certainly. Then if we can do it with words of fonetic brevity and compactness, why keep the present cumbersome forms? But can we? Yes. I hold in my hand the proof of it. Here is a letter written by a woman, right out of her heart of hearts. I think she never saw a spelling book in her life. The spelling is her own. There isn't a waste letter in it anywhere. It reduces the fonetics to the last gasp—it squeezes the surplusage out of every word—there's no spelling that can begin with it on this planet outside of the White House. And as for the punctuation, there isn't any. It is all one sentence, eagerly and breathlessly uttered, without break or pause in it anywhere. The letter is absolutely genuine—I have the proofs of that in my possession[1]. I can't stop to spell the words for you, but you can take the letter presently and comfort your eyes with it. I will read the letter:

"Miss ——— dear friend I took some Close into the armerry and give them to you to Send too the suffrers out to California and i Hate to truble you but i got to have one of them Back it was a black oll wolle Shevyott With a jacket to Mach trimed Kind of Fancy no 38 Burst measure and passy menterry acrose the front And the color i woodent Trubble you but it belonged to my brothers wife and she is Mad about it i thoght she was willing but she want she says she want done with it and she was going to Wear it a Spell longer she ant so free harted as what i am and she Has got more to do with Than i have having a Husband to Work and slave For her i gess you remember Me I am shot and stout and light complected i torked with you quite a spell about the suffrars and said it was orful about that erth quake I shoodent wondar if they had another one rite off seeine general Condision of the country is Kind of Explossive i hate to take that Black dress away from the suffrars but i will hunt round And see if i can get

[1] Unfortunately for this statement, the letter later proved to be a clever hoax, the work of Miss Grace Donworth.

Mark Twain enjoyed the joke and urged the author to continue the letters and gather them in a book, which she did later.

another One if i can i will call to the armerry for it if you will jest lay it aside so no more at present from your True freind
i liked your
appearance very Much"

Now you see what simplified spelling can do. It can convey any fact you need to convey; and it can pour out emotions like a sewer. I beg you, I beseech you, to adopt our spelling, and print all your despatches in it.

Now I wish to say just one entirely serious word:

I have reached a time of life, seventy years and a half, where none of the concerns of this world have much interest for me personally. I think I can speak dispassionately upon this matter, because in the little while that I have got to remain here I can get along very well with these old-fashioned forms, and I don't propose to make any trouble about it at all. I shall soon be where they won't care how I spell so long as I keep the Sabbath.

There are eighty-two millions of us people that use this orthography, and it ought to be simplified in our behalf, but it is kept in its present condition to satisfy one million people who like to have their literature in the old form. That looks to me to be rather selfish, and we keep the forms as they are while we have got one million people coming in here from foreign countries every year and they have got to struggle with this orthography of ours, and it keeps them back and damages their citizenship for years until they learn to spell the language, if they ever do learn. This is merely sentimental argument.

People say it is the spelling of Chaucer and Spencer and Shakespeare and a lot of other people who do not know how to spell anyway, and it has been transmitted to us and we preserved it and wish to preserve it because of its ancient and hallowed associations.

Now, I don't see that there is any real argument about that. If that argument is good, then it would be a good argument not to banish the flies and the cockroaches from hospitals because they have been there so long that the patients have got used to them and they feel a tenderness for them on account of the associations.

Now, you see before you the wreck and ruin of what was once a young person like yourselves. I am exhausted by the heat of the day. I must take what is left of this wreck and run out of your presence and carry it away to my home and spread it out there and sleep the sleep of the righteous. There is nothing much left of me but my age and my righteousness, but I leave with you my love and my blessing, and may you always keep your youth.

COPYRIGHT

When the present copyright law was under discussion, Mr. Clemens appeared in Washington, and sent Speaker Cannon the following letter:

December 7, 1906.

"Dear Uncle Joseph,—Please get me the thanks of Congress, not next week but right away. It is very necessary. Do accomplish this for your affectionate old friend right away—by persuasion if you can, by violence if you must, for it is imperatively necessary that I get on the floor of the House for two or three hours and talk to the members, man by man, in behalf of support, encouragement, and protection of one of the nation's most valuable assets and industries—its literature. I have arguments with me—also a barrel with liquid in it.

"Give me a chance. Get me the thanks of Congress. Don't wait for others—there isn't time; furnish them to me yourself and let Congress ratify later. I have stayed away and let Congress alone for seventy-one years and am entitled to the thanks. Congress knows this perfectly well, and I have long felt hurt that this quite proper and earned expression of gratitude has been merely felt by the House and never publicly uttered.

"Send me an order on the sergeant-at-arms quick. When shall I come?

"With love and a benediction,

"Mark Twain."

Later in the day with Mr. Howells, Edward Everett Hale, Thomas Nelson Page, and a number of other authors, Mr. Clemens appeared before the copyright committee. The new Bill contemplated an author's copyright for the term of his life and for fifty years thereafter, applying also for the benefit of artists, musicians, and others, but the authors did most of the talking. F. D. Millet made a speech for the artists, and John Philip Sousa for the musicians.

Mr. Clemens was the last speaker of the day, and its chief feature.

I HAVE read this bill. At least I have read such portions as I could understand. Nobody but a practiced legislator can read the bill and thoroughly understand it, and I am not a practiced legislator.

I am interested particularly and especially in the part of the bill which concerns my trade. I like that extension of copyright life to the author's life and fifty years afterward. I think that would satisfy any reasonable author, because it would take care of his children. Let the grandchildren take care of themselves. That would take care of my daughters, and after that I am not particular. I shall then have long been out of this struggle, independent of it, indifferent to it.

It isn't objectionable to me that all the trades and professions in the United States are protected by the bill. I like that. They are all important and worthy, and if we can take care of them under the Copyright law I should like to see it done. I should like to see oyster culture added, and anything else.

I am aware that copyright must have a limit, because that is required by the Constitution of the United States, which sets aside the earlier Constitution, which we call the decalogue. The decalogue says you shall not take away from any man his profit. I don't like to be obliged to use the harsh term. What the decalogue really says is, "Thou shalt not steal," but I am trying to use more polite language.

The laws of England and America do take it away, do select but one class, the people who create the literature of the land. They always talk handsomely about the literature of the land, always what a fine,

They had all perished before they were ten years old. It is only one book in 1000 that can outlive the forty-two-year limit. Therefore why put a limit at all? You might as well limit the family to twenty-two children.

If you recall the Americans in the nineteenth century who wrote books that lived forty-two years you will have to begin with Cooper; you can follow with Washington Irving, Harriet Beecher Stowe, Edgar Allan Poe, and there you have to wait a long time. You come to Emerson, and you have to stand still and look further. You find Howells and T. B. Aldrich, and then your numbers begin to run pretty thin, and you question if you can name twenty persons in the United States who in a whole century have written books that would live forty-two years. Why, you could take them all and put them on one bench there [pointing]. Add the wives and children and you could put the result on two or three more benches.

One hundred persons—that is the little, insignificant crowd whose bread and butter is to be taken away for what purpose, for what profit to anybody? You turn these few books into the hands of the pirate and of the legitimate publisher, too, and they get the profit that should have gone to the wife and children.

When I appeared before that committee of the House of Lords the chairman asked me what limit I would propose. I said, "Perpetuity." I could see some resentment in his manner, and he said the idea was illogical, for the reason that it has long ago been decided that there can be no such thing as property in ideas. I said there was property in ideas before

Queen Anne's time; they had perpetual copyright. He said, "What is a book? A book is just built from base to roof on ideas, and there can be no property in it."

I said I wished he could mention any kind of property in this planet that had a pecuniary value which was not derived from an idea or ideas. He said real estate. I put a supposititious case, a dozen Englishmen who travel through South Africa and camp out, and eleven of them see nothing at all; they are mentally blind. But there is one in that party who knows what this harbor means and what the lay of the land means. To him it means that some day a railway will go through here, and there on that harbor a great city will spring up. That is his idea. And he has another idea, which is to go and trade his last bottle of Scotch whiskey and his last horse-blanket to the principal chief of that region and buy a piece of land the size of Pennsylvania. That was the value of an idea that the day would come when the Cape to Cairo Railway would be built.

Every improvement that is put upon the real estate is the result of an idea in somebody's head. The skyscraper is another idea; the railroad is another; the telephone and all those things are merely symbols which represent ideas. An andiron, a washtub, is the result of an idea that did not exist before.

So if, as that gentleman said, a book does consist solely of ideas, that is the best argument in the world that it is property, and should not be under any limitation at all. We don't ask for that. Fifty years from now we shall ask for it.

I hope the bill will pass without any deleterious amendments. I do seem to be extraordinary interested in a whole lot of arts and things that I have got nothing to do with. It is a part of my generous, liberal nature; I can't help it. I feel the same sort of charity to everybody that was manifested by a gentleman who arrived at home at two o'clock in the morning from the club and was feeling so perfectly satisfied with life, so happy, and so comfortable, and there was his house weaving, weaving, weaving around. He watched his chance, and by and by when the steps got in his neighborhood he made a jump and climbed up and got on the portico.

And the house went on weaving and weaving and weaving, but he watched the door, and when it came around his way he plunged through it. He got to the stairs, and when he went up on all fours the house was so unsteady that he could hardly make his way, but at last he got to the top and raised his foot and put it on the top step. But only the toe hitched on the step, and he rolled down and fetched up on the bottom step, with his arm around the newel-post, and he said: "God pity the poor sailors out at sea on a night like this."

EDUCATING THEATRE-GOERS

The children of the Educational Alliance gave a performance of "The Prince and the Pauper" on the afternoon of April 14, 1907, in the theatre of the Alliance Building in East Broadway. The audience was composed of nearly one thousand children of the neighborhood. Mr. Clemens, Mr. Howells, and Mr. Daniel Frohman were among the invited guests.

I HAVE not enjoyed a play so much, so heartily, and so thoroughly since I played Miles Hendon twenty-two years ago. I used to play in this piece ("The Prince and the Pauper") with my children, who, twenty-two years ago, were little youngsters. One of my daughters was the Prince, and a neighbor's daughter was the Pauper, and the children of other neighbors played other parts. But we never gave such a performance as we have seen here to-day. It would have been beyond us.

My late wife was the dramatist and stage-manager. Our coachman was the stage-manager, second in command. We used to play it in this simple way, and the one who used to bring in the crown on a cushion—he was a little fellow then—is now a clergyman way up high—six to seven feet high—and growing higher all the time. We played it well, but not as well as you see it here, for you see it done by practically trained professionals.

I was especially interested in the scene which we have just had, for Miles Hendon was my part. I did it as well as a person could who never remembered his part. The children all knew their parts. They did not mind if I did not know mine. I could thread a needle nearly as well as the player did whom you saw to-day. The words of my part I could supply on the spot. The words of the song that Miles Hendon sang here I did not catch. But I was great in that song.

It was so fresh and enjoyable to make up a new set of words each time that I played the part.

If I had a thousand citizens in front of me, I would like to give them information, but you children already know all that I have found out about the Educational Alliance. It's like a man living within thirty miles of Vesuvius and never knowing about a volcano. It's like living for a lifetime in Buffalo, eighteen miles from Niagara, and never going to see the Falls. So I lived in New York and knew nothing about the Educational Alliance.

This theatre is a part of the work, and furnishes pure and clean plays. This theatre is an influence. Everything in the world is accomplished by influences which train and educate. When you get to be seventy-one and a half, as I am, you may think that your education is over, but it isn't.

If we had forty theatres of this kind in this city of four millions, how they would educate and elevate! We should have a body of educated theatre-goers.

It would make better citizens, honest citizens. One of the best gifts a millionaire could make would be a theatre here and a theatre there. It would make of you a real Republic, and bring about an educational level.

THE EDUCATIONAL THEATRE

On November 19, 1907, Mr. Clemens entertained a party of six or seven hundred of his friends, inviting them to witness the representation of "The Prince and the Pauper," played by boys and girls of the East Side at the Children's Educational Theatre, New York.

JUST a word or two to let you know how deeply I appreciate the honor which the children who are the actors and frequenters of this cozy playhouse have conferred upon me. They have asked me to be their ambassador to invite the hearts and brains of New York to come down here and see the work they are doing. I consider it a grand distinction to be chosen as their intermediary. Between the children and myself there is an indissoluble bond of friendship.

I am proud of this theatre and this performance—proud, because I am naturally vain—vain of myself and proud of the children.

I wish we could reach more children at one time. I am glad to see that the children of the East Side have turned their backs on the Bowery theatres to come to see the pure entertainments presented here.

This Children's Theatre is a great educational institution. I hope the time will come when it will be part of every public school in the land. I may be pardoned in being vain. I was born vain, I guess.

[At this point the stage-manager's whistle interrupted Mr. Clemens.] That settles it; there's my cue to stop. I was to talk until the whistle blew, but it blew before I got started. It takes me longer to get started than most people. I guess I was born at slow speed. My time is up, and if you'll keep quiet for two minutes I'll tell you something about Miss Herts, the woman who conceived this splendid idea. She is the originator and the creator of this theatre. Educationally, this institution coins the gold of young hearts into external good.

[*On April 23, 1908, he spoke again at the same place.*]

I will be strictly honest with you; I am only fit to be honorary president. It is not to be expected that I should be useful as a real president. But when it comes to things ornamental I, of course, have no objection. There is, of course, no competition. I take it as a very real compliment because there are thousands of children who have had a part in this request. It is promotion in truth.

It is a thing worth doing that is done here. You have seen the children play. You saw how little Sally reformed her burglar. She could reform any burglar. She could reform me. This is the only school in which can be taught the highest and most difficult lessons—morals. In other schools the way of teaching morals is revolting. Here the children who come in thousands live through each part.

They are terribly anxious for the villain to get his bullet, and that I take to be a humane and proper sentiment. They spend freely the ten cents that is

to myself—a terrible thing—for his *Joan of Arc*, a book of chivalry, of nobility, and of manly sincerity for which I take this opportunity of thanking him. But you can all drink this toast, each one of you with his own intention. You can get into it what meaning you like. Mark Twain is a man whom English and Americans do well to honor. He is the true consolidator of nations. His delightful humor is of the kind which dissipates and destroys national prejudices. His truth and his honor, his love of truth, and his love of honor, overflow all boundaries. He has made the world better by his presence. We rejoice to see him here. Long may he live to reap the plentiful harvest of hearty, honest human affection!"

PILGRIMS, I desire first to thank those undergraduates of Oxford. When a man has grown so old as I am, when he has reached the verge of seventy-two years, there is nothing that carries him back to the dreamland of his life, to his boyhood, like recognition of those young hearts up yonder. And so I thank them out of my heart. I desire to thank the Pilgrims of New York also for their kind notice and message which they have cabled over here. Mr. Birrell says he does not know how he got here. But he will be able to get away all right—[pointing at Mr. Birrell's empty glass] he has not drunk anything since he came here. I am glad to know about those friends of his, Otway and Chatterton—fresh, new names to me. I am glad of the disposition he has shown to rescue them from the evils of poverty, and if they are still in London, I hope to have a talk with them. For a while I thought he was going to tell us the effect which my book had upon his growing manhood. I thought he was going to tell us how much that effect amounted to, and whether it really made him what he now is, but with the discretion born of Parliamentary experience he dodged that, and we do not know now whether he read the book or not. He did that very neatly. I could not do it any better myself.

My books have had effects, and very good ones, too, here and there, and some others not so good. There is no doubt about that. But I remember one monumental instance of it years and years ago. Professor Norton, of Harvard, was over here, and when he came back to Boston I went out with Howells to call on him. Norton was allied in some way by marriage with Darwin. Mr. Norton was very gentle in what he had to say, and almost delicate, and he said: "Mr. Clemens, I have been spending some time with Mr. Darwin in England, and I should like to tell you something connected with that visit. You were the object of it, and I myself would have been very proud of it, but you may not be proud of it. At any rate, I am going to tell you what it was, and to leave to you to regard it as you please. Mr. Darwin took me up to his bedroom and pointed out certain things there—pitcher plants, and so on, that he was measuring and watching from day to day—and he said: 'The chambermaid is permitted to do what she pleases in this room, but she must never touch those plants and never touch those books on that table by that candle. With those books I read myself to sleep every night.' Those were your own books." I said: "There is no question to my mind as to whether I should regard that as a compliment or not. I do regard it as a very great compliment and a very high honor that that great mind, laboring for the whole human race, should rest itself on my books. I am proud that he should read himself to sleep with them."

Now, I could not keep that to myself—I was so proud of it. As soon as I got home to Hartford I called up my oldest friend—and dearest enemy on occasion—the Rev. Joseph Twichell, my pastor, and I told him about that, and, of course, he was full of interest and venom. Those people who get no compliments like that feel like that. He went off. He did not issue any applause of any kind, and I did not hear of that subject for some time. But when Mr. Darwin passed away from this life, and some time after Darwin's *Life and Letters* came out, the Rev. Mr. Twichell procured an early copy of that work and found something in it which he considered applied to me. He came over to my house—it was snowing, raining, sleeting, but that did not make any difference to Twichell. He produced the book, and turned over and over, until he came to a certain place, when he said: "Here, look at this letter from Mr. Darwin to Sir Joseph Hooker." What Mr. Darwin said—I give you the idea and not the very words—was this: I do not know whether I ought to have devoted my whole life to these drudgeries in natural history and the other sciences or not, for while I may have gained in one way I have lost in another. Once I had a fine perception and appreciation of high literature, but in me that quality is atrophied. "That was the reason," said Mr. Twichell, "he was reading your books."

Mr. Birrell has touched lightly—very lightly, but

so that before I got home I had a much higher opinion of myself than I have ever had before or since. And there is in that very connection an incident which I remember at that old date which is rather melancholy to me, because it shows how a person can deteriorate in a mere seven years. It is seven years ago. I have not that hat now. I was going down Pall-Mall, or some other of your big streets, and I recognized that that hat needed ironing. I went into a big shop and passed in my hat, and asked that it might be ironed. They were courteous, very courteous, even courtly. They brought that hat back to me presently very sleek and nice, and I asked how much there was to pay. They replied that they did not charge the clergy anything. I have cherished the delight of that moment from that day to this. It was the first thing I did the other day to go and hunt up that shop and hand in my hat to have it ironed. I said when it came back, "How much to pay?" They said, "Ninepence." In seven years I have acquired all that worldliness, and I am sorry to be back where I was seven years ago.

But now I am chaffing and chaffing and chaffing here, and I hope you will forgive me for that; but when a man stands on the verge of seventy-two you know perfectly well that he never reached that place without knowing what this life is—heartbreaking bereavement. And so our reverence is for our dead. We do not forget them; but our duty is toward the living; and if we can be cheerful, cheerful in spirit, cheerful in speech and in hope, that is a benefit to those who are around us.

My own history includes an incident which will always connect me with England in a pathetic way, for when I arrived here seven years ago with my wife and my daughter—we had gone around the globe lecturing to raise money to clear off a debt—my wife and one of my daughters started across the ocean to bring to England our eldest daughter. She was twenty-four years of age and in the bloom of young womanhood, and we were unsuspecting. When my wife and daughter—and my wife has passed from this life since—when they had reached mid-Atlantic, a cablegram—one of those heartbreaking cablegrams which we all in our days have to experience—was put into my hand. It stated that that daughter of ours had gone to her long sleep. And so, as I say, I cannot always be cheerful, and I cannot always be chaffing; I must sometimes lay the cap and bells aside, and recognize that I am of the human race like the rest, and must have my cares and griefs. And, therefore, I noticed what Mr. Birrell said—I was so glad to hear him say it—something that was in the nature of these verses here at the top of this menu.

> "He lit our life with shafts of sun
> And vanquished pain.
> Thus two great nations stand as one
> In honoring Twain."

I am very glad to have those verses. I am very glad and very grateful for what Mr. Birrell said in that connection. I have received since I have been here, in this one week, hundreds of letters from all conditions of people in England—men, women, and children—and there is in them compliment, praise, and, above all and better than all, there is in them a note of affection. Praise is well, compliment is well, but affection—that is the last and final and most precious reward that any man can win, whether by character or achievement, and I am very grateful to have that reward. All these letters make me feel that here in England—as in America—when I stand under the English flag, I am not a stranger. I am not an alien, but at home.

INDEPENDENCE DAY

The American Society in London gave a banquet, July 4, 1907, at the Hotel Cecil. Ambassador Choate called on Mr. Clemens to respond to the toast "The Day We Celebrate."

MR. CHAIRMAN, MY LORD, AND GENTLEMEN,—Once more it happens, as it has happened so often since I arrived in England a week or two ago, that instead of celebrating the Fourth of July properly as has been indicated, I have to first take care of my personal character.

Sir Mortimer Durand still remains unconvinced. Well, I tried to convince these people from the beginning that I did not take the Ascot Cup; and as I have failed to convince anybody that I did not take the cup, I might as well confess I did take it and be done with it. I don't see why this uncharitable feeling should follow me everywhere, and why I should have that crime thrown up to me on all occasions. The tears that I have wept over it ought to have created a different feeling than this—and, besides, I don't think it is very right or fair that, considering England has been trying to take a cup of ours for forty years—I don't see why they should take so much trouble when I tried to go into the business myself.

Sir Mortimer Durand, too, has had trouble, through going to a dinner here, and he has told you what he suffered in consequence. But what did he suffer? He only missed his train and one night of discomfort, and he remembers it to this day. Oh! if you could only think what I have suffered from a similar circumstance. Two or three years ago, in New York, with that Society there which is made up of people from all British Colonies, and from Great Britain generally, who were educated in British colleges and British schools, I was on hand to respond to a toast of some kind or other, and I did then what I have been in the habit of doing, from a selfish motive, for a long time, and that is, I got myself placed No. 3 in the list of speakers—then you get home early.

I had to go five miles upriver, and had to catch a particular train or not get there. But see the magnanimity which is born in me, which I have cultivated all my life. A very famous and very great British clergyman came to me presently, and he said: "I am away down in the list; I have got to catch a certain train this Saturday night; if I don't catch that train I shall be carried beyond midnight and break the Sabbath. Won't you change places with me?" I said: "Certainly I will." I did it at once. Now, see what happened. Talk about Sir Mortimer Durand's sufferings for a single night! I have suffered ever since because I saved that gentleman from breaking the Sabbath—yes, saved him. I took his place, but I lost my train, and it was I who broke the Sabbath. Up to that time I never had broken the Sabbath in my life, and from that day to this I never have kept it.

Oh! I am learning much here to-night. I find I

didn't know anything about the American Society—that is, I didn't know its chief virtue. I didn't know its chief virtue until his Excellency our Ambassador revealed it—I may say, exposed it. I was intending to go home on the 13th of this month, but I look upon that in a different light now. I am going to stay here until the American Society pays my passage.

Our Ambassador has spoken of our Fourth of July and the noise it makes. We have got a double Fourth of July—a daylight Fourth and a midnight Fourth. During the day in America, as our Ambassador has indicated, we keep the Fourth of July properly in a reverent spirit. We devote it to teaching our children patriotic things—reverence for the Declaration of Independence. We honor the day all through the daylight hours, and when night comes we dishonor it. Presently—before long—they are getting nearly ready to begin now—on the Atlantic coast, when night shuts down, that pandemonium will begin, and there will be noise, and noise, and noise—all night long—and there will be more than noise—there will be people crippled, there will be people killed, there will be people who will lose their eyes, and all through that permission which we give to irresponsible boys to play with firearms and fire-crackers, and all sorts of dangerous things. We turn that Fourth of July, alas! over to rowdies to drink and get drunk and make the night hideous, and we cripple and kill more people than you would imagine.

We probably began to celebrate our Fourth-of-July night in that way one hundred and twenty-five years ago, and on every Fourth-of-July night since these horrors have grown and grown, until now, in our five thousand towns of America, somebody gets killed or crippled on every Fourth-of-July night, besides those cases of sick persons whom we never hear of, who die as the result of the noise or the shock. They cripple and kill more people on the Fourth of July in America than they kill and cripple in our wars nowadays, and there are no pensions for these folk. And, too, we burn houses. Really we destroy more property on every Fourth-of-July night than the whole of the United States was worth one hundred and twenty-five years ago. Why, our Fourth of July is our day of mourning, our day of sorrow! Fifty thousand people who have lost friends, or who have had friends crippled, receive that Fourth of July, when it comes, as a day of mourning for the losses they have sustained in their families.

I have suffered in that way myself. I have had relatives killed in that way. One was in Chicago years ago—an uncle of mine, just as good an uncle as I have ever had, and I had lots of them—yes, uncles to burn, uncles to spare. This poor uncle, full of patriotism, opened his mouth to hurrah, and a rocket went down his throat. Before that man could ask for a drink of water to quench that thing, it blew up and scattered him all over the forty-five States, and—really, now, this is true—I know about it myself—twenty-four hours after that it was raining buttons, recognizable as his, on the Atlantic seaboard. A person cannot have a disaster like that and be entirely cheerful the rest of his life. I had another uncle, on an entirely different Fourth of

July, who was blown up that way, and really it trimmed him as it would a tree. He had hardly a limb left on him anywhere. All we have left now is an expurgated edition of that uncle. But never mind about these things; they are merely passing matters. Don't let me make you sad.

Sir Mortimer Durand said that you, the English people, gave up your colonies over there—got tired of them—and did it with reluctance. Now I wish you just to consider that he was right about that, and that he had his reasons for saying that England did not look upon our Revolution as a foreign war, but as a civil war fought by Englishmen.

Our Fourth of July which we honor so much, and which we love so much, and which we take so much pride in, is an English institution, not an American one, and it comes of a great ancestry. The first Fourth of July in that noble genealogy dates back seven centuries lacking eight years. That is the day of the Great Charter—the Magna Charta—which was born at Runnymede in the next to the last year of King John, and portions of the liberties secured thus by those hardy Barons from that reluctant King John are a part of our Declaration of Independence, of our Fourth of July, of our American liberties. And the second of those Fourths of July was not born until four centuries later, in Charles the First's time, in the Bill of Rights, and that is ours, that is part of our liberties. The next one was still English, in New England, where they established that principle which remains with us to this day, and will continue to remain with us—no taxation without representation. That is always going to stand, and that the English Colonies in New England gave us.

The Fourth of July, and the one which you are celebrating now, born in Philadelphia on the 4th of July, 1776—that is English, too. It is not American. Those were English colonists, subjects of King George III, Englishmen at heart, who protested against the oppressions of the Home Government. Though they proposed to cure those oppressions and remove them, still remaining under the Crown, they were not intending a revolution. The revolution was brought about by circumstances which they could not control. The Declaration of Independence was written by a British subject, every name signed to it was the name of a British subject. There was not the name of a single American attached to the Declaration of Independence—in fact, there was not an American in the country in that day except the Indians out on the plains. They were Englishmen, all Englishmen—Americans did not begin until seven years later, when that Fourth of July had become seven years old, and then the American Republic was established. Since then there have been Americans. So you see what we owe to England in the matter of liberties.

We have, however, one Fourth of July which is absolutely our own, and that is that great proclamation issued forty years ago by that great American to whom Sir Mortimer Durand paid that just and beautiful tribute—Abraham Lincoln. Lincoln's proclamation, which not only set the black slaves free, but set the white man free also. The owner was set free from the burden and offence, that sad condition of things where he was in so many instances a master and owner of slaves when he did not want to be. That proclamation set them all free. But even in this matter England suggested it, for England had set her slaves free thirty years before, and we followed her example. We always followed her example, whether it was good or bad.

And it was an English judge that issued that other great proclamation, and established that great principle that, when a slave, let him belong to whom he may, and let him come whence he may, sets his foot upon English soil, his fetters by that act fall away and he is a free man before the world. We followed the example of 1833, and we freed our slaves as I have said.

It is true, then, that all our Fourths of July, and we have five of them, England gave to us, except that one that I have mentioned—the Emancipation Proclamation, and, lest we forget, let us all remember that we owe these things to England. Let us be able to say to Old England, this great-hearted, venerable old mother of the race, you gave us our Fourths of July that we love and that we honor and revere, you gave us the Declaration of Independence, which is the Charter of our rights, you, the venerable Mother of Liberties, the Protector of Anglo-Saxon Freedom—you gave us these things, and we do most honestly thank you for them.

THE SAVAGE CLUB DINNER

A portrait of Mr. Clemens, signed by all the members of the club attending the dinner, was presented to him, July 6, 1907, and in submitting the toast "The Health of Mark Twain" Mr. J. Scott Stokes recalled the fact that he had read parts of Doctor Clemens's works to Harold Frederic during Frederic's last illness.

MR. CHAIRMAN AND FELLOW-SAVAGES,—I am very glad indeed to have that portrait. I think it is the best one that I have ever had, and there have been opportunities before to get a good photograph. I have sat to photographers twenty-two times to-day. Those sittings added to those that have preceded them since I have been in Europe—if we average at that rate—must have numbered one hundred to two hundred sittings. Out of all those there ought to be some good photographs. This is the best I have had, and I am glad to have your honored names on it. I did not know Harold Frederic personally, but I have heard a great deal about him, and nothing that was not pleasant and nothing except such things as lead a man to honor another man and to love him. I consider that it is a misfortune of mine that I have never had the luck to meet him, and if any book of mine read to him in his last hours made those hours easier for him and more comfortable, I am very glad and proud of that. I call to mind such a case many years ago of an English authoress, well known in her day, who wrote such beautiful child tales, touching and lovely in every possible way. In a little biographical sketch of her I found that her last hours were spent partly in reading a book of mine, until she was no longer able to read. That has always remained in my mind, and I have always cherished it as one of the good things of my life. I had read what she had written, and had loved her for what she had done.

Stanley apparently carried a book of mine feloniously away to Africa, and I have not a doubt that it had a noble and uplifting influence there in the wilds of Africa—because on his previous journeys he never carried anything to read except Shakespeare and the Bible. I did not know of that circumstance. I did not know that he had carried a book of mine. I only noticed that when he came back he was a reformed man. I knew Stanley very well in those old days. Stanley was the first man who ever reported a lecture of mine, and that was in St. Louis. He did it so thoroughly that I could never use that lecture in St. Louis again. I met Stanley here when he came back from that first expedition of his which closed with the finding of Livingstone. You remember how he would break out at the meetings of the British Association, and find fault with what people said, because Stanley had notions of his own, and could not contain them. They had to come out or break him up—and so he would go round and address geographical societies. He was always on the war-path in those days, and people always had to have Stanley contradicting their geography for them and improving it. But he always came back and sat drinking beer with me in the hotel up to two in the morning, and he was then one of the most civilized human beings that ever was.

I saw in a newspaper this evening a reference to an interview which appeared in one of the papers the other day, in which the interviewer said that I characterized Mr. Birrell's speech the other day at the Pilgrims' Club as "bully." Now, if you will excuse me, I never use slang to an interviewer or anybody else. That distresses me. Whatever I said about Mr. Birrell's speech was said in English, as good English as anybody uses. If I could not describe Mr. Birrell's delightful speech without using slang I would not describe it at all. I would close my mouth and keep it closed, much as it would discomfort me.

Now that comes of interviewing a man in the first person, which is an altogether wrong way to interview him. It is entirely wrong because none of you, I, or anybody else, could interview a man—could listen to a man talking any length of time and then go off and reproduce that talk in the first person. It can't be done. What results is merely that the interviewer gives the substance of what is said and puts it in his own language and puts it in your mouth. It will always be either better language than you use or worse, and in my case it is always worse. I have a great respect for the English language. I am one of its supporters, its promoters, its elevators. I don't degrade it. A slip of the tongue would be the most that you would get from me. I have always tried hard and faithfully to improve my English and never to degrade it. I always try to use the best

English to describe what I think and what I feel, or what I don't feel and what I don't think.

I am not one of those who in expressing opinions confine themselves to facts. I don't know anything that mars good literature so completely as too much truth. Facts contain a deal of poetry, but you can't use too many of them without damaging your literature. I love all literature, and as long as I am a doctor of literature—I have suggested to you for twenty years I have been diligently trying to improve my own literature, and now, by virtue of the University of Oxford, I mean to doctor everybody else's.

Now I think I ought to apologize for my clothes. At home I venture things that I am not permitted by my family to venture in foreign parts. I was instructed before I left home and ordered to refrain from white clothes in England. I meant to keep that command fair and clean, and I would have done it if I had been in the habit of obeying instructions, but I can't invent a new process in life right away. I have not had white clothes on since I crossed the ocean until now.

In these three or four weeks I have grown so tired of gray and black that you have earned my gratitude in permitting me to come as I have. I wear white clothes in the depth of winter in my home, but I don't go out in the streets in them. I don't go out to attract too much attention. I like to attract some, and always I would like to be dressed so that I may be more conspicuous than anybody else.

If I had been an ancient Briton, I would not have contented myself with blue paint, but I would have bankrupted the rainbow. I so enjoy gay clothes in which women clothe themselves that it always grieves me when I go to the opera to see that, while women look like a flower-bed, the men are a few gray stumps among them in their black evening dress. These are two or three reasons why I wish to wear white clothes. When I find myself in assemblies like this, with everybody in black clothes, I know I possess something that is superior to everybody else's. Clothes are never clean. You don't know whether they are clean or not, because you can't see.

Here or anywhere you must scour your head every two or three days or it is full of grit. Your clothes must collect just as much dirt as your hair. If you wear white clothes you are clean, and your cleaning bill gets so heavy that you have to take care. I am proud to say that I can wear a white suit of clothes without a blemish for three days. If you need any further instruction in the matter of clothes I shall be glad to give it to you. I hope I have convinced some of you that it is just as well to wear white clothes as any other kind. I do not want to boast. I only want to make you understand that you are not clean.

As to age, the fact that I am nearly seventy-two years old does not clearly indicate how old I am, because part of every day—it is with me as with you—you try to describe your age, and you cannot do it. Sometimes you are only fifteen; sometimes you are twenty-five. It is very seldom in a day that I am seventy-two years old. I am older now sometimes than I was when I used to rob orchards; a thing which I would not do to-day—if the orchards were watched. I am so glad to be here to-night. I am so glad to renew with the Savages that now ancient time when I first sat with a company of this club in London in 1872. That is a long time ago. But I did stay with the Savages a night in London long ago, and as I had come into a very strange land, and was with friends, as I could see, that has always remained in my mind as a peculiarly blessed evening, since it brought me into contact with men of my own kind and my own feelings.

I am glad to be here, and to see you all again, because it is very likely that I shall not see you again. It is easier than I thought to come across the Atlantic. I have been received, as you know, in the most delightfully generous way in England ever since I came here. It keeps me choked up all the time. Everybody is so generous, and they do seem to give you such a hearty welcome. Nobody in the world can appreciate it higher than I do. It did not wait till I got to London, but when I came ashore at Tilbury the stevedores on the dock raised the first welcome—a good and hearty welcome from the men who do the heavy labor in the world, and save you and me having to do it. They are the men who with their hands build empires and make them prosper. It is because of them that the others are wealthy and can live in luxury. They received me with a "Hurrah!" that went to my heart. They are the men that build civilization, and without them no civilization can be built. So I came first to the authors and creators of civilization, and I blessedly end this happy meeting with the Savages who destroy it.

CHARITY AND ACTORS

Address at the Actors' Fund Fair in the Metropolitan Opera House, New York, May 6, 1907

Mr. Clemens, in his white suit, formally declared the fair open. Mr. Daniel Frohman, in introducing Mr. Clemens, said:

"We intend to make this a banner week in the history of the Fund, which takes an interest in every one on the stage, be he actor, singer, dancer, or workman. We have spent more than $40,000 during the past year. Charity covers a multitude of sins, but it also reveals a multitude of virtues. At the opening of the former fair we had the assistance of Edwin Booth and Joseph Jefferson. In their place we have to-day that American institution and apostle of wide humanity—Mark Twain."

As Mr. Frohman has said, charity reveals a multitude of virtues. This is true, and it is to be proved here before the week is over. Mr. Frohman has told you something of the object and something of the character of the work. He told me he would do this—and he has kept his word! I had expected to hear of it through the newspapers. I wouldn't trust anything between Frohman and the newspapers—except when it's a case of charity!

You should all remember that the actor has been your benefactor many and many a year. When you have been weary and downcast he has lifted your heart out of gloom and given you a fresh impulse. You are all under obligation to him. This is your opportunity to be his benefactor—to help provide for him in his old age and when he suffers from infirmities.

At this fair no one is to be persecuted to buy. If you offer a twenty-dollar bill in payment for a purchase of $1 you will receive $19 in change. There is to be no robbery here. There is to be no creed here—no religion except charity. We want to raise $250,000—and that is a great task to attempt.

The President has set the fair in motion by pressing the button in Washington. Now your good wishes are to be transmuted into cash.

By virtue of the authority in me vested I declare the fair open. I call the game. Let the transmuting begin!

FULTON DAY, JAMESTOWN

ADDRESS DELIVERED SEPTEMBER 23, 1907

Lieutenant-Governor Ellyson, of Virginia, in introducing Mr. Clemens, said:

"The people have come here to bring a tribute of affectionate recollection for the man who has contributed so much to the progress of the world and the happiness of mankind." As Mr. Clemens came down to the platform the applause became louder and louder, until Mr. Clemens held out his hand for silence. It was a great triumph, and it was almost a minute after the applause ceased before Mr. Clemens could speak. He attempted it once, and when the audience noticed his emotion, it cheered again loudly.

LADIES AND GENTLEMEN,—I am but human, and when you give me a reception like that I am obliged to wait a little while I get my voice. When you appeal to my head, I don't feel it; but when you appeal to my heart, I do feel it.

We are here to celebrate one of the greatest events of American history, and not only in American history, but in the world's history.

Indeed it was—the application of steam by Robert Fulton.

It was a world event—there are not many of them. It is peculiarly an American event, that is true, but the influence was very broad in effect. We should regard this day as a very great American holiday. We have not many that are exclusively American holidays. We have the Fourth of July, which we regard as an American holiday, but it is nothing of the kind. I am waiting for a dissenting voice. All great efforts that led up to the Fourth of July were made, not by Americans, but by English residents of America, subjects of the King of England.

They fought all the fighting that was done, they shed and spilt all the blood that was spilt, in securing to us the invaluable liberties which are incorporated in the Declaration of Independence; but they were not Americans. They signed the Declaration of Independence; no American's name is signed to that document at all. There never was an American such as you and I are until the Revolution, when it had all been fought out and liberty secured, after the adoption of the Constitution, and the recognition of the Independence of America by all powers.

While we revere the Fourth of July—and let us always revere it, and the liberties it conferred upon us—yet it was not an American event, a great American day.

It was an American who applied that steam successfully. There are not a great many world events, and we have our full share. The telegraph, telephone, and the application of steam to navigation—these are great American events.

To-day I have been requested, or I have requested myself, not to confine myself to furnishing you with information, but to remind you of things, and to introduce one of the nation's celebrants.

Admiral Harrington here is going to tell you all that I have left untold. I am going to tell you all that I know, and then he will follow up with such rags and remnants as he can find, and tell you what he knows.

No doubt you have heard a great deal about Robert Fulton and the influences that have grown from his invention, but the little steamboat is suffering neglect.

You probably do not know a great deal about that boat. It was the most important steamboat in the world. I was there and saw it. Admiral Harrington was there at the time. It need not surprise you, for he is not as old as he looks. That little boat was interesting in every way. The size of it. The boat was one [consults Admiral], he said ten feet long. The breadth of that boat [consults Admiral], two hundred feet. You see, the first and most important detail is the length, then the breadth, and then the depth; the depth of that boat was [consults again]—the Admiral says it was a flat boat. Then her tonnage—you know nothing about a boat until you know two more things: her speed and her tonnage. We know the speed she made. She made four miles—and sometimes five miles. It was on her initial trip, on August 11, 1807, that she made her initial trip, when she went from [consults Admiral] Jersey City—to Chicago. That's right. She went by way of Albany. Now comes the tonnage of that boat. Tonnage of a boat means the amount of displacement; displacement means the amount of water a vessel can shove in a day. The tonnage of man is estimated by the amount of whiskey he can displace in a day.

Robert Fulton named the *Clermont* in honor of his bride, that is, Clermont was the name of the county seat.

I feel that it surprises you that I know so much. In my remarks of welcome of Admiral Harrington I am not going to give him compliments. Compliments always embarrass a man. You do not know anything to say. It does not inspire you with words. There is nothing you can say in answer to a compliment. I have been complimented myself a great many times, and they always embarrass me—I always feel that they have not said enough.

The Admiral and myself have held public office, and were associated together a great deal in a friendly way in the time of Pocahontas. That incident where Pocahontas saves the life of Smith from her father, Powhatan's club, was gotten up by the Admiral and myself to advertise Jamestown.

At that time the Admiral and myself did not have the facilities of advertising that you have.

I have known Admiral Harrington in all kinds of situations—in public service, on the platform, and in the chain gang now and then—but it was a mistake. A case of mistaken identity. I do not think it is at all a necessity to tell you Admiral Harrington's public history. You know that it is in the histories. I am not here to tell you anything about his public life, but to expose his private life.

I am something of a poet. When the great poet laureate, Tennyson, died, and I found that the place was open, I tried to get it—but I did not get it. Anybody can write the first line of a poem, but it is a very difficult task to make the second line rhyme with the first. When I was down in Australia there were two towns named Johnswood and Par-am. I made this rhyme:

> "The people of Johnswood are pious and good;
> The people of Par-am they don't care a ——."

I do not want to compliment Admiral Harrington, but as long as such men as he devote their lives to the public service the credit of the country will never cease. I will say that the same high qualities, the same moral and intellectual attainments, the same graciousness of manner, of conduct, of observation, and expression have caused Admiral Harrington to be mistaken for me—and I have been mistaken for him.

A mutual compliment can go no further, and I now have the honor and privilege of introducing to you Admiral Harrington.

THE ALPHABET AND SIMPLIFIED SPELLING

ADDRESS AT THE DINNER GIVEN TO MR. CARNEGIE AT THE DEDICATION OF THE NEW YORK ENGINEERS' CLUB, DECEMBER 9, 1907

Mr. Clemens was introduced by the president of the club, who, quoting from the Mark Twain autobiography, recalled the day when the distinguished writer came to New York with three dollars in small change in his pockets and a ten-dollar bill sewed in his clothes.

IT seems to me that I was around here in the neighborhood of the Public Library about fifty or sixty years ago. I don't deny the circumstances, although I don't see how you got it out of my autobiography, which was not to be printed until I am dead, unless I'm dead now. I had that three dollars in change, and I remember well the ten dollars which was sewed in my coat. I have prospered since. Now I have plenty of money and a disposition to squander it, but I can't. One of those trust companies is taking care of it.

Now, as this is probably the last time that I shall be out after nightfall this winter, I must say that I have come here with a mission, and I would make my errand of value.

Many compliments have been paid to Mr. Carnegie to-night. I was expecting them. They are very gratifying to me.

I have been a guest of honor myself, and I know what Mr. Carnegie is experiencing now. It is embarrassing to get compliments and compliments and only compliments, particularly when he knows as well as the rest of us that on the other side of him there are all sorts of things worthy of our condemnation.

Just look at Mr. Carnegie's face. It is fairly scintillating with fictitious innocence. You would think, looking at him, that he had never committed a crime in his life. But no—look at his pestiferous simplified spelling. You can't any of you imagine what a crime that has been. Torquemada was nothing to Mr. Carnegie. That old fellow shed some blood in the Inquisition, but Mr. Carnegie has brought destruction to the entire race. I know he didn't mean it to be a crime, but it was, just the same. He's got us all so we can't spell anything.

The trouble with him is that he attacked orthography at the wrong end. He meant well, but he attacked the symptoms and not the cause of the disease. He ought to have gone to work on the alphabet. There's not a vowel in it with a definite value, and not a consonant that you can hitch anything to. Look at the "h's" distributed all around. There's "gherkin." What are you going to do with the "h" in that? What the devil's the use of "h" in gherkin, I'd like to know. It's one thing I admire the English for: they just don't mind anything about them at all.

But look at the "pneumatics" and the "pneumonias" and the rest of them. A real reform would settle them once and for all, and wind up by giving us an alphabet that we wouldn't have to spell with at all. Why, there isn't a man who doesn't have to throw out about fifteen hundred words a day when he writes his letters because he can't spell them! It's like trying to do a St. Vitus's dance with wooden legs.

Now I'll bet there isn't a man here who can spell "pterodactyl," not even the prisoner at the bar. I'd like to hear him try once—but not in public, for it's too near Sunday, when all extravagant histrionic entertainments are barred. I'd like to hear him try in private, and when he got through trying to spell "pterodactyl" you wouldn't know whether it was a fish or a beast or a bird, and whether it flew on its legs or walked with its wings. The chances are that he would give it tusks and make it lay eggs.

Let's get Mr. Carnegie to reform the alphabet, and we'll pray for him—if he'll take the risk.

If we had adequate, competent vowels, with a system of accents, giving to each vowel its own soul and value, so every shade of that vowel would be shown in its accent, there is not a word in any tongue that we could not spell accurately. That would be competent, adequate, simplified spelling, in contrast to the clipping, the hair punching, the carbuncles, and the cancers which go by the name of simplified spelling. If I ask you what b-o-w spells you can't tell me unless you know which b-o-w I mean, and it is the same with r-o-w, and the whole family of words which were born out of lawful wedlock and don't know their own origin.

Now, if we had an alphabet that was adequate

and competent, instead of inadequate and incompetent, things would be different. Spelling reform has only made it bald-headed and unsightly. There is the whole tribe of them, "row" and "read" and "lead" —a whole family who don't know who they are. I ask you to pronounce s-o-w, and you ask me what kind of a one.

If we had a sane, determinate alphabet, instead of a hospital of comminuted eunuchs, you would know whether one referred to the act of a man casting the seed over the ploughed land or whether one wished to recall the lady hog and the future ham.

It's a poor alphabet. I appoint Mr. Carnegie to get after it, and leave simplified spelling alone. Simplified spelling brought about sun spots, the San Francisco earthquake, and the recent business depression, which we would never have had if spelling had been left all alone.

Now, I hope I have soothed Mr. Carnegie and made him more comfortable than he would have been had he received only compliment after compliment, and I wish to say to him that simplified spelling is all right, but, like chastity, you can carry it too far.

THE LAST LOTOS CLUB SPEECH

DELIVERED JANUARY 11, 1908

In introducing Mr. Clemens, Frank B. Lawrence, the President of the Lotos Club, recalled the fact that the first club dinner in the present club-house, some fourteen years ago, was in honor of Mark Twain.

I WISH to begin this time at the beginning, lest I forget it altogether; that is to say, I wish to thank you for this welcome that you are giving, and the welcome which you gave me seven years ago, and which I forgot to thank you for at that time. I also wish to thank you for the welcome you gave me fourteen years ago, which I also forgot to thank you for at the time.

I hope you will continue this custom to give me a dinner every seven years before I join the hosts in the other world—I do not know which world.

Mr. Lawrence and Mr. Porter have paid me many compliments. It is very difficult to take compliments. I do not care whether you deserve the compliments or not, it is just as difficult to take them. The other night I was at the Engineers' Club, and enjoyed the sufferings of Mr. Carnegie. They were complimenting him there; there it was all compliments, and none of them deserved. They say that you cannot live by bread alone, but I can live on compliments.

I do not make any pretence that I dislike compliments. The stronger the better, and I can manage to digest them. I think I have lost so much by not making a collection of compliments, to put them away and take them out again once in a while. When in England I said that I would start to collect compliments, and I began there and I have brought some of them along.

The first one of these lies—I wrote them down and preserved them—I think they are mighty good and extremely just. It is one of Hamilton Mabie's compliments. He said that La Salle was the first one to make a voyage of the Mississippi, but Mark Twain was the first to chart, light, and navigate it for the whole world.

If that had been published at the time that I issued that book [*Life on the Mississippi*], it would have been money in my pocket. I tell you, it is a talent by itself to pay compliments gracefully and have them ring true. It's an art by itself.

Here is another compliment by Albert Bigelow Paine, my biographer. He is writing four octavo volumes about me, and he has been at my elbow two and one-half years.

I just suppose that he does not know me, but says he knows me. He says "Mark Twain is not merely a great writer, a great philosopher, a great man; he is the supreme expression of the human being, with every human strength—and weakness." What a talent for compression! It takes a genius in compression to compact as many facts as that.

W.D.Howells spoke of me as first of Hartford, and ultimately of the solar system, not to say of the universe.

You know how modest Howells is. If it can be proved that my fame reaches to Neptune and Saturn, that will satisfy even me. You know how modest and retiring Howells seems to be, but deep down he is as vain as I am.

Mr. Howells had been granted a degree at Oxford, whose gown was red. He had been invited to an exercise at Columbia, and upon inquiry had been told that it was usual to wear the black gown. Later he had found that three other men wore bright gowns, and he had lamented that he had been one of the black mass, and not a red torch.

Edison wrote: "The average American loves his family. If he has any love left over for some other person, he generally selects Mark Twain."

Now here's the compliment of a little Montana girl which came to me indirectly. She was in a room in which there was a large photograph of me. After gazing at it steadily for a time, she said:

"We've got a John the Baptist like that." She also said: "Only ours has more trimmings."

I suppose she meant the halo. Now here is a gold miner's compliment. It is forty-two years old. It was my introduction to an audience to which I lectured in a log school-house. There were no ladies there. I wasn't famous then. They didn't know me. Only the miners were there, with their breeches tucked into their boot-tops and with clay all over them. They wanted some one to introduce me, and they selected a miner, who protested, saying:

"I don't know anything about this man. Anyhow, I only know two things about him. One is, he has never been in jail, and the other is, I don't know why."

There's one thing I want to say about that English trip. I knew his Majesty the King of England long years ago, and I didn't meet him for the first time then. One thing that I regret was that some newspapers said I talked with the Queen of England with my hat on. I don't do that with any woman. I did not put it on until she asked me to. Then she *told* me to put it on, and it's a command there. I thought I had carried my American democracy far enough. So I put it on. I have no use for a hat, and never did have.

Who was it who said that the police of London knew me? Why, the police know me everywhere. There never was a day over there when a policeman did not salute me, and then put up his hand and stop the traffic of the world. They treated me as though I were a duchess.

The happiest experience I had in England was at a dinner given in the building of the *Punch* publication, a humorous paper which is appreciated by all Englishmen. It was the greatest privilege ever allowed a foreigner. I entered the dining-room of the building, where those men get together who have been running the paper for over fifty years. We were about to begin dinner when the toastmaster said: "Just a minute; there ought to be a little ceremony." Then there was that meditating silence for a while, and out of a closet there came a beautiful little girl dressed in pink, holding in her hand the original of a cartoon of me, published in the previous week's paper, Mr. Punch, offering me welcome to England. It broke me all up. I could not even say "Thank you." That was the prettiest incident of the dinner, the delight of all that wonderful table. When she was about to go, I said, "My child, you are not going to leave me; I have hardly got acquainted with you." She replied, "You know I've got to go; they never let me come in here before, and they never will again." That is one of the beautiful incidents that I cherish.

[At the conclusion of his speech, and while the diners were still cheering him, Colonel Porter brought forward the red-and-gray gown of the Oxford "doctor," and Mr. Clemens was made to don it. The diners rose to their feet in their enthusiasm. With the mortar board on his head, and looking down admiringly at himself, Mr. Twain said:]

I like that gown. I always did like red. The redder it is the better I like it. I was born for a savage. Now, whoever saw any red like this? There is no red outside the arteries of an archangel that could compare with this. I know you all envy me. I am going to have luncheon shortly with ladies—just ladies. I will be the only lady of my sex present, and I shall put on this gown and make those ladies look dim.

[Mr. Clemens then, by request, gave the closing remarks of an address which he had delivered at a farewell dinner tendered him, July 10, 1907, by the Lord Mayor of Liverpool.]

Home is dear to us all, and now I am departing to my own home beyond the ocean. Oxford has conferred upon me the loftiest honor that has ever fallen to my share of this life's prizes. It is the very one I would have chosen, as outranking all and any others, the one more precious to me than any and all others, within the gift of man or state. During my four weeks' sojourn in England I have had another lofty honor, a continuous honor, an honor which has flowed serenely along, without halt or obstruction, through all these twenty-six days, a most moving and pulse-stirring honor—the heartfelt grip of the hand, and the welcome that does not descend from the pale-gray matter of the brain, but rushes up with the red blood from the heart. It makes me proud, and sometimes it makes me humble, too . . . Many and many a year ago I gathered an incident from Dana's *Two Years Before the Mast.* It was like this: There was a presumptuous little self-important skipper in a coasting sloop, engaged in the dried-apple and kitchen-furniture trade, and he was always hailing every ship that came in sight. He did it just to hear himself talk and to air his small grandeur. One day a majestic Indiaman came ploughing by with course on course of canvas towering into the sky, her decks and yards swarming with sailors, her hull burdened to the Plimsoll line with a rich freightage of precious spices, lading the breezes with gracious and mysterious odors of the Orient. It was a noble spectacle, a sublime spectacle! Of course, the little skipper popped into the shrouds and squeaked out a hail, "Ship ahoy! What ship is that? And whence and whither?" In a deep and thunderous bass the answer came back through the speaking trumpet, "The *Begum*, of

Bengal, one hundred and forty-two days out from Canton, homeward bound! What ship is that?" Well, it just crushed that poor little creature's vanity flat, and he squeaked back most humbly, "Only the *Mary Ann*, fourteen hours out from Boston, bound for Kittery Point—with nothing to speak of!" Oh, what an eloquent word, that "only," to express the depths of his humbleness! That is just my case. During just one hour in the twenty-four—not more—I pause and reflect in the stillness of the night with the echoes of your English welcome still lingering in my ears, and then I am humble. Then I am properly meek, and for that little while I am only the *Mary Ann*, fourteen hours out, cargoed with vegetables and tinware; but during all the twenty-three hours my vain self-complacency rides high on the white crest of your approval, and then I am a stately Indiaman, ploughing the great seas under a cloud of canvas and laden with the kindest words that have ever been vouchsafed to any wandering alien in this world, I think; then my twenty-six fortunate days on this old mother soil seem to be multiplied by six, and *I* am the *Begum* of Bengal, one hundred and forty-two days out from Canton, homeward bound!

BOOKSELLERS

Address at banquet on Wednesday evening, May 20, 1908, of the American Booksellers' Association, which included most of the leading booksellers of America, held at the rooms of the Aldine Association, New York.

THIS annual gathering of booksellers from all over America comes together ostensibly to eat and drink, but really to discuss business; therefore I am required to talk shop. I am required to furnish a statement of the indebtedness under which I lie to you gentlemen for your help in enabling me to earn my living. For something over forty years I have acquired my bread by print, beginning with *The Innocents Abroad*, followed at intervals of a year or so by *Roughing It*, *Tom Sawyer*, *Gilded Age*, and so on. For thirty-six years my books were sold by subscription. You are not interested in those years, but only in the four which have since followed. The books passed into the hands of my present publishers at the beginning of 1904, and you then became the providers of my diet. I think I may say, without flattering you, that you have done exceedingly well by me. Exceedingly well is not too strong a phrase, since the official statistics show that in four years you have sold twice as many volumes of my venerable books as my contract with my publishers bound you and them to sell in five years. To your sorrow you are aware that frequently, much too frequently, when a book gets to be five or ten years old its annual sale shrinks to two or three hundred copies, and after an added ten or twenty years ceases to sell. But you sell thousands of my moss-backed old books every year—the youngest of them being books that range from fifteen to twenty-seven years old, and the oldest reaching back to thirty-five and forty.

By the terms of my contract my publishers had to account to me for 50,000 volumes per year for five years, and pay me for them whether they sold them or not. It is at this point that you gentlemen come in, for it was your business to unload 250,000 volumes upon the public in five years if you possibly could. Have you succeeded? Yes, you have—and more. For in four years, with a year still to spare, you have sold the 250,000 volumes, and 240,000 besides.

Your sales have increased each year. In the first year you sold 90,328; in the second year, 104,851; in the third, 133,975; in the fourth year—which was last year—you sold 160,000. The aggregate for the four years is 500,000 volumes, lacking 11,000.

Of the oldest book, *The Innocents Abroad*,—now forty years old—you sold upward of 46,000 copies in the four years; of *Roughing It*—now thirty-eight years old, I think—you sold 40,334; of *Tom Sawyer*, 41,000. And so on.

And there is one thing that is peculiarly gratifying to me: the *Personal Recollections of Joan of Arc* is a serious book; I wrote it for love, and never expected it to sell, but you have pleasantly disappointed me in that matter. In your hands its sale has increased each year. In 1904 you sold 1726 copies; in 1905 2445; in 1906, 5381; and last year, 6574.

Last February, when Rudyard Kipling was ill in America, the sympathy which was poured out to him was genuine and sincere, and I believe that which cost Kipling so much will bring England and America closer together. I have been proud and pleased to see this growing affection and respect between the two countries. I hope it will continue to grow, and, please God, it will continue to grow. I trust we authors will leave to posterity, if we have nothing else to leave, a friendship between England and America that will count for much. I will now confess that I have been engaged for the past eight days in compiling a toast. I have brought it here to lay at your feet. I do not ask your indulgence in presenting it, but for your applause.

Here it is: "Since England and America may be joined together in Kipling, may they not be severed in 'Twain.'"

EDUCATION AND CITIZENSHIP

On the evening of May 14, 1908, the alumni of the College of the City of New York celebrated the opening of the new college buildings at a banquet in the Waldorf-Astoria. Mr. Clemens followed Mayor McClellan.

I AGREED when the Mayor said that there was not a man within hearing who did not agree that citizenship should be placed above everything else, even learning.

Have you ever thought about this? Is there a college in the whole country where there is a chair of good citizenship? There is a kind of bad citizenship which is taught in the schools, but no real good citizenship taught. There are some which teach insane citizenship, bastard citizenship, but that is all. Patriotism! Yes; but patriotism is usually the refuge of the scoundrel. He is the man who talks the loudest.

You can begin that chair of citizenship in the College of the City of New York. You can place it above mathematics and literature, and that is where it belongs.

We used to trust in God. I think it was in 1863 that some genius suggested that it be put upon the gold and silver coins which circulated among the rich. They didn't put it on the nickels and coppers because they didn't think the poor folks had any trust in God.

Good citizenship would teach accuracy of thinking and accuracy of statement. Now, that motto on the coin is an overstatement. Those Congressmen had no right to commit this whole country to a theological doctrine. But since they did, Congress ought to state what our creed should be.

There was never a nation in the world that put its whole trust in God. It is a statement made on insufficient evidence. Leaving out the gamblers, the burglars, and the plumbers, perhaps we do put our trust in God after a fashion. But, after all, it is an overstatement.

If the cholera or black plague should come to these shores, perhaps the bulk of the nation would pray to be delivered from it, but the rest would put their trust in the Health Board of the City of New York.

I read in the papers within the last day or two of a poor young girl who they said was a leper. Did the people in that populous section of the country where she was—did they put their trust in God? The girl was afflicted with the leprosy, a disease which cannot be communicated from one person to another.

Yet, instead of putting their trust in God, they harried that poor creature, shelterless and friendless, from place to place, exactly as they did in the Middle Ages, when they made lepers wear bells, so that people could be warned of their approach and avoid them. Perhaps those people in the Middle Ages thought they were putting their trust in God.

The President ordered the removal of that motto from the coin, and I thought that it was well. I thought that overstatement should not stay there. But I think it would better read, "Within certain judicious limitations we trust in God," and if there isn't enough room on the coin for this, why, enlarge the coin.

Now I want to tell a story about jumping at conclusions. It was told to me by Bram Stoker, and it concerns a christening. There was a little clergyman who was prone to jump at conclusions sometimes. One day he was invited to officiate at a christening. He went. There sat the relatives—intelligent-looking relatives they were. The little clergyman's instinct came to him to make a great speech. He was given to flights of oratory that way—a very dangerous thing, for often the wings which take one into clouds of oratorical enthusiasm are wax and melt up there, and down you come.

But the little clergyman couldn't resist. He took the child in his arms, and, holding it, looked at it a moment. It wasn't much of a child. It was little like a sweet potato. Then the little clergyman waited impressively, and then: "I see in your countenances," he said, "disappointment of him. I see you are disappointed with this baby. Why? Because he is so little. My friends, if you had but the power of looking into the future you might see that great things may come of little things. There is the great ocean, holding the navies of the world, which comes from little drops of water no larger than a woman's tears. There are the great constellations in the sky, made up of little bits of stars. Oh, if you could consider his future you might see that he might become the greatest poet of the universe, the greatest warrior the world has ever known, greater than Cæsar, than Hannibal, than—er—er" (turning to the father)—"what's his name?"

The father hesitated, then whispered back: "His name? Well, his name is Mary Ann."

DINNER TO WHITELAW REID

ADDRESS AT THE DINNER IN HONOR OF AMBASSADOR REID, GIVEN BY THE PILGRIMS' CLUB OF NEW YORK ON FEBRUARY 19, 1908

I AM very proud to respond to this toast, as it recalls the proudest day of my life. The delightful hospitality shown me at the time of my visit to Oxford I shall cherish until I die. In that long and distinguished career of mine I value that degree above all other honors. When the ship landed even the stevedores gathered on the shore and gave an English cheer. Nothing could surpass in my life the pleasure of those four weeks. No one could pass by me without taking my hand, even the policemen. I've been in all the principal capitals of Christendom in my life, and have always been an object of interest to policemen. Sometimes there was suspicion in their eyes, but not always. With their puissant hand they would hold up the commerce of the world to let me pass.

I noticed in the papers this afternoon a despatch from Washington, saying that Congress would immediately pass a bill restoring to our gold coinage the motto "In God We Trust." I'm glad of that; I'm glad of that. I was troubled when that motto was removed. Sure enough, the prosperities of the whole nation went down in a heap when we ceased to trust in God in that conspicuously advertised way. I knew there would be trouble. And if Pierpont Morgan hadn't stepped in[1]—Bishop Lawrence may now add to his message to the old country that we are now trusting in God again. So we can discharge Mr. Morgan from his office with honor.

Mr. Reid said an hour or so ago something about my ruining my activities last summer. They are not ruined, they are renewed. I am stronger now—much stronger. I suppose that the spiritual uplift I received increased my physical power more than anything I ever had before. I was dancing last night at 12.30 o'clock.

Mr. Choate has mentioned Mr. Reid's predecessors. Mr. Choate's head is full of history, and some of it is true, too. I enjoyed hearing him tell about the list of the men who had the place before he did. He mentioned a long list of those predecessors, people I never heard of before, and elected five of them to the Presidency by his own vote. I'm glad and proud to find Mr. Reid in that high position, because he didn't look it when I knew him forty years ago. I was talking to Reid the other day, and he showed me my autograph on an old paper twenty years old. I didn't know I had an autograph twenty years ago. Nobody ever asked me for it.

I remember a dinner I had long ago with Whitelaw Reid and John Hay at Reid's expense. I had another last summer when I was in London at the

[1] Refers to the panic of 1907 when J. Pierpont Morgan, George F. Baker, and other downtown bankers tided the country through a financial crisis.

embassy that Choate blackguards so. I'd like to live there.

Some of us don't appreciate what this country can do. There's John Hay, Reid, Choate, and me. This is the only country in the world where youth, talent and energy can reach such heights. It shows what we could do without means, and what people can do with talent and energy when they find it in people like us.

When I first came to New York they were all struggling young men, and I am glad to see that they have got on in the world. I knew John Hay when I had no white hairs in my head and more hair than Reid has now. Those were days of joy and hope. Reid and Hay were on the staff of the *Tribune.* I went there once in that old building, and I looked all around, and I finally found a door ajar and looked in. It wasn't Reid or Hay there, but it was Horace Greeley. Those were the days when Horace Greeley was a king. That was the first time I ever saw him and the last. I only stayed a minute. I could have stayed longer if I had wanted to, but I didn't want to.

I was admiring him when he stopped and seemed to realize that there was a fine presence there somewhere. He looked at me a moment, and said: "What in H— do you want?"

Well, I couldn't think of what I wanted, so I retired.

But later Hay rose, and you know what summit Whitelaw Reid has reached, and you see me. Those two men have regulated troubles of nations and conferred peace upon mankind. And in my humble way, of which I am quite vain, I was the principal moral force in all those great international movements. These great men illustrated what I say. Look at us great people—we all come from the dregs of society. That's what can be done in this country. That's what this country does for you.

Choate here—he hasn't got anything to say, but he says it just the same, and he can do it so felicitously, too. I said long ago he was the handsomest man America ever produced. May the progress of civilization always rest on such distinguished men as it has in the past!

COURAGE

At a beefsteak dinner, given by artists, caricaturists, and humorists of New York City, April 18, 1908, Mr. Clemens, Mr. H. H. Rogers, and Mr. Patrick McCarren were the guests of honor. Each wore a white apron, and each made a short speech.

IN the matter of courage we all have our limits. There never was a hero who did not have his bounds. I suppose it may be said of Nelson and all the others whose courage has been advertised that there came times in their lives when their bravery knew it had come to its limit.

I have found mine a good many times. Sometimes this was expected—often it was unexpected. I know a man who is not afraid to sleep with a rattlesnake, but you could not get him to sleep with a safety-razor.

I never had the courage to talk across a long, narrow room. I should be at the end of the room facing all the audience. If I attempt to talk across a room I find myself turning this way and that, and thus at alternate periods I have part of the audience behind me. You ought never to have any part of the audience behind you; you never can tell what they are going to do.

I'll sit down.

ROGERS AND RAILROADS

At a Banquet Given Mr. H. H. Rogers by the Business Men of Norfolk, Va., Celebrating the Opening of the Virginian Railway, April 3, 1909

Toastmaster:

"I have often thought that when the time comes, which must come to all of us, when we reach that Great Way in the Great Beyond, and the question is propounded, 'What have you done to gain admission into this great realm?' if the answer could be sincerely made, 'I have made men laugh,' it would be the surest passport to a welcome entrance. We have here to-night one who has made millions laugh—not the loud laughter that bespeaks the vacant mind, but the laugh of intelligent mirth that helps the human heart and the human mind. I refer, of course, to Doctor Clemens. I was going to say Mark Twain, his literary title, which is a household phrase in more homes than that of any other man, and you know him best by that dear old title."

I THANK you, Mr. Toastmaster, for the compliment which you have paid me, and I am sure I would rather have made people laugh than cry, yet in my time I have made some of them cry; and before I stop entirely I hope to make some more of them cry. I like compliments. I deal in them myself. I have listened with the greatest pleasure to the compliments which the chairman has paid to Mr. Rogers and that road of his to-night, and I hope some of them are deserved.

It is no small distinction to a man like that to sit here before an intelligent crowd like this and to be classed with Napoleon and Cæsar. Why didn't he say that this was the proudest day of his life? Napoleon and Cæsar are dead, and they can't be here to defend themselves. But I'm here!

The chairman said, and very truly, that the most lasting thing in the hands of man are the roads which Cæsar build, and it is true that he built a lot of them; and they are there yet.

Yes, Cæsar built a lot of roads in England, and you can find them. But Rogers has only built one road, and he hasn't finished that yet. I like to hear my old friend complimented, but I don't like to hear it overdone.

I didn't go around to-day with the others to see what he is doing. I will do that in a quiet time, when there is not anything going on, and when I shall not be called upon to deliver intemperate compliments on a railroad in which I own no stock.

They proposed that I go along with the committee and help inspect that dump down yonder. I didn't go. I saw that dump. I saw that thing when I was coming in on the steamer, and I didn't go because I was diffident, sentimentally diffident, about going and looking at that thing again—that great, long, bony thing; it looked just like Mr. Rogers's foot.

The chairman says Mr. Rogers is full of practical wisdom, and he is. It is intimated here that he is a very ingenious man, and he is a very competent financier. Maybe he is now, but it was not always so. I know lots of private things in his life which people don't know, and I know how he started; and it was not a very good start. I could have done better myself. The first time he crossed the Atlantic he had just made the first little strike in oil, and he was so young he did not like to ask questions. He did not like to appear ignorant. To this day he doesn't like to appear ignorant, but he can look as ignorant as anybody. On board the ship they were betting on the run of the ship, betting a couple of shillings, or half a crown, and they proposed that this youth from the oil regions should bet on the run of the ship. He did not like to ask what a half crown was, and he didn't know; but rather than be ashamed of himself he did bet half a crown on the run of the ship, and in bed he could not sleep. He wondered if he could afford that outlay in case he lost. He kept wondering over it, and said to himself: "A king's crown must be worth $20,000, so half a crown would cost $10,000." He could not afford to bet away $10,000 on the run of the ship, so he went up to the stakeholder and gave him $150 to let him off.

I like to hear Mr. Rogers complimented. I am not stingy in compliments to him myself. Why, I did it to-day when I sent his wife a telegram to comfort her. That is the kind of person I am. I knew she would be uneasy about him. I knew she would be solicitous about what he might do down here, so I did it to quiet her and to comfort her. I said he was doing well for a person out of practice. There is nothing like it. He is like I used to be. There were times when I was careless—careless in my dress when I got older. You know how uncomfortable your wife can get when you are going away without her superintendence. Once when my wife could not go with me (she always went with me when she could—I always did meet that kind of luck), I was going to Washinton once, a long time ago, in Mr. Cleveland's first administration, and she could not go; but, in her anxiety that I should not desecrate the house, she made preparation. She knew that there was to be a reception of those authors at the White House at seven o'clock in the evening. She said, "If I should tell you now what I want to ask of you, you would forget it before you get to Washington, and therefore, I have written it on a card, and you will find it in your dress-vest pocket when you are dressing at the Arlington—when you are dressing to see the President." I never thought of it again until I was dressing, and I felt in that pocket and took it out, and it said, in a kind of imploring way. "Don't wear your artics in the White House."

You complimented Mr. Rogers on his energy, his foresightedness, complimented him in various ways, and he has deserved those compliments, although I say it myself; and I enjoy them all. There is one side of Mr. Rogers that has not been mentioned. If you will leave that to me I will touch upon that. There was a note in an editorial in one of the Norfolk papers this morning that touched upon that very thing, that hidden side of Mr. Rogers, where it spoke of Helen Keller and her affection for Mr. Rogers, to whom she dedicated her life book. And she has a right to feel that way, because, without the public knowing anything about it, he rescued, if I may use that term, that marvellous girl, that wonderful

Southern girl, that girl who was stone deaf, blind, and dumb from scarlet fever when she was a baby eighteen months old; and who now is as well and thoroughly educated as any woman on this planet at twenty-nine years of age. She is the most marvellous person of her sex that has existed on this earth since Joan of Arc.

That is not all Mr. Rogers has done; but you never see that side of his character, because it is never protruding; but he lends a helping hand daily out of that generous heart of his. You never hear of it. He is supposed to be a moon which has one side dark and the other bright. But the other side though you don't see it, is not dark; it is bright, and its rays penetrate, and others do see it who are not God.

I would like this opportunity to tell something that I have never been allowed to tell by Mr. Rogers, either by my mouth or in print, and if I don't look at him I can tell it now.

In 1893, when the publishing company of Charles L. Webster, of which I was financial agent, failed, it left me heavily in debt. If you will remember what commerce was at that time you will recall that you could not sell anything, and could not buy anything, and I was on my back; my books were not worth anything at all, and I could not give away my copyrights. Mr. Rogers had long enough vision ahead to say, "Your books have supported you before, and after the panic is over they will support you again," and that was a correct proposition. He saved my copyrights, and saved me from financial ruin. He it was who arranged with my creditors to allow me to roam the face of the earth for four years and persecute the nations thereof with lectures, promising that at the end of four years I would pay dollar for dollar. That arrangement was made; otherwise I would now be living out-of-doors under an umbrella, and a borrowed one at that.

You see his white mustache and his head trying to get white (he is always trying to look like me— I don't blame him for that). These are only emblematic of his character, and that is all. I say, without exception, hair and all, he is the whitest man I have ever known.

DINNER TO MR. JEROME

A dinner to express their confidence in the integrity and good judgment of District Attorney Jerome was given at Delmonico's by his admirers on the evening of May 7, 1909

INDEED, that is very sudden. I was not informed that the verdict was going to depend upon my judgment, but that makes not the least difference in the world when you already know all about it. It is not any matter when you are called upon to express it; you can get up and do it, and my verdict has already been recorded in my heart and in my head as regards Mr. Jerome and his administration of the criminal affairs of this county.

I agree with everything Mr. Choate has said in his letter regarding Mr. Jerome; I agree with everything Mr. Shepard has said; and I agree with everything Mr. Jerome has said in his own commendation. And I thought Mr. Jerome was modest in that. If he had been talking about another officer of this county, he could have painted the joys and sorrows of office and his victories in even stronger language than he did.

I voted for Mr. Jerome in those old days, and I should like to vote for him again if he runs for any office. I moved out of New York, and that is the reason, I suppose, I cannot vote for him again. There may be some way, but I have not found it out. But now I am a farmer—a farmer up in Connecticut, and winning laurels. Those people already speak with such high favor, admiration, of my farming, and they say that I am the only man that has ever come to that region who could make two blades of grass grow where only three grew before.

Well, I cannot vote for him. You see that. As it stands now, I cannot. I am crippled in that way and to that extent, for I would ever so much like to do it. I am not a Congress, and I cannot distribute pensions, and I don't know any other legitimate way to buy a vote. But if I should think of any legitimate way, I shall make use of it, and then I shall vote for Mr. Jerome.

THE END